Fighting Proud

The Untold Story of the Gay Men
who Served in Two World Wars

STEPHEN BOURNE

I.B. TAURIS

LONDON · NEW YORK

New paperback edition published in 2018 by
I.B.Tauris & Co. Ltd
London • New York
www.ibtauris.com

First published in hardback in 2017 by I.B.Tauris & Co. Ltd

ISBN: 978 1 78831 346 9
eISBN: 978 1 78672 215 7
ePDF: 978 1 78673 215 6

A full CIP record for this book is available from the British Library
A full CIP record is available from the Library of Congress

Library of Congress Catalog Card Number: available

Typeset by JCS Publishing Services Ltd, jcs-publishing.co.uk
Printed and bound in Sweden by ScandBook AB

n Bourne is a writer and historian. An expert on black and British history, he has written for *BBC History Magazine* *listory Today* and is a regular contributor to the *Oxford Dictionary of National Biography*. His most recent Amazon-bestselling book *Black Poppies* (2014), a history of the contribution of black men and women to World War I, won the Southwark Arts Forum Award for Literature. He has also written widely on homosexual representations in film. In 2017 Stephen was awarded an Honorary Fellowship from London South Bank University for his contribution to diversity.

'Stephen Bourne brings great natural scholarship and passion to largely hidden stories. He is highly accessible, accurate, and surprising. You always walk away from his work knowing something that you didn't know, that you didn't even suspect.'

Bonnie Greer

'A magnificent piece of work. I was gripped throughout; laughed out loud at times; became blazingly angry at the injustice, hypocrisy and expediency ... and sheer waste. And, at times, delighted by the courage and refusal of many to bow down to prejudice or to dampen our full potential as human beings.'

Keith Howes, author of *Broadcasting It: An Encyclopaedia of Homosexuality on Film, Radio and TV 1923–1993*

Contents

List of Illustrations	vii
Acknowledgements	ix
Author's Note	xi
Preface	xiii
Introduction	1

Part I: World War I, 1914–1918

1	Lord Kitchener	5
2	Unfortunate Fellows	11
3	Edward Brittain	19
4	James Whale, R. C. Sherriff and *Journey's End*	23
5	Ralph and Monty: The Man I Love	31

Part II: World War II, 1939–1945

The Army

6	Kiss Me Goodnight, Sergeant Major	43
7	Prisoners of War Part 1: Dudley Cave	53
8	Prisoners of War Part 2	61

The Navy

9	Rum, Bum and Concertina	67
10	Terri Gardener: Behind Enemy Lines	75

The RAF

11 The Killing Skies   85
12 Richard Rumbold: The Flyer   91
13 Ian Gleed: The Hero   97
14 Hector Bolitho: The Writer   105

The Home Front

15 Brief Encounters in the Blackout   115
16 Against the Law   121
17 Lily Law Goes to War   127

Entertainment on the Home Front

18 Noël Coward and *In Which We Serve*   137
19 'Snakehips' Swings into the Blitz   145
20 Brian Desmond Hurst 'Old Twank'   155

Part III: Not Forgotten

21 1914–1918   165
22 1939–1945   175
23 My Friend Ken   187

Conclusion   197
Appendix: Cinema and Television   201

Notes   207
Bibliography   223
About the Author   229
Index   233

Illustrations

World War I

Front cover: A Private and a Lance-Corporal from the East Kent Mounted Rifles (Courtesy of James Gardiner and Neil Bartlett Collection/Wellcome Library)

1 Lord Kitchener (Author's Collection)

2, 3, 4 'Is a Soldier Married a Soldier Spoiled?', *Home Chat*, 11 June 1910 (Courtesy of George Pagliero)

5 The final resting place of Edward Brittain in Granezza British Cemetery, Italy (Courtesy of the War Graves Photographic Project)

6 R. C. Sherriff (Author's Collection)

7 HMS *Erin*, 1917 (Courtesy of Geoff Cunnington)

8 HMS *Barham* visitors' day with sailors dancing (Courtesy of Geoff Cunnington)

9 HMS *Bellerophon*, 11 November 1918 (Courtesy of Geoff Cunnington)

10 Aberdeen, 1919 (Author's Collection)

11 Montague Glover (Courtesy of James Gardiner and Neil Bartlett Collection)

12 Soldiers photographed by Montague Glover (Courtesy of James Gardiner and Neil Bartlett Collection)

13 Wilfred Owen (Photo taken in 1916 by John Gunston; courtesy of the National Portrait Gallery. Ref. P515)

14 Roger Casement (Author's Collection)
15 Ivor Novello (Author's Collection)
16 Fred Barnes (Author's Collection)

World War II

17 Ralph Hall (Courtesy of James Gardiner and Neil Bartlett Collection)
18 *Kiss Me Goodnight, Sergeant Major* music sheet (Author's Collection)
19 World War II postcard (Author's Collection)
20, 21 'Christmas in the Tropics, 1940'. Unidentified seamen aboard the *Queen of Bermuda* (Courtesy of the Hull family)
22 Richard Rumbold (Courtesy of Terry Bolas)
23 Christopher Gotch (Courtesy of Terry Bolas)
24 Wing Commander Ian Gleed (Courtesy of the Imperial War Museum. Ref. CM5005)
25 The final resting place of Wing Commander Ian Gleed in Enfidaville War Cemetery, Tunisia (Courtesy of the War Graves Photographic Project)
26 Hector Bolitho (Photo by Howard Coster; courtesy of the National Portrait Gallery. Ref. X10394)
27 The cover of Hector Bolitho's *A Penguin in the Eyrie* (Author's Collection)
28 Quentin Crisp in his Chelsea flat (Courtesy of Popperfoto/ Getty Images)
29 PC Harry Daley and friend from *This Small Cloud* (1986)
30 Berto Pasuka (Author's Collection)
31 Ken 'Snakehips' Johnson music sheet (Author's Collection)
32 Noël Coward entertaining the forces on BBC radio in 1943 (Photo by Felix Mann/Picture Post; courtesy of Getty Images)
33 Brian Desmond Hurst (Author's Collection)
34 Alan Turing (Courtesy of the National Portrait Gallery. Ref. X82217)

Acknowledgements

Andrew Bird
The late Terry Bolas
Geoff Cunnington
Andrew Davies
Peter Devitt, Assistant Curator, RAF Museum London
James Gardiner
Nick Goodall
David Hankin
Tina Horsley
Keith Howes
Linda Hull
Molly Hull
Richard Norman
Terence Pepper
John Webber
Adrian Woodhouse

British Library
Commonwealth War Graves Commission
Imperial War Museum London
National Archives
RAF Museum London
Surrey Heritage Centre
The War Graves Photographic Project

Author's Note

*F*ighting Proud should not be read in isolation. Readers will find a comprehensive bibliography at the end of this book. However, there are a few titles that I would like to recommend personally which I feel are worth locating and reading. In 1985 John Costello's *Love, Sex and War: Changing Values 1939–45* (Guild Publishing) was a groundbreaking study of changing sexual relations in World War II, and Costello included an informative chapter about gay and lesbian servicemen and women called 'Comrades in Arms'. I remember accessing this book from my local library in the 1980s and being influenced by this chapter, which opened up the subject for me and gave me my first insights into gay men's wartime experiences, good and bad.

In 1989 the Hall Carpenter Archives Gay Men's Oral History Group's *Walking After Midnight: Gay Men's Life Stories* (Routledge) appealed to my interest in firsthand testimonies. This was how I began my own career as an author. My first book, *Aunt Esther's Story* (1991), included the firsthand testimony of my adopted aunt. *Walking After Midnight* proved to be extremely useful for its original interviews with several men who spoke about their wartime experiences, especially Dudley Cave, who eloquently recounted his life as a prisoner of war.

I have often felt that the 1990s was a watershed decade, a 'golden period', for gay histories both in print and on television. The decade began promisingly with the superb documentary *Comrades in Arms* which was shown in Channel 4's Out on Tuesday series in

1990. In *Comrades in Arms* the director Stuart Marshall movingly re-examined World War II through the eyes of a group of real-life gay servicemen and servicewomen whose experiences ranged from ENSA-style entertainment to the River Kwai prison camp. Personal reminiscences, archive material and staged recreations of gay romances which were shot in the style of 1940s black-and-white movies were combined in a humorous reclamation of a hitherto unrecorded history.

The following year Kevin Porter and Jeffrey Weeks edited a compilation of interviews entitled *Between the Acts: Lives of Homosexual Men 1885–1967* (Routledge), and this included reminiscences by several interviewees about the two world wars. In 1992 James Gardiner's indispensable and beautifully written and illustrated *A Class Apart: The Private Pictures of Montague Glover* was published by Serpent's Tail. In 1997 came Alkarim Jivani's *It's Not Unusual: A History of Lesbian and Gay Britain in the Twentieth Century*, published by Michael O'Mara to coincide with BBC2's outstanding documentary series which included World War II. In 1998 BBC2's *Timewatch: Sex and War* drew upon gay men's bravery during World War II to highlight the campaign to lift the ban in the armed services.

Since the 'golden age' of the 1990s very few books have surfaced that cover the lives of gay men in the two world wars. Neither Matt Houlbrook's *Queer London: Perils and Pleasures in the Sexual Metropolis, 1918–1957* (2005) or Emma Vickers's *Queen and Country: Same-Sex Desire in the British Armed Forces, 1939–45* (2013) include World War I, but they do cover World War II. They are rich in detail and superb resources for anyone interested in gay men's history.

Preface

In Nazi Germany on 4 April 1938, a dictate ordered that homosexuals be incarcerated in concentration camps and over the next seven years more than 100,000 men suspected of homosexuality were arrested, of whom half were convicted and sentenced to internal exile within the prison and concentration camp system. Most were thoroughly respectable citizens – their only crime was that they were attracted to other men, yet regardless of age or background each was forced to wear a pink triangle denoting sexual deviancy […] The pink triangle was seen as a badge of dishonour that earned the wearer particularly harsh treatment in camps, where an estimated 60 percent of homosexuals perished – far more than in any other Nazi-deemed 'anti-social' group.[1]

My father-in-law tells the story of the debate on the Wolfenden Report in the House of Lords. Apparently, Field-Marshal Viscount Montgomery of Alamein rose to state categorically that he was quite convinced that no homosexuality had ever occurred among any of the hundreds of thousands of men under his command during the war. The statement produced a moment of astonished silence followed by suppressed snorts of disbelief and then an uproar of laughter.[2]

Over five million men served in the British armed forces during World War II. Of these, it's likely that at least 250,000 were gay or bisexual (based on projections from the 1990–91 National Survey of

Sexual Attitudes and Lifestyles which found that six per cent of men report having had homosexual experiences).[3]

In the 1970s I was completely unaware that, as a gay teenager, I had a history. Then something happened to change this. In 1980 I borrowed a book from my local library called *The Men with the Pink Triangle* by Heinz Heger. It had been reprinted from the German original by the Gay Men's Press and it told the story of the homosexuals who had been persecuted, arrested, imprisoned, tortured and exterminated in Nazi Germany. Reading this book changed my life. I was aware of Anne Frank and the fate of 6 million Jews in Germany, known as the Holocaust, but no one had informed me that at least another 5 million 'others' had perished in Nazi concentration camps and throughout occupied Europe, and these would have included communists, lesbians, gay men, Jehovah's Witnesses, Gypsies and people with physical or mental disabilities. Jews wore the yellow star. Gay men were forced to wear the pink triangle. This discovery shocked and horrified me but it led me to the realisation that gay men had existed in history.

When I 'came out' to my parents in the 1980s they could not have been more supportive. I'm not sure if they had guessed that I was gay, but the disclosure marked an important turning point in our relationship. We had always been close, they had always been kind and loving parents, but now we could be more open and honest. No more secrets and lies. Not only did my parents learn something new about me, I gradually began to learn new things about them. To reassure me that being gay was fine with him, my dad mentioned a sergeant he had known in his National Service days, in the Royal Air Force, in the early 1950s. He told me that the sergeant was known to be gay, but it didn't bother anyone because he was liked and respected. I asked my dad questions about this gay military man in his early life, but he couldn't recall anything else, not even the sergeant's name. It was all so long ago. This man existed at a time when homosexuality was a criminal offence – he could have been court-martialled and thrown out of the RAF –

but I felt reassured that my dad didn't remember anything nasty happening to the sergeant. It was my first realisation that, in those difficult, troubled times for gay men in Britain – and it was the time of the homosexual 'witch hunt' – some of us were still accepted, and respected, even in the closed, 'macho' worlds of the armed services. The existence of the gay sergeant also made me see that this gentleman could have been old enough to have served in World War II. I was intrigued because, if the gay sergeant *had* served in the war, there would have been others. So I kept my eyes and ears open and, over time, I gradually found what I was hoping to find: fragments about gay men's lives in the armed services. Consequently a picture began to build.

By 2012 I had a sufficient awareness and understanding of the subject to be commissioned to write a feature about gay men's lives in World War II for *BBC History Magazine*. This led to an offer from I.B.Tauris to write *Fighting Proud*. Thanks to Tomasz Hoskins, the editor who read the feature and commissioned me, I was happy to take responsibility for the project. It was agreed that I should avoid attempting to rewrite the stories of some of the iconic gay figures from the two world wars that *are* well known. These included Wilfred Owen, Lawrence of Arabia, Roger Casement, Ivor Novello and Alan Turing. These men are well served by biographers and other media. Instead, you can find short profiles about them in a separate section entitled 'Not Forgotten'. This book is about exploring and highlighting the many stories about gay men's lives in the two world wars which have never been grouped together and published in one volume. Most of the stories I had uncovered were fragments I had come across through the years, references in books I had been reading since I became interested in gay men's history. Neither is *Fighting Proud*, in spite of its title, intended to be a book specifically about gay servicemen, because I wanted to embrace a much wider range of gay men's lives, and include the home front as well as the front line. All these men played their part, even the gays who enjoyed brief encounters with American GIs in the London blackout.

Due to the availability of material, World War II is given more prominence than World War I.

While researching *Fighting Proud* I discovered that I had something in common with some of the older generations of working-class gay men who also came from loving, caring families like mine. They had lived in tight-knit communities in which they were *accepted* and this really comes across in the interviews given by Alex Purdie and 'John' in Chapter 6. In writing this book I have discovered that it was mostly the working classes who were willing to accept people's differences – rather than so-called 'educated' people. My adopted Aunt Esther once told me about a couple of gay men in her community, close to North End Road, Fulham, who dressed up as women. This would have been in the 1930s.

> They used to wear the most beautiful picture hats. We used to sit on the kerb, and the organ man would come round, and directly that organ pulled up, so these blokes used to come along dressed as women. And they used to dance and we'd sit on the kerb watching them for hours. Yes, that was marvellous. It was lovely.

As a black woman, Esther also told me how *she* was accepted in her community, especially in wartime when everyone pulled together. It appears that in *some* close-knit, working-class communities, gay men and black citizens *were* accepted and protected.

The publication of *Fighting Proud* was scheduled to coincide with the fiftieth anniversary of the Sexual Offences Act. It is my intention to provide part of the 'back story' to this landmark occasion. On 27 July 1967 the Sexual Offences Act became law and partially decriminalised male homosexual acts. However, it only applied to men who were over the age of 21 and not those in the armed services. The ban in the armed services was not lifted until 2000. Though gay adult men could live without the threat of arrest and prison, decriminalisation was not seen as an approval of homosexuality. The campaign to lift the ban in the armed services intensified in the 1990s and attracted a good deal of media attention. *The Times* reported:

> To the utter disgust of the nation's military, four of Britain's best-known soldiers from two world wars will be the target of a bizarre protest [...] which will allege they were homosexual. The statues in Whitehall of field marshals Haig, Kitchener, Montgomery and the Earl Mountbatten will be decked with pink garlands by the gay rights group Outrage. The protest is against attitudes to homosexuality in the armed forces, where it remains a court martial offence. The demonstration [...] has drawn a furious response from some of Britain's leading military figures. Field Marshal Lord Carver says: 'It is a ridiculous protest, which is in bad taste. It does nothing but harm to their cause. But our great soldiers will hardly be turning in their graves: they faced far worse on the battlefields.' [...] incensed General Sir John Hackett, who was wounded three times in the last war and knew both Montgomery and Mountbatten well says 'It is unforgivable. But Mountbatten would have laughed at them, which is what we should do.'[4]

In 1996 I made a small contribution to the campaign. Prompted by a request in the gay newspaper *Capital Gay* for their readers to make contact with the Ministry of Defence, I wrote to them to complain about the draconian ban. I mentioned my dad telling me that, during his National Service days in the RAF in the 1950s, his sergeant was known to be gay and was liked and respected by the recruits. They did not have an issue with it, even though it was a criminal offence. In a letter dated 18 June 1996, Lieutenant Commander A. J. Kirkpatrick of the Royal Navy replied:

> Thank you for your letter concerning homosexuality in the Armed Forces. I would like to emphasise that it is the Department's view, that in situations of imposed communal living, where facilities are shared, space is minimal and privacy at a premium, the mere fact of homosexual orientation can cause unease amongst other personnel.

As a result, relationships can become polarised, morale adversely affected and discipline undermined to the detriment of operational efficiency. We do not believe that a code of conduct, however rigorously enforced, would adequately address these issues, and it would be neither possible, nor desirable, to provide separate facilities for homosexuals and heterosexuals. The prime concern of the Armed Forces in their policy on homosexuality is the maintenance of operational effectiveness. It is not a question of moral judgement, but rather a practical assessment of the effect of homosexuality on military life.

With regard to your observations about the 'minority of bigots' and their comments concerning homosexuality, I would like to make clear that there is, in fact, no evidence to show that the Armed Forces are any more or less prejudiced or homophobic than any other section of the community, nor is such a view supported by the recent Homosexuality Policy Assessment. What does emerge very strongly is the ability of Service personnel to differentiate quite clearly between their own personal views on homosexuality – which, in many cases, are both sympathetic and tolerant – and what they nevertheless perceive as the effect of homosexuality in the operational environment. As you rightly perceive, there is a widespread acceptance by Service personnel that, within the civilian community, homosexuality is a private matter for the individual; it is only the special circumstances of military life that for many render homosexuality unacceptable.

In your letter you mention your father's views on this matter and are correct in suggesting that homosexuals have served in the Armed Forces. Homosexual activity was, however, a criminal offence until 1967 for all males, whether civilians or Servicemen. In the circumstances, it is unlikely that many homosexuals were prepared to reveal their sexual orientation publicly for fear of the legal consequences; they would therefore have been very discreet about their orientation and activities in order not to attract the attention of the civilian or military authorities. Nevertheless, where personnel were found to be homosexual, they were discharged from the Armed

Forces. I hope that this has clarified our position, and I thank you for
the interest that you have shown in this matter.

In reality the situation could be very different. John Webber, a
friend of mine who served in the Merchant Navy from 1963 to 1985,
recalls:

Although homosexuality was illegal there was a tolerance exercised
in all but the most extreme situations. To be honest, some of the best
ship mates I had were openly homosexual. As one, a former Royal
Marine who always wanted to be called Alice, said, 'If they want it
they can have it but we are not here to rape anybody.' Alice, like the
vast majority of gays I sailed with, was exceedingly loyal. In 1982 I
went to the Falklands with Maggie's Army. We transported troops
out to the islands. The Queen's Own Highlanders. Very aptly named
as it turned out! During the three-week voyage south there were
several incidents when some of the lads got too close to each other.
As a civilian ship requisitioned by the MOD we had the ultimate
responsibility for safety, however, as soon as we passed Ascension
Islands we came under the Articles of War and naval discipline was
enforced. There was no leeway as far as Queen's Regulations were
concerned and any homosexual acts which came to light, were dealt
with quite severely. We had a brig on the ship and a couple of the
lads finished the voyage to the Falklands languishing in there. I got
into some quite animated 'discussions' with the Senior Naval Officer,
the Major from the Queen's Own Highlanders, and the Senior RAF
Officer we had on board with us, about the rigorous implementation
of regulations. Their argument was simply 'you can't have men
playing with each other like this, what if you're being attacked
and they are busy taking care of each other's desires.' I found the
attitude antiquated and did tell them about Alice, and several other
ex-marines I sailed with, and who could be more macho than
a Marine? I knew who I would rather have behind me when the
chips were down and it wasn't one of the 'Ruperts' (military slang
for officers).

Introduction

At the end of World War II the British public wanted to get back to 'normal'. Women who had joined the services or worked in war factories were expected to return to the kitchen and cook their husband's tea. Black service personnel and factory workers recruited from their homelands in West Africa and the West Indies were expected to go back and live under colonial rule. However, their lives had been changed forever. They had been liberated from the kitchen and the colonies, and both of these oppressed groups had discovered a sense of freedom.

After the war gay men who had served their King and country found themselves subjected to a vigorous enforcement of the draconian law that would put them in prison if found guilty. But, as John Costello wrote in *Love, Sex and War: Changing Values 1939–45* (1985), the military experience of gay men in World War II had 'chipped away some of the old taboos'. He added that servicemen living in close proximity were made aware that men who chose to have sexual relationships with other men were *not* suffering from sexual perversion or a deadly disease, nor were they cowards or the stereotypical limp-wristed effeminates. More importantly, 'Many thousands of homosexuals discovered a new consciousness of their collective identity in the sub-culture of bars and camaraderie which expanded to meet the wartime demand.'[1]

Fighting Proud is about equality: being equally brave, scared, decisive, uniformed, wounded, and equally dead. War is the great leveller in which we are tested, tried and traumatised. No one ever emerges from war quite the same, whether it is battleground, air raid or that telegram with its irrevocable news. The two world wars proved, incontrovertibly, that there should never be another; both times that message has been ignored. The difference is that today, in some countries, men and women who are required to defend territory and kill other humans are now allowed to tell their mates and officers who they really are when on the parade ground or out of uniform. In the case of gay male servicemen they can now exist openly with the comradeship of their heterosexual counterparts, in the fullest, most supportive, most intimate sense. Fighting proud is heart-thumping and rousing; loving proud should be the same. May the second be humanity's legacy, not the former.

PART I
WORLD WAR I
1914–1918

Lord Kitchener

On 5 June 2016, the centenary of the death of Lord Kitchener, I visited his statue in Horse Guards Parade off Whitehall to pay my respects. As I approached the statue, I noticed two armed police officers standing in front of it. As I came closer to the officers, they looked very serious, and one of them asked: 'Can we help you, sir?' I smiled and explained that I had come to see Lord Kitchener's statue because I had written about him in my latest book. The same officer asked: 'What is your book about?' I informed him it was about gay men's lives in the two world wars. He looked surprised (while his colleague looked suspicious), and he asked: 'Was Lord Kitchener gay?' 'Well, no one is certain, but he never married, lived with a younger male colleague for a number of years, and in his spare time he enjoyed flower arranging.' The officer burst out laughing, his colleague broke into a smile, 'But surely flower arranging doesn't make Lord Kitchener gay?' I agreed and replied: 'Well, I did say no one is certain.' It broke the ice, and I spent an enjoyable time learning from them about some of the other historical landmarks and buildings in Horse Guards Parade. When I departed, the two officers shook my hand and wished me luck.

It could be argued, with some confidence, that Lord Kitchener, or General Viscount Herbert Kitchener of Khartoum (1850–1916), was the most famous and celebrated military leader of World War I. The War Secretary's moustachioed face and pointing finger adorned the famous recruiting poster, 'Your Country Needs You' and this is, without doubt, the best-known and iconic image of the 1914–18 war. In Max Arthur's *Forgotten Voices of the Great War* (2002), Private Thomas McIndoe of the 12th Battalion, Middlesex Regiment, said that he was inspired to join up because of the recruiting poster: 'It was seeing the picture of Kitchener and his finger pointing at you – any position that you took up the finger was always pointing at you – it was a wonderful poster really.'[1]

Jeremy Paxman has summarised Kitchener's pre-World War I achievements in *Great Britain's Great War* (2013): 'suppressor of the Boers in South Africa, commander of the Indian Army, governor of Egypt, slayer of rebels in Sudan' and adds that he had 'a look of imperial invincibility about him [...] Autocratic, taciturn, generally unsmiling and often morose, he became the first serving soldier to sit in cabinet since the middle of the seventeenth century.'[2] However, Paxman remains unconvinced that Kitchener was homosexual and he responded negatively to the gay activist Peter Tatchell who, some years earlier, had informed the *Guardian* that Kitchener and 'Fitz', Captain Oswald Fitzgerald, his faithful and devoted companion, were lovers who 'died in each other's arms when the HMS *Hampshire* struck a mine off Orkney in 1916.'[3] Paxman responded in the *Daily Mail*: 'There is not a shred of evidence to support this claim.' Paxman acknowledges that Kitchener never married and spent nine years with 'Fitz', but 'that hardly adds up to conclusive evidence [...] homosexual activity in the Army was a court martial offence.' But he does accept that 'homosexuals were, and are, almost certainly as well represented in the Army as in any other walk of life.'[4]

The conflict here is often repeated: many historians fail to acknowledge that some homosexuals in the Army (until the ban was lifted in 2000) *would* have been sexually active, in spite of the laws and restrictions imposed on their lifestyle. There is no real, plausible reason to assume that Kitchener and 'Fitz', living together for nine years, were celibate. They lived as a couple in dangerous times, not long after the 1895 trial of the dramatist Oscar Wilde which led to his public humiliation, imprisonment and death in 1900. Jad Adams wrote in *History Today*:

> It would have been a very serious charge. No gentleman in Kitchener's lifetime could tolerate a public accusation of this type. Oscar Wilde's fall came about because he felt obliged to sue for libel at being accused of 'posing as a sodomite' – he was not even being called a sodomite, just that he was acting like one.[5]

This would have had an impact on Kitchener and 'Fitz', and led to them being extremely secretive and careful. Adams adds, 'Someone as discreet as Kitchener, who destroyed all his own papers and was never accused of a sexual crime, would be unlikely to leave any direct evidence.'

Almost without exception, Kitchener's biographers have referred to the possibility of his homosexuality, and all of them, like Paxman, have dismissed it as unfounded rumour. In 1970 H. Montgomery Hyde mentioned Kitchener's 'abnormal condition' (an unfortunate description) in *The Other Love*, his survey of homosexuality in Britain. He also drew upon Kitchener's 1958 biographer, Philip Magnus to highlight the devotion 'Fitz' had for the older man: 'their intimate association was happy and fortunate. Fitzgerald, like Kitchener, was a bachelor and celibate; he devoted the whole of the rest of his life exclusively to Kitchener.'[6] So, while stating that the two men had a happy 'intimate association', it is impossible for Magnus to acknowledge that they could have taken that intimacy into the bedroom and had sexual relations. Hyde also quotes Queen Victoria, as many of Kitchener's biographers do: 'They say he dislikes women but I can only say he was very nice to me.'

In *The Kitchener Enigma* (1985), Trevor Royle describes 'Fitz' as Kitchener's 'constant companion and paladin who put his chief's interests above all others. Many resented the aura of quarantine

"Fitz" brought to Kitchener's entourage.' Royle said that Prime Minister Herbert Asquith 'contemptuously dismissed him as Kitchener's "familiar"; others thought the relationship more physical than spiritual and hinted at a homosexual relationship.' 'Fitz', a quiet, orderly man who was 25 years younger than Kitchener, provided the older man with companionship. Their shared interests included fine arts, and they became partners in East African estates and property enterprise. In 1916 'Fitz' even shared Kitchener's death.[7]

However, John Pollock, in his 1998 biography, *Kitchener: The Road to Omdurman*, felt it necessary to add an appendix entitled 'Kitchener and Sex'. Pollock takes great pains to refute the claim that Kitchener was homosexual and criticises Frank Richardson, a retired medical major-general, for including Kitchener in his 1981 book *Mars Without Venus: A Study of Some Homosexual Generals*: 'He suggested that Kitchener's passion for porcelain and his love of flower arranging were symptoms of homosexuality. Porcelain is not the preserve of homosexual collectors.'[8] From a gay perspective, it would be difficult if not impossible to accept anything that Pollock said on Kitchener and homosexuality. He was, in fact, Reverend John Pollock, an Anglican clergyman, a devout Christian who was the devoted friend and official biographer of the American evangelist Billy Graham. This leads one to suspect that he was no friend of the gay community. When the gay historian Rictor Norton reviewed Pollock's book, he said:

Pollock virtually defines homosexuality in terms of physical acts rather than by desire or a mindset. He does not countenance the concept of the chaste homosexual, though I would have thought that a Christian biographer would be aware that 'non-practicing' homosexuals burdened with a duty to God were quite common, that celibacy and homosexuality are not incompatible, that Kitchener might just possibly have been sober, upright, chaste and gay [...] His love of flower arranging and interior decorating is rightly dismissed as insufficient proof that he was gay, but Pollock holds up a similarly risible theory that his platonic friendships with older married women in later life suggests that he was *not* gay![9]

Regarding Kitchener's sexuality, the final comments in *Fighting Proud* will go to two gay historians: James Gardiner and Keith Howes. In an email to the author (28 November 2015), Gardiner says:

Strikes me there is no hard evidence either way. Just because a man never marries, devotes his entire life to an exclusively masculine uniformed career, collects porcelain and is interested in flower arranging and spends the last decade of his life in the exclusive company of a beautiful young man many years his junior, just doesn't make him a poof, does it?

In an email to the author (29 November 2015), Howes says: 'Lord Kitchener (or "Kitty" as we'll dub him) may have been a devoted husband who had sex with his wife every night or a celibate Christian or an asexual man. None of the above prevents him from being attracted to men or, in Kitty's case, one particular male.'

On 5 June 1916 HMS *Hampshire*, the cruiser on which Lord Kitchener and his beloved 'Fitz' were travelling on a mission to Russia, hit a mine and sank. Kitchener and 'Fitz' were among those who perished. The body of 'Fitz' was recovered and there followed a full military funeral in his hometown of Eastbourne. Kitchener's body was not found, adding to the nation's sense of grief. His unexpected death generated an extraordinary outpouring of love and respect for the military leader throughout the country. Said John Pollock in his epilogue to *Kitchener* (2001):

A stunned British public could hardly believe that he was gone [...] On the Western Front in France the troops felt the same bewilderment and shock at Kitchener's death [...] yet perhaps it was a mercy that he did not live to learn that no fewer than 19,000 British soldiers died on the first day of the Battle of the Somme on 1 July 1916 less than one month after his death.[10]

Jeremy Paxman wrote:

> the reaction to Kitchener's disappearance had about it some of the
> characteristics of the death of Princess Diana. Kitchener – tall,
> tough, cold-hearted – was a hero of a different age, the man the
> politicians had sent for when war was inevitable, and many people
> found it impossible to imagine winning the war without him.[11]

A memorial service at St Paul's Cathedral was delayed until 15
June 1916 in case Kitchener's body was washed up, thus making it
possible for a funeral to take place. His body was never found. The
service at St Paul's, attended by King George V and Queen Mary,
was a fitting tribute. Afterwards, the King described the service
as 'most impressive. Mama and all the family were there, all the
Govt., Ambassadors and ministers and thousands of soldiers.'[12]
The 'family' included Edward, Prince of Wales who, ten years later,
unveiled Kitchener's statue on Horse Guards Parade. He said: 'It
will always be within just surmise that had the span of his life been
but a little extended the forger of the great weapon of war would
have been a great architect of peace.'[13]

A British soldier who was lost at sea in World War I, Kitchener
has no known grave and yet, while he has gradually faded from
the memory of the British public, there are memorials all over
the country. London alone has quite a few: a memorial cross
for Kitchener was unveiled at St Botolph's Church in 1916 (near
Liverpool Street Station), perhaps one of the first memorials of
World War I in England; the North-West Chapel of All Souls at
St Paul's Cathedral was rededicated the Kitchener Memorial in
1925; an English Heritage Blue Plaque was erected to mark where
Kitchener lived at 2 Carlton Gardens, St James's, Westminster. And
then there is the impressive statue in Horse Guards Parade.[14]

2

Unfortunate Fellows

I n 1998 Niall Ferguson said in *The Pity of War*, 'In the period 1914–19 twenty-two officers and 270 other ranks were court-martialled for "indecency" with another man. Generally homosexual officers slept with officers and men with men.'[1] In 2004 Richard Holmes in *Tommy: The British Soldier* noted, 'the number of courts martial for "indecency" is surprisingly low' and this reflects several facts:

> Firstly, some homosexual officers and men sublimated their desires, at what cost we will never know. Secondly, there was often a clear understanding that soldiers in monogamous relationships ought not to be penalised. David Jones wrote movingly of a homosexual couple in his company [in *In Parenthesis*, 1961] [...] And thirdly, it was often easy enough for officers to masturbate in a two-man room in a hut, or for private soldiers to do the same in the dark recesses of a tent or dugout. 'Brook, Jackson and myself all had some homosexual tendencies,' wrote Eric Hiscock [in *The Bells of Hell Go Ting-a-Ling*, 1976] 'and in the days and nights of stress we masturbated, but kisses on unshaven faces were rare, and then only at moments of acute danger'.[2]

Among those who found themselves involved in courts martial that concerned homosexual acts was Raymond Asquith, Oxford

scholar, English barrister and the son of H. H. Asquith, the then
prime minister (1908–16). When Raymond joined the Army in
December 1914 he was commissioned as a second lieutenant into
the 16th (County of London) Battalion, London Regiment. He was
transferred to the 3rd Battalion, Grenadier Guards, on 14 August
1915 and assigned as a staff officer. During his time as a staff officer,
he reluctantly became involved in a court martial case involving an
officer who had been accused of homosexual offences. In a letter to
Lady Diana Manners dated 27 August 1916, Raymond described
himself as a man of 'wide sympathies', but he hoped to persuade Sir
Edward Carson, who had successfully prosecuted Oscar Wilde, to
take the case from him:

> All the morning I have spent conferring with a bn. Officer
> who wants me to defend him at a Court Martial on a charge
> of 'homosexualism', as these overeducated soldiers persist in
> misnaming these elementary departures from the strict letters of
> 'Infantry Training 1914'. His story seemed a very queer one even to
> me who esteem myself a man of wide sympathies. But I am hoping
> to persuade Sir E. Carson to take my place, as I think the situation
> demands a deeper reservoir of cant than anyone but an Ulster
> covenanter can extemporarily command.[3]

On 12 September Raymond wrote to his wife Katharine Asquith,
informing her of the outcome of the court martial at which the
accused had been found guilty and given an extremely harsh
sentence:

> My client in the Court Martial was an unfortunate fellow […] He
> was convicted on 4 out of the 5 charges and sentenced not only to be
> cashiered but to serve one year's imprisonment – most barbarous I
> call it. His buttons were cut off in the Orderly room yesterday and he
> was taken off to Rouen by the military police, poor devil. His father
> was killed earlier in the war and he is the 6th consecutive generation
> of his family to hold a commission in the Grenadiers.[4]

Three days later Raymond was dead. He had made a request to return to active duty with his battalion and while leading his men into battle on 15 September at the Battle of Flers-Courcelette, he was fatally wounded.

Sources of information about the lives of gay men in the armed services in World War I are hard to find. However, in *Jamaican Volunteers in World War I* (2004), Richard Smith describes what happened to Ernest Dunn, a white Jamaican officer who was cashiered for homosexuality in 1917. A former 'minor' civil servant, Ernest enlisted as a private in the East Surrey Regiment. In March 1915 he earned a commission as a second lieutenant in the 3rd Battalion of the Northumberland Fusiliers but suffered concussion and shrapnel wounds in August 1916. After recuperating for almost a year, Ernest returned to his unit in July 1917. However, within weeks of his return, he was denounced by a fellow officer, Second Lieutenant Yates, for mutual sexual acts while the two men shared a billet. Richard Smith explains:

> Dunn fiercely denied that such contact had taken place, both during and in the wake of the case. However, aside from the sexual aspects of the case, it is evident that Dunn was quite open about his need for comfort and emotional support due to his continuing fragile mental condition; a need to which his accuser seems to have initially responded positively. The military authorities seem to have been as much concerned about this display of male vulnerability and affection, and the boundaries of male friendship, as about the alleged instances of sexual contact. While comradely and platonic friendship between a younger and older male were highly regarded in the masculine culture of the period, any intimation of sexual contact was held to diminish such relationships. Although there was insufficient evidence for a court martial, Dunn was stripped of his commission and dismissed from the army. As a result, he also lost his peacetime position in the Jamaican civil service, although he subsequently enlisted in the Royal Naval Air Service for the remainder of the war without disclosing his recent army service. Yates on the other hand had his commission

reinstated on the personal intervention of Lord Derby, Secretary of
State for War, on the grounds that he had been 'led astray'.[5]

It was not always the end of the road for men who were caught
in compromising situations. Solicitors could find ways of getting
some of them off the hook. In the Imperial War Museum Sound
Archive, a former sailor called Joseph Vine, interviewed in 1976,
recalls an incident on board his ship, HMS *London*. Joseph said that
there were a large number of courts martial on board his ship in the
year 1913–14. He explains there was not enough for the sailors to
do and it led to arguments. Joseph recalls one of the courts martial
was for 'sodomy'. An officer had seen two sailors, one older, one
younger, in a compromising situation and a court martial followed.
But the 'Canteen Committee' had asked the captain for a solicitor
to defend the older sailor. At the trial the solicitor asked: 'Were
the lights on?' 'No,' was the reply. Then the solicitor proved that it
would be impossible for the officer (witness) to see the two men in
a compromising situation because the lights were not on. So, Joseph
said, 'the two men got off.'[6]

Newspapers of the period occasionally reported stories about
'effeminate' servicemen who found themselves in trouble. Private
William Edward Mason of the 2/5th King's Liverpool Regiment
shot himself in camp at Aldershot and in August 1916 the *Dover
and East Kent News* informed its readers what was disclosed at the
inquest in a detailed report which began, 'Curious evidence, says the
Military Mail, published at Aldershot, was heard regarding a young
soldier's strange effeminate ways at an inquest held at Aldershot.'
When Corporal Lonsdale gave evidence he stated that he had heard
the report of a rifle from the tent of the deceased. On entering, he
found the deceased lying on his back, and asked him what the matter
was. Private Mason just raised his hand to his chest and said, 'It's no
use, Corporal, I'm done,' and died almost immediately from a bullet
wound to the chest a few inches from his heart. Private Mason had
enlisted on 15 February 1915 and had not been abroad. He was 22
years old, and unmarried. He was an effeminate man who had been

away from the regiment for three days, during which time he was arrested in Dover after being discovered masquerading in women's clothes and had been sentenced to 107 days' military detention. He had never threatened suicide. In the newspaper report it said,

> Corporal Mercer, 2/5th King's Liverpool Regiment, stated that the deceased was in his section, and occupied the same tent. He was a good worker, and was quite normal excepting his effeminate ideas. He was ragged a little, but nothing out of the ordinary. The men in the regiment knew of the Dover episode, and he was chaffed a good deal over it, but there was no serious ragging.[7]

A verdict of 'Suicide during temporary insanity' was returned at the inquest.

In June 1916 the *North-Eastern Daily Gazette* reported on the sad tale of a soldier who deserted and, dressed as a woman, tried to find a position as a lady's companion. In a report entitled 'Soldier's Masquerade – Disowned by Sisters for his Effeminate Ways', the *Gazette* explained that, at Highgate, 22-year-old Frederick Wright of Percy Road, North Finchley, dressed in smart female attire for his court appearance,

> was charged on remand with being an idle and disorderly person found in female clothes, with giving false particulars when registering at a boarding-house, and also, in his own confession, with being a deserter from the Royal Fusiliers. When the police called on him Wright protested that he was Kathleen Woodhouse, but ultimately admitted his sex, saying that he loved beautiful clothes. It was now proved that he failed to return to his regiment on June 5th, when his pass expired, and Detective Inspector Ferrier said that Wright was bound over on March 7th at Marylebone for attempting suicide by taking veronal tablets. His two sisters refused to have anything to do with him because of his effeminate ways. The Chairman: Did he join the Army voluntarily? Inspector Ferrier: No, that was a condition of being bound over. He was taken by a detective to the Attestation

Station to enlist right away. When he took lodgings at Finchley, he said that he wanted to live a quiet life, and that he was endeavouring to find a situation as a companion to a lady. (Laughter). Wright was remanded to await an escort, the Chairman remarking that he did not suppose he would be of much use in the Army. In the meantime the police might put him into proper garb. 'I should not send him to the Army in this condition,' the Chairman added.[8]

Files at The National Archives can provide some information about homosexuals in the Great War. 'Prisoner 214428 R. Hulme' was another soldier who is described as 'effeminate'. Before the war he worked as a 'girl mimic' in music halls, but he faced difficulties after joining the Army. He is described in a short report dated 7 July 1917 by Captain H. Yellowlees of the Royal Army Medical Corps as:

a degenerate, very hysterical, somewhat depraved patient, with an extremely bad family history. He is quite unfit for service at present, and it is a matter for surprise that he has been able to carry on for so long. He is unstrung, effeminate, and emotional, and I suspect that at one time he has been a homosexual. The 'self-inflicted wounds' are simply superficial scratches, and were in no sense an attempt to injure or incapacitate himself, in my opinion. In any case, I think he should be regarded as having been quite irresponsible at the time, and should be dealt with as an ordinary case and evacuated either to D. Block, Netley, or to the 4th London General Hospital in due course, as his condition at time may warrant. I expect that he may shortly become fit for the latter destination.[9]

Further investigation reveals that Hulme was Private 214428 Robert Hulme who served with the York Light Infantry and the Royal Engineers throughout World War I. He may have been described as a 'degenerate' and 'depraved', but Robert received the British War Medal and Victory Medal for his services to King and country.

When Tommy Keele was interviewed for the Imperial War Museum's Sound Archive in 1991, he was 98 years old with a clear memory of the time he spent on the Western Front in the Great War. However, although he was heterosexual, Tommy spent part of the war dressed as a woman. For the first three years he was an ordinary lance corporal in the Middlesex Regiment but, in 1917, he joined a concert party called the Ace of Spades. Using the stage name 'Dot Keele', Tommy took female parts in theatres behind the lines and provided entertainment for sex-starved soldiers. He said, 'The audience never imagined that during the war years, in France, they would see variety acts like us. People didn't always know I was a man dressed as a woman. I was wearing a very low-cut evening dress.' When a colonel refused to believe Tommy was a 'Tommy', he had to go along to the colonel's barracks 'to prove I was a little lance corporal in the Middlesex Regiment. He was disgusted.'[10] When Joshua Levine wrote about Tommy for the *Telegraph* in 2013, he said, 'Occasional disgust was balanced by the adoration of Tommy's fans, the soldiers. He happily remembers their requests for signed photos which brought him "a nice little income" [...] The tapes reveal Tommy to be a lively storyteller [...] For an oral historian such as myself, they are gold dust.'[11]

Even at nearly 100 years old, Tommy was determined not to be mistaken for a homosexual or, as he put it, a 'sissy'. Said Joshua Levine:

> his voice rises in anger, and he recounts an episode from his earlier Army career when he had offered a sergeant, exhausted from the trenches, a share of 'a very nice bedroom with a double bed'. In the middle of the night, Tommy felt the sergeant's hand wandering near his bottom. He brushed the hand away, but it returned. 'Don't you dare!' said Tommy, but the sergeant did dare, and Tommy woke a little later to find the man on top of him. 'So', says Tommy, 'I really battered his head and face.' The sergeant threatened him with a court martial – so he shouted back that buggery carried the death penalty. 'But,' says Tommy, 'I was a bit sorry for him afterwards. There was no such thing as real girls around, and anything was good enough. But if I was good enough, I didn't want to be!'[12]

3

Edward Brittain

When the film *Testament of Youth* was released in 2015 I was aware that it was based on Vera Brittain's book of the same name, published in 1933. In this acclaimed 'Autobiographical Study', as she termed it, the author wrote movingly about the impact of World War I on the women of Britain, and the country's middle-class civilians. I knew that Vera's book was considered a landmark in feminist literature for its depiction of the difficulties she faced as an educated woman in a male-dominated society. It has also played a major part in the way the Great War is remembered and understood. I found the film version of Vera's memoir absorbing, well-crafted and beautifully acted. During World War I Vera had to cope with the tragic losses of the three most important men in her life: her fiancé, Roland Leighton, a poet and soldier who was killed in action in 1915 (shot by a sniper); her friend Victor Richardson, wounded in action, who died in 1917; and her beloved brother Edward Brittain, an Army officer who was killed in action in 1918. Vera and Roland's relationship was the main focus of the film, though her close relationship with and adoration of Edward was also depicted. While watching the story unfold, I felt very strongly that something important was missing, but I was unable to work out what the filmmakers were suppressing. I had been unaware of Edward Brittain's existence until I saw *Testament of Youth* yet it was *his* character that intrigued me. I sensed that the filmmakers were hiding something about Edward, especially in the hospital scene with his sister Vera and the reading of a letter from his friend Geoffrey Thurlow, but it just wasn't made clear. When Nigel Jones wrote about Edward and the film in the *Mail on Sunday*, he said: 'Edward had met and formed an intimate relationship with Geoffrey Thurlow, a sensitive scholar who wanted to become a priest, but had returned to the front despite being badly shell-shocked.'[1] Geoffrey was killed in action in 1917. After viewing the film, I researched Edward and discovered not only that claims had been made that he was homosexual, but that it is possible his death was suicide.

Captain Edward Brittain of the Sherwood Foresters was described by Richard Holmes in *Soldiers* (2011) as 'a classic member of the sparkling generation swept away by the war'.[2] Holmes acknowledged that we can never be sure of the circumstances of Edward's death, but it could have been suicide. During the war, mail was censored and 'in a letter to a former officer of his company – opened in a random check – Brittain had described homosexual relationships with private soldiers'.[3] Edward's commanding officer warned the young man he should be more cautious. Edward realised, to his horror, that if this case was investigated and he was found guilty, he could face a sentence of dismissal and imprisonment as well as public humiliation for himself and his family. In 1916 Edward had been awarded the Military Cross 'for conspicuous gallantry and leadership during an attack' on the first day of the Battle of the Somme. It was pinned to his chest by King George V at Buckingham Palace. However, Edward's bravery on the front line would not have made a difference to his case.

Officially, Edward was killed in action in June 1918 on the Asiago Plateau in northern Italy while leading a counter-offensive against an Austrian attack. But in a book that was written by Mark Bostridge to coincide with the release of the film *Testament of Youth*, the truth was finally revealed. Bostridge explained that Edward's tragic death led Vera to make contact with his commanding officer: 'For several months she pursued him relentlessly, convinced he knew far more about Edward's part in the action than he was prepared to tell. However, it was all to no avail, and Edward's final hours remained cloaked in mystery.'[4] Vera recounted as much in *Testament of Youth*. An Austrian sniper had shot him, the colonel told Vera, just after the counter-attack: 'I looked at him in silent reproach, for I frankly did not believe him.'[5] Mark Bostridge explained that, in 1934, after the publication of Vera's book, and 15 years after Edward's death, the commanding officer had a change of heart and, unexpectedly, wrote to her. He confirmed what she had suspected in 1918: 'he had withheld certain facts of a personal nature about Edward's death.'[6]

The commanding officer, unable to write down the facts, requested that they meet. But here the trail goes cold, for whatever information the commanding officer shared with Vera remained with her until she died in 1970. No written record of their meeting was ever found. However, not long after this encounter, Vera wrote a novel, *Honourable Estate* (1936), in which she depicted a homosexual character called Richard Alleyndene, the brother of the heroine. To avoid a court martial for homosexuality, Richard becomes involved in the Gallipoli campaign with the intention of being killed. In *Honourable Estate*, Richard writes a farewell letter to his sister: 'I can't confront Father and Mother with the fact that their son is what they would call vicious and immoral instead of a virtuous patriotic hero.'

In the detailed 'Afterword' to his book, Mark Bostridge finally revealed the truth about what had happened to Edward. After establishing that the commanding officer was Colonel Charles Hudson, a career soldier and holder of the Victoria Cross, Bostridge made contact with Hudson's son. The son informed him that his father, who had died in 1959, had recorded all that he knew about the circumstances of Edward's death in his unpublished memoirs. Hudson's son was happy for Bostridge to read the manuscript, but requested that he first seek the permission of Vera Brittain's daughter Shirley Williams. When this was eventually achieved, Bostridge was given access to the manuscript. He said:

On 12 June 1918, Edward's commanding officer, Colonel Hudson, had received a communication from the Provost Marshal, the head of the Military Police, informing him that a letter written by one of his officers, while on leave, to another officer in the battalion, had been intercepted and censored at the Base. The contents of this letter made it plain that the two officers were involved in homosexual relations with men in their company. The more senior of the two was Captain Brittain. [Hudson] had a conversation with Edward in which he gave him a warning [...] Edward turned white and made no comment. But it was clear he had understood. Edward was the only officer killed on 15 June. After the battle, Hudson had reached the terrible conclusion that, faced in all likelihood with the prospect of a court martial when they came out of the line, imprisonment and the subsequent disgrace that would ensue, Edward had either shot himself or deliberately courted death by presenting himself as an easy target for a sniper's bullet.[7]

The subject is not really touched upon in the film version of *Testament of Youth*, except obliquely. Perhaps the filmmakers felt that a treatment of Edward Brittain's sexuality and the part it may have played in the events leading to his death would have been a diversion from the major themes of Vera Brittain's memoir. Mark Bostridge says:

The film is only two hours long and many more salient events and details had to be omitted. I don't myself believe that Edward and Geoffrey Thurlow had a homosexual relationship. You could look at their letters, if you haven't done so already, in *Letters from a Lost Generation* (1998). *Vera Brittain: A Life* by myself and Paul Berry (1995), especially chapter 3, offers a much more considered treatment of the subject of Edward Brittain's friendships and his last days than the short book published in the wake of the film.[8]

4

James Whale, R. C. Sherriff and
Journey's End

It has not been easy to find information about homosexuals in World War I. Historians have barely acknowledged the existence of gay men in the military and the trenches. However, a few years *after* the war, in 1925, the homosexual dramatist J. R. Ackerley succeeded in staging his play, *The Prisoners of War*, set during World War I, at the Lyric, Hammersmith. Censors failed to identify the homosexual theme of the play, which focused on Captain Conrad, a prisoner of war who is attracted to the handsome young Lieutenant Grayle. Ackerley's drama was a critical and commercial success. Three years later, R. C. Sherriff's play *Journey's End* was first staged in London and, though homosexuality is not *explicit* in the story, this most celebrated and popular of theatrical ventures succeeded in placing *homosocial* relationships centre stage.

Journey's End was directed by James Whale, who was also responsible for directing the American stage and film versions. Set in the British trenches in 1918, the drama focuses on the relationships of a group of British officers sharing a dugout just before a German attack. Sherriff's anti-war message is partly related by the tortured, helpless and confused Captain Stanhope. Theatre critics applauded the play. One of the toughest, James Agate, from the *Sunday Times*, also reviewed plays for BBC Radio and told listeners: 'I cannot believe that there was any single member of the audience this afternoon who was not only deeply moved but also exalted and even exhilarated by this tragedy.' Agate became the play's 'most powerful advocate'.[1] In time it had its detractors. The left-wing theatre director Joan Littlewood, famous for the anti-war stage musical *Oh! What a Lovely War* (1963), hated it. In his diary Kenneth Williams referred to the play, when it was revived in 1972, as 'uninspired pedestrian muck'.[2] If the play achieved greatness in 1928 it was in the writing of Sherriff and the direction of Whale. Through them, *Journey's End* became a haunting, poetic vision of male bonding.

James Whale was at ease with his homosexuality and, since his death in 1957, this has been acknowledged by his biographers, including Mark Gatiss in *James Whale: A Biography or The Would-Be Gentleman* (1995), and in the film *Gods and Monsters* (1998), starring Ian McKellen as Whale. However, Sherriff's sexuality remains a mystery, although he was more than likely a closeted, celibate homosexual, like the film director Anthony Asquith (see 'Not Forgotten'). Born in Hampton Wick, on the Thames, Robert Cedric Sherriff was working as a clerk in an insurance office at the start of the war, and in 1915 he was commissioned into the 9th Battalion of the East Surrey Regiment as a second lieutenant. He saw active service in France from September 1916 to August 1917, when he was severely wounded at Passchendaele near Ypres. Sherriff was demobbed in 1919 with the rank of captain and remained a 'confirmed bachelor' until the end of his life. He died in 1975.

It was not until the publication, in 2013, of Robert Gore-Langton's *Journey's End: The Classic War Play Explored*, that Sherriff's homosexuality was confirmed, though 'non-practising'. Gore-Langton described Sherriff as:

> gentle, straitlaced, highly sporty, hero-worshipping, deeply conservative and proudly unintellectual [...] His love life is a total

mystery […] He never married and lived with his mother nearly all her life. Most people connected to the play today seem to have intuited that he was gay – a likely hunch I'd say. He seems to have diverted all his bachelor energies entirely into his work, his garden and his coin collection.[3]

Three years later, Sherriff's biographer, Roland Wales, commented:

Throughout his entire life there is no evidence of Sherriff entering into any kind of physical relationship with anyone. He would always remain most comfortable in the company of men – and frequently young men, especially through coaching them in rowing clubs – but most likely because he thought in the same way that they did, rather than that he was attracted to them (although that can never be wholly ruled out).[4]

In October 1915 Whale left art school to enlist in the Inns of Court Officer Training Corps as an officer cadet – quite an achievement for the son of a working-class blast furnaceman from Dudley in the Black Country area of the West Midlands. In the summer of 1916 he was commissioned as a second lieutenant in the 2nd Battalion of the 7th Worcestershire Regiment in France, serving on the Somme, and at Arras and Ypres. Mark Gatiss describes Whale as a modest man who would bring his intimate knowledge of dugout life to Sherriff's *Journey's End*. He was:

inclined to make light of the time he spent in action […] Furthermore, the war presented the chance to escape from Dudley and see something of the world […] It would also have given him his first experience of close contact with other men and, in all probability, his sexuality.[5]

In August 1917 Whale was taken prisoner of war on the Western Front in Flanders. He spent the next 15 months in a POW camp with 1,400 other men before being repatriated in December 1918.

While imprisoned, he pursued his artistic interests: acting, writing and designing sets for amateur stage productions which took place in the camp.

As a result of the success of *Journey's End* in London and New York, Universal offered Whale an opportunity to direct a film version, made in Hollywood in 1930. Whale knew exactly what he wanted. Just before filming commenced he said:

> When it comes to human emotions people are the same [...] and the simpler a big situation is presented to them the harder it strikes. The whole foundation of *Journey's End*, to my mind, is that it presents an unusual situation in a most appealing way. Some critics have said that it violates the ethics of the drama. It does not, because the essential element in all drama is truth.[6]

One of the most striking features of *Journey's End* is the intimacy in the relationships of its male characters. Though homosexuality is not *explicit* in *Journey's End*, the intense relationships of the soldiers in the trenches sometimes bring to the surface deeper feelings. Stanhope, an alcoholic, has spent three traumatic years at the Front. He is suffering from stress and looks to the older, calmer Osborne, affectionately known as 'Uncle', for advice, comfort and reassurance. The male bonding or homosocial relationship between Stanhope and his beloved 'Uncle' continues to develop throughout the drama. They share a close, intimate friendship within the claustrophobic confines of their dugout, and this occasionally brings to the surface deeper feelings and emotions. For example, at the beginning of the play, 'Uncle' defends Stanhope to Captain Hardy, who has criticised him: 'You don't know him as I do. I love that fellow. I'd go to hell with him.' Taken aback, the captain responds with 'Oh, you sweet sentimental old darling.' There are several intimate and tender exchanges between 'Uncle' and Stanhope. This freedom of expression is made possible by the interplay between the two men, and the camaraderie they enjoy. When 'Uncle' puts the exhausted, drunken Stanhope to bed, the latter exclaims 'Kiss me Uncle!' To which 'Uncle' replies, 'Kiss you be hanged.'

Stanhope is angered by the arrival of the young second lieutenant, Harry Raleigh, who not only went to the same school as Stanhope, but has hero-worshipped him ever since. Stanhope treats Raleigh with contempt, and this creates further tension in the dugout. However, after 'Uncle' is tragically killed in a raid, Stanhope suffers a breakdown, and in doing so he subjects Raleigh to a hysterical outburst after the young man has accused him of not caring about 'Uncle's' death. 'You think I don't care?' he cries, 'The one man I could trust. My best friend. The one man I could talk to as a man to a man, who understood everything. And you think I don't care. You little fool.' It is an outburst one would expect from someone who has lost a lover, not a fellow officer in wartime. After Raleigh leaves the room, Stanhope breaks down and sobs uncontrollably. It is the drama's most powerful and emotionally charged moment, with Stanhope's loss, confusion and desperation powerfully expressed.

The role of Stanhope was perfectly suited to Colin Clive, who had played the role on stage before being cast in the film. Clive had attended the Royal Military Academy Sandhurst, but a knee injury disqualified him from military service. He was a complex and confused man whose alcoholism had been caused partly by his inability to come to terms with his homosexuality. Whale had deliberately cast him as Stanhope because of the close parallels of his tortured private life with the character created by Sherriff.

After making *Journey's End*, Whale continued directing films in Hollywood for just over a decade. He enjoyed Hollywood, and a long-term contract with Universal that paid him well. In her autobiography the character actress Elsa Lanchester, who worked with Whale, recalled that her husband, the actor Charles Laughton, who was a closeted and self-loathing homosexual, shared her opinion of Whale's talents as a film director, but thought him vulgar and a snob. Laughton referred to him as The Would-Be Gentleman, taken from the title of a play Whale had once acted in. Said Lanchester: 'Jimmy Whale said, "You will love it here in Hollywood, Charles. I'm pouring the gold through my hair and enjoying every minute of it!" Charles was horrified by that. But Jimmy did love money. He came from a poverty-stricken family.'[7] According to the British film magazine *Picturegoer* in 1934: 'When he started work on *Journey's End* Whale was earning £15 for the whole job of producing the play. He came away from America after directing the film, with a contract for £15,000 a picture in his pocket.'[8]

A recurring theme in Whale's films is the plight of social outcasts, the most famous example being the 'monster' played by Boris Karloff in *Frankenstein* (1931). Whale became famous for *Frankenstein* and several other Gothic fantasy films where he displayed 'a genius for finding beauty and humour in horror, and through his intelligent use of wilful scenic distortion, expressionistic lighting and witty musical scores, realised both the spirituality and pathos of the creatures and the fear and loathing they evoked'.[9] There are other notable outcasts in his films, such as the doomed streetwalker Myra in the melodrama *Waterloo Bridge* (1931), the scientist Dr Jack Griffin in *The Invisible Man* (1933), scripted by R. C. Sherriff, and the African American singer Julie, who is discovered passing for white and subjected to virulent racism in America's South, in the musical *Show Boat* (1936). With Captain Stanhope in *Journey's End*, these characters reveal Whale's understanding of and empathy with men and women who are considered social outcasts and victimised for being different.

It seems that in the 1940s Whale became a victim himself, of Hollywood's homophobia. Unlike other gay directors, who stayed in the closet, Whale remained dangerously indiscreet, as the film director Robert Aldrich later observed:

> Jimmy Whale was the first guy [in Hollywood] who refused to stay in the closet [...] all those other guys played it straight, and they were onboard, but Whale said 'Fuck it, I'm a great director and I don't have to put up with this bullshit' – and he *was* a great director. And he was unemployed after that – never worked again.[10]

Whale 'retired' from film directing in 1941, supposedly to concentrate on his painting. Commenting on the end of his life, Elsa Lanchester said:

The poet Shelley had written that 'poetry turns all things to loveliness; it exalts the beauty of that which is most beautiful, and it adds beauty to that which is most deformed.' James Whale seemed to carry out this thought, giving his monsters spiritual beauty and pathos, over and above the horror [...] And then, in 1957, James Whale was found dead 'under mysterious circumstances' – floating in his large pool at the foot of his hillside garden.[11]

5

Ralph and Monty: The Man I Love

In the last century there existed a gay couple who lived together for several decades, in spite of the repressive law that existed until 1967 and would have seen them in prison. Middle-class Monty and working-class Ralph managed to escape detection because Monty, the elder of the two, 'employed' Ralph as his personal manservant and chauffeur. Many gay couples who wanted to live together avoided detection in this way, but it meant that they had to lead double-lives. Monty and Ralph met in the 1930s and were devoted to each other, but what is really extraordinary about this couple is the legacy they left: numerous photographs and over 300 of Ralph's wartime letters to Monty. The latter are a treasure trove which should be valued more widely; a small selection can be found at the end of this chapter. The love and devotion these two men had for each other were no different from those of a heterosexual couple. We should be thankful that the letters have survived; many gay men, in fear of being exposed, destroyed such personal things: letters, diaries, private papers. They are gone forever. So Monty and Ralph have been placed at the very heart of this book, which is where they belong. This chapter helps to bridge the gap between the two world wars, for Monty served in the British Army in World War I and Ralph served in the RAF in World War II.

When Ralph Hall was drafted into the RAF in 1940 he knew all about the joys of gay sex and what it was like to have a long and loving relationship with another man. Ralph was still in his teens in 1930 when he met Montague 'Monty' Glover, a World War I veteran. They fell in love and lived together for over 50 years until Monty died in 1983. In his later years, Monty was described by his friends as a charming, if somewhat reserved man, and Ralph as an outgoing, cheerful 'cockney'. After Ralph died in 1987, their house, known as 'Little Windovers', near the village of Balsall Heath, between Coventry and Leamington Spa, was put up for sale. Miraculously Monty's diaries, scrapbooks and vast photograph collection as well as wartime letters from Ralph were saved.

Montague Charles Glover was born in Leamington Spa in 1898 into a middle-class family and in 1916 he joined the Army, the Artists' Rifles Regiment. Appointed to a commission as second lieutenant in the Territorial Force, Monty was posted to the 6th Warwickshire Regiment. While serving in Italy in 1918 he was awarded the Military Cross for bravery. After the war, Monty worked as an architect for 30 years and based himself in London. During World War II, he was employed by the government.

In London, Monty had many sexual encounters with 'rough trade': builders, road-workers, dockers, labourers, young military men, including guardsmen, and the 'rent boys' (prostitutes) who hung around Trafalgar Square. In his spare time Monty enjoyed keeping scrapbooks of magazine pictures of body builders, sportsmen and soldiers. He was also a keen and prolific photographer and found great pleasure in photographing some of the young men he met. Every year of his life with Ralph is documented in snapshots by Monty of his young lover. In 1988 Ralph's next of kin put Monty's possessions up for auction and one lot, purchased by the gay ephemera collector James Gardiner, was a cardboard box that contained much of Monty's collection. The precious store included negatives from photographs Monty had taken since serving in World War I, as well as journals and Ralph's World War II correspondence. A selection of these were later published in Gardiner's superb book, *A Class Apart: The Private Pictures of Montague Glover* (1992).[1]

Ralph Edward Hall was born in 1913, not in London's East End, as some sources claim, but across the river in South London. His birth certificate confirms that Ralph was born in Vine Street Buildings off Tooley Street in Bermondsey (now in the London Borough of Southwark). Ralph came from a poor working-class family, had eight brothers and sisters, and his father worked as a wharf labourer and served in the Army during World War I. This class difference was not an issue for Monty and Ralph who shared a life together at 'Little Windovers', as James Gardiner explained in *A Class Apart*:

> Monty and Ralph were both 'ordinary' men, from different social back-grounds, but well-adjusted to their sexuality. They were lucky enough to be able to make a life together with relative ease because Monty was sufficiently well-off and socially placed to 'employ' Ralph as a live-in servant, thus providing plausible cover for their actual relationship.[2]

Gardiner continued:

> What knowledge we have of gay men's lives in the early twentieth century has generally come to us via middle-class and upper-class intellectuals, writers and diarists for the most part badly adjusted to, even tortured by, their sexuality, certainly not able to express it unequivocally in their work. This work can therefore give us little idea of the lives of gay men who considered themselves ordinary or sexually well-adjusted. All too often, the evidence of happiness – private diaries, personal photographs, letters revealing intimate feelings – has been destroyed for fear of blackmail or legal recrimination and the resultant shame and scandal.[3]

Monty and Ralph's domestic life and happiness was interrupted by the outbreak of World War II. In August 1940 Ralph was drafted into the RAF and it was their first real separation. Neither of them realised that it would last over four long years. Ralph's first posting to RAF Waddington in Lincolnshire meant that he was close enough to Monty to spend the occasional weekend leave with him. James Gardiner writes: 'Realising that sooner or later Ralph might get posted overseas, Monty took a protracted leave from his job with the Ministry of Work (claiming 'nervous exhaustion' as a surviving letter testifies), so that he could be close by when Ralph got his infrequent weekends off.'[4]

Letters from Ralph Hall to Montague Glover

Ralph wrote to his beloved Monty on a regular basis, and all of his wartime letters have miraculously survived, over three hundred of them. Here is a selection, reprinted from *A Class Apart* with James Gardiner's permission:

RAF Waddington
10 November 1940

My dear,

We had a raid the other night. It was about an hour raid and they did no damage, my dear. They put about twenty bombs on the turnips in the field at the back of the block and the place seem to lift off the ground and the next morning we had another one but we brought it down my dear. I did not go out as they did not call us out. The cake has just arrived my darling and it is lovely and I will be able to have some for tea on sunday. I have been on three night running this week my dear and I have just been told that I am on again tonight. Well it all is a lifetime my dear. The lads all love our cake my Darling, we had some for tea my dear.

I will be with you tonight Darling.

Love Ralph

20 November 1940

My dear Monty

I have just got your letter telling me about the raid at Coventry and I was glad to hear that it is allright at home. With your letters dear you are always speaking to me and I read them over and over again my dear. The lads say that they think we are going out soon, one just said that and came in dear. So you say you went round the site with me and I can see you now walking round. I go back all over the days we had at Richmond and Esher and Drunken Bidford and Leamington along the river. Do you remember the old days when we first started darling. I went back all over it again last night. What a time we had in them days and I am sorry to say I am crying I cannot hold it back no more my Darling. I love you my old Darling. I do miss you ever such a lot my dear as you know my dear. I hope this finds you in good health my dear and all the rest at home. I get over to you as soon as I can my Darling. I love you Monty. Lots of love to my old Darling Monty. I miss you. Goodnight dear.

Ralph xxxxxxx a ring of them for you.

9 May 1941

My darling

How can you forgive me for forgetting your birthday you know I wish you all the best in the world my darling. I thought it was the 12 of this month darling. But I tell you the truth darling I would have forgotten as I have been troubled by this going overseas. Darling you don't know how I miss you darling. I might as well tell you the truth. I have been letting myself go and I have been crying over you Darling and calling out for you. The lads say who is Monty? to me and I say what do you mean and they say I was calling out for you in my drunkenness Darling. You old darling I am going to get drunk again tonight too darling and I am with you down at the Bear in Esher darling and please forgive me darling for what I have done

darling and forgot your birthday darling, you know I love you darling
ALWAYS DARLING Goodnight my love and I will be with you
for ever and ever you old Darling and the one and only

RALPH TO MONTY XXXXXXXXXXXXX

[from aboard ship, ca. October 1941]

My darling

I wish you could have seen me off but it was impossible to. I hope
you got my telegram allright and the last letter. We are passing a lot
of islands you and I done in the crosswords my dear. A lot of the
lads are feeling sick and I feel sorry for them my dear […] On the
night I sent the telegram I was off the next morning, and off like a
shot as they say. And I was thinking of you my dear in your office
and at home and all the rest my darling. The wrist watch has gone
again my dear, it just starts when it likes every hour, I dropped it. I
am just bedding down for the night my darling and dont I just wish
I was with you, old darling. I can see you lying there sweetheart.
Goodnight darling XXXXX All the lads are guessing where we are
going darling. I only know I am going away from the man I love, the
one and only you old darling. But I know I will come back darling to
you, and it will only be a dream darling.

Hut 192 Heliopolis
23 March 1942

Darling,

I would love to be in the garden today. It is just like English
spring and I know what it is like down your end, the lads tell me all
the news when they come out. The garden should be looking nice
when this reaches you my Sweetheart. My work is just finished for
today and it is 9 o'clock the 20 march and it is just started to rain and
it is very cold at night. I hope you are in good health my darling and
all at home and I wish I was coming on the boat to you darling. I
miss you so much Monty xxxxx you old sweetheart of mine.

18 December 1942

Hallo Darling,

[…] You don't know how much I miss you […] I kiss the photo every night. so you are in bed with me after all. I would rather have you with me. I was up the blue in the desert for a week and was it hell. Just sand and more sand. Lets get back to the old days my dear as soon as this war is over. . . Cairo is just a smell. I cant think of a good thing to say about it all so lets get home.

[Egypt]
   19 December 1942

Darling

I have not had a letter from you yet and the lads that came out here with me have had a lot. I hope everything is all right at home. Look after yourself darling and try to do something for me, you know what I mean my darling. Think of me Monty, You are the only one that ever gave me a frill and you still do. Darling I can see me and you on the bed now you old darling and well be there again don't worry my darling. It is six days before Xmas. Just think of me in the desert with the lads on guard. You are always in my thoughts and I know you will think better of me when this war is over you old darling. Dont I wish I was there with you now darling. I am feeling so strong tonight my sweet. I would love you all night darling.

I am in the guardroom waiting to do my 4th guard my dear and I can see you all at home round the table for Xmas and I know you will miss me darling. This is a XMASxxxxxGIFT from your one and only darling. You don't know how much I miss you Monty. I love you darling so think good of me my sweetheart.

All my love and a merry Xmas
and a HAPPY NEW YEAR TO THEM ALL
        LOVE
            Ralph

[Telegram, December 1942]

GREETINGS TELEGRAM to MR GLOVER

MY DARLING

ALL LETTERS ARE ARRIVING AND WHAT LOVELY LETTERS. ALL MY LOVE AND BEST WISHES FOR XMAS DARLING

RALPH TO MONTY I MISS YOU DARLING

PART II
WORLD WAR II
1939—1945

The Army

6

Kiss Me Goodnight, Sergeant Major

Although they were exposed to homophobic attitudes and living a knife-edge existence, fearful of being found out and court-martialled, it is surprising how many gay men were able to assert themselves and avoid trouble in the wartime armed services. While researching this chapter, the story of Len and William brought home how some gay men were accepted and embraced by their Army pals. Neil 'Bunny' Roger's outrageous and camp exploits on the battlefield, while facing the enemy and death, will make the reader laugh out loud. And we are fortunate to have Bruce Copp's informative and entertaining autobiography that reveals how some gay men were accepted 'without reservation'. These stories will upset the preconception that all servicemen who were found out to be gay or who asserted themselves were victims of homophobia. In *Love, Sex and War: Changing Values 1939–45* (1985) John Costello said that the military experience of gay men in World War II 'chipped away some of the old taboos'. He added that, in the British Army, King's Regulations stated 'confirmed homosexuals whose rehabilitation is unlikely should be removed from the Army by the most expeditious and appropriate means'. However, 'formal charges were usually only instituted in the British armed forces for those sexual transgressors who had committed a flagrant breach of discipline, especially between officers and other ranks, or civilians'.[1] In wartime, tolerance

or 'turning a blind eye' was practised because the potential loss of
soldiers would have left front-line regiments badly under strength.

There can be no better example of the changing attitudes in
wartime than that highlighted in Jeremy Seabrook's *A Lasting
Relationship: Homosexuals and Society* (1976). Seabrook's interview
with Len and William, a 'happy couple' in their fifties, living in
North London, is very revealing and deeply moving. They had been
brought up in the slums of Deptford in South London and they
were in their early twenties and working as dockers in Rotherhithe
when they became a couple. They were both called up in 1939, and
conscripted into the Army, but this meant a separation. Len became
a cook:

> peeling potatoes and so on. Do you know, all the officers knew I
> was gay, and they all accepted it. I had a picture of William by my
> bed; and I wrote to him and he wrote to me every day. Of course,
> with the post being so erratic, I sometimes got six letters in a day
> and then none for a week. One day I was in the kitchen, and one of
> the batmen comes up behind me and puts his hand over my eyes,
> and says 'Don't look, there's a surprise for you.' And I said 'What
> surprise?', and there in the doorway stood Will. I was overjoyed.
> They let us have the rest of the day to ourselves; so that shows how
> sympathetic they were to us, it proves they didn't have any prejudice.[2]

When the couturier and dandy Neil 'Bunny' Roger was a little
boy he asked for a doll's house, and got it. At the age of six he
was given a fairy costume with diaphanous skirts and butterfly
wings. At Oxford he was considered a 'beauty' but was 'sent down'
(expelled) after being accused of homosexual practices. In 1937,
when he was still in his twenties, he established his popular fashion
house, known as Neil Roger, in London's Great Newport Street.
One of his clients was the film star Vivien Leigh. During the war
he was a hero in battle. Bunny served in Italy and North Africa
in the Rifle Brigade. When the Germans were approaching him
and his comrades, he apparently told a sergeant, 'When in doubt,

powder heavily.' As an infantry officer in 1944, he was decorated for charging a machine-gun post at the famous Battle of Monte Cassino in Italy in the attempt to make a breakthrough to Rome. Bunny showed tremendous bravery on the battlefield but, when he ran into an old friend in the bombed-out monastery of Monte Cassino, he was wearing a silk chiffon scarf and a copy of *Vogue* magazine was stuffed into his pocket. When his friend asked him what the hell he was doing, Bunny just looked at him and said 'shopping'.[3]

Bruce Copp's entertaining autobiography *Out of the Firing Line ... Into the Foyer* (2015) is also one of the most revealing testaments to the gay goings on in the British Army during World War II. Being subjected to homophobia and living with the constant fear of exposure and a court martial was part of the daily existence of gay soldiers. Copp acknowledges that the majority of gays and bisexuals tried to conceal their sexual preferences, but there were those who took risks, and they were not necessarily men who identified as gay. Copp makes reference to the heterosexual commandos he was stationed with at a camp near Algiers who enjoyed a bit of man-on-man action away from the battlefields: 'They were the toughest men in the Army, but we were sleeping in pup tents, which housed two soldiers each. Well, every tent was heaving about and bursting at the seams, and you could hear everything that was going on.'[4] Bruce's friend Ronald Benge wrote him a letter explaining that their battalion, the West Kents, known as the 'Buffs', was 'taken over' by a 'fifth column' of homosexuals – a higher percentage than average. Benge said: 'They were good soldiers and devoted to their comrades. One was either a good fellow or not and prejudices disappeared and gays were accepted without reservation.' Copp wrote:

> I'm not sure about 'a fifth column' – I think that might have been a slight exaggeration – but it's true that the Buffs were famous for having more than their fair share of gay men. Our company commander, a courageous man and much admired by those under

him, was very open about his homosexuality, and once he inspected us on horseback while wearing a lot of slap! In fact, I don't think he joined the Army so that he could see the world; he was so conceited that he actually signed up so the world could see him![5]

When Copp was taken ill on the front line, he was taken to a field hospital where he befriended a 'wonderfully camp' male nurse:

He was completely over the top, extravagantly gay and he would have definitely been a drag queen in civilian life. I think we called him 'Fanny' or 'Gladys' or something like that. He was responsible for about fifty wounded or sick soldiers […] He looked after us all, tending to us, bringing us food and providing so much care. He was quite wonderful, and everybody adored him – even though he was so camp. He made no secret of being homosexual, but the boys all accepted him because he was such a marvellous nurse. I'll never forget him.[6]

Bravery was not the preserve of fighting men – there were others who had to keep a stiff upper lip when they were confronted by the horrors of war. Alex Purdie discovered this after he joined the Army. When Alex received his call-up papers his gay friends in the West End told him he did not have to join up. 'Tell 'em you're queer!' they said, but Alex didn't want to avoid conscription: 'I said, "Get out of it? I wanna get *in*!" My father was a soldier in the fourteen war. My youngest brother was a soldier in this war and I wasn't going to be out of that. I was determined to do my duty.'[7] Little did he know he was going to spend half his Army career in a dress and high heels! Alex was born in Deptford in 1914 into a working-class family. His father was a fishmonger. Matt Houlbrook in *Queer London: Perils and Pleasures in the Sexual Metropolis, 1918–1957* (2005) observed that, in the working-class neighbourhoods of East and South London, gay men were 'most firmly integrated into everyday life'. He discovered that, from an early age, Alex, with his flamboyantly camp persona:

was accepted by family, friends and neighbours. He always had a boyfriend. When he worked on his parents' market stall 'the customers loved me. I gave them a first class performance.' Purdie never wore a public mask – he didn't need to: 'It was,' he remembered, 'my world.' Like many other queens, Purdie was not only accepted but treated with real warmth by his local community.[8]

The feeling of solidarity between East Enders and their gay sons was described by 'John', born in 1917, when he was interviewed in Kevin Porter and Jeffrey Weeks's *Between the Acts: Lives of Homosexual Men 1885–1967* (1991):

> Homosexuality in the East End of London had always been absolutely accepted. I mean, going back to my early days, we used to go to the East End occasionally to one of the pubs where the mums and dads used to go. And they used to refer to the boys by their camp name, Hello Lola, love. How are you dear? You going to give us a song? The East End of London, which had very tightly-knit families living in their streets of terraced houses, in and out of one anothers, they knew about their sons and it was accepted.[9]

In the gay world of London's West End, Alex Purdie learned a secret language. It was called Polari. Alex explained:

> Heterosexual people didn't know what we were talking about – thought it was Chinese or something. We didn't want people to know. Didn't want to say there's a copper coming in the bar. You just say there's a sharpy omi. And if you spotted a pretty boy you say vada di omi-oh bona omi.[10]

Alex recalled that he was a 'swine' for makeup. He wore lipstick, eye shadow, rouge, powder and painted his fingernails. He also wore scent: 'my perfume was called Soir de Paris. If I could scrounge together half a crown to have a bottle of this my day was made.' Before they went out, gay men like Alex carefully checked each other's appearance:

If you had too much slap on when you went out your mates would say too much slap on your ecaf. Yeah. Oh really girl? Yes. Go in the lavs here and have a look. And they would look in the mirror, take some off. Or put some on sometimes.

In the 1930s the flamboyantly camp Alex, with his slap and Soir de Paris, said he was barred from nearly every pub in the West End.[11]

On joining the Army, Alex was posted to Harrow:

I was interviewed by the officer and he said what did you do in civilian life and I told him I was a ballet dancer so he offered me a job on the telephones, plugging in and all that. Last thing in the world I knew anything about. He put me on the telephones and I was in touch with all the gun sites but I was plugging in all the wrong gun sites. I'm sure I was the cause of the Blitz on London![12]

Alex was quickly removed from the Army's telephone exchange and moved to a job in catering. Eventually he auditioned as a female impersonator for the Garrison Theatre. Wearing 'lashes and slap', he was accepted for the Bengal Entertainment Services Association (BESA), which was a troupe of Army entertainers who were dispatched to the most remote and dangerous parts of India, where it was not safe for civilians and women to be sent. By the middle of 1943, BESA's all-male casts of about 100 servicemen were touring in 12 productions. Said Andy Merriman in *Greasepaint and Cordite: How ENSA Entertained the Troops During World War II* (2013): 'Travelling was arduous, communication was complicated and parties were repeatedly lost and frequently late.'[13] BESA's command area covered hundreds of thousands of square miles. 'It was very difficult,' Alex said:

we had the minimum of props. We played two or three shows a day. No changing rooms. We could be in the middle of a paddy field. Of course it was dangerous but I just didn't think about things like that. I had a job to do and I was determined to do it.

Alex went with BESA to many field hospitals, where he entertained 'these lovely boys who had had terrible things done to them and were trying to clap and laugh at me. That wasn't very nice. They're the things I try to forget. It was too awful.'[14]

On the home front it was relatively easy for a gay man to pick up a soldier. Interviewed in *Between the Acts*, 'Norman', a Londoner, was in his forties at the outbreak of hostilities and he discovered that, during the war, there were a lot of soldiers in the metropolis who needed a place to bed down:

> So, of course, it was quite easy to say, well come and sleep with me. I had a room in Marble Arch. I've been rather amused, because it's a great triumph to get people who are not a bit interested, to accept all this nonsense. I picked up a lovely boy in Hyde Park, a soldier, from Grimsby. I took him home and I began sucking him off. And do you know what he said? I wouldn't let anyone else do this to me except you.[15]

John Alcock, from Birmingham, was conscripted into the Army towards the end of the war, but he had tried to avoid it, moving to different addresses with his parents. Eventually the police caught up with him, and off to war he went. Soon after joining, although he hated basic training ('I couldn't hold a gun: it terrified me'), young John, still in his late teens, realised there was fun to be had wearing his uniform:

> On my first leave I found myself in the West End of London and I met two other queer soldiers in Leicester Square and I remember we walked arm-in-arm, our berets cocked at a jaunty angle [...] Places to go in those days were a bit thin on the ground, but the Regent Palace hotel had a men-only bar called the Shake Up Bar so I went there. I was sitting at the bar and I became aware of the amount of officers that were standing around, including two from my own battalion in Portsmouth, and all the officers were homosexual and it gave me a tremendous lift to realize that other ranks were queer the same as I was.[16]

When they were lads, two of Britain's best-loved comedy entertainers, Larry Grayson and Kenneth Williams, had different experiences of the war. Using the stage name 'Billy Breen', Larry had started to earn a living as a stage performer and also enjoyed entertaining the American GIs, the 'Yanks', at home with his family. This meant they were showered with gifts of chewing gum and tins of fruit. But one day Larry's call-up papers arrived requesting him to attend a medical examination. Mike Malyon, Larry's great-nephew and biographer, described what happened:

> As he walked into the room, mincing theatrically as if he was making a stage entrance, Billy was met by a stern-faced orderly who took one look at him and said: 'Oh, no, the war's not *that* bad!' Probably because of his pasty pallor – and even maybe due to the fact that he had not completely wiped away the stage make-up from the previous night's concert party – Billy was marked down as a grade four, which made him exempt for National Service, but also excluded him from joining ENSA – the forces' entertainment regiment, which is what he'd set his sights on. Billy was never given any official reason why he failed the military medical [...] 'What a shame – the army never knew what they missed.'[17]

Kenneth Williams was just 18 years old in 1944, working as an apprentice draughtsman, when he was drafted into the Army. He became a sapper in the Engineers Survey section. Interviewed by the popular talk-show host Michael Parkinson on BBC television in the 1970s, he recalled:

> I'd been brought up in the Christian faith, and the idea of holding guns and killing people was abhorrent to me, quite apart from the fact that I'm not really born for that kind of thing. I don't look good with a gun. Some people can hold them, trying to look tough, and it really isn't my forte. You have to accept it's just part of one's limitations. I went to my father and said, 'I don't want to join the Army,' and he said, 'Look, this country's facing a tyrant.' He said

Hitler was an evil man and the situation had become such in Europe that the only thing to do was to fight, and I believed what he said was true, because I thought him in a better position to judge. I was only eighteen, and he was considerably wiser and had been through another war, which he thought was for good reasons at that time, but he certainly thought this was an even better reason. So I joined the Army and spent three years of my life there, which of course was an awful thing for me to do. Not only did I not believe in killing […] it also infringed my freedom and involved a way of life I'd never faced. I'd never undressed in public and I didn't like it. I did not like taking my clothes off in front of a lot of people, and in barrack rooms I had to. So I used to arrange the shirt to cover the dick, and then they checked. They'd shout at you and say, 'Go on, show us your willy,' and accused you of a lack of manhood because you didn't show it. So eventually I got exhibitionistic and started going, 'Yeah!'[18]

Some gay men went to great lengths to conceal their sexual feelings. One sad case involved a 42-year-old sergeant who was a highly regarded soldier who had repressed his homosexuality to the point of mental instability. He left letters from a fictitious son lying about the barracks but the fear that he would be exposed eventually led to a suicide attempt. While hospitalised, he demanded to be castrated or imprisoned.[19]

John Costello acknowledged that while some duration-only officers with little or no service experience 'treated every sexual offender strictly by the book, the professional officer corps, many of whom had seen service in India where homosexual activity, particularly among the Sikh regiments, was not uncommon, were prepared to be more lenient'.[20] In 1942, just before the Battle of El Alamein in Egypt, one British Army major recalled how a potentially embarrassing court martial was hushed up:

A sergeant in our brigade was discovered masturbating with a private in a tent, and they were both put on a charge by the sergeant major. Our colonel, who was himself a homosexual, was absent, and so the case went right up to brigade headquarters. The brigadier [...] dismissed both men with a reprimand. The colonel was absolutely furious that it had got as far as it did. 'The battalion's been out here for two years, these two youngsters had never had home leave,' he stormed afterwards in the mess. 'Out in India when I was in the ranks, reveille brought every man tumbling out of everyone else's bunks. What the hell do they want the men to do for sexual relief, go down to the brothels in the bazaar, chase Arab women and catch syphilis?'[21]

7

Prisoners of War Part 1: Dudley Cave

In the 1990s Stonewall, a British LGBT rights pressure group, was at the forefront of challenging and asking for the lifting of the ban on openly lesbian and gay people serving in the military. In 1998 the organisation was approached by Jeanette Smith, who had been thrown out of the Royal Air Force, and Duncan Lustig Prean, a Royal Navy commander who was in the process of being dismissed. Jeannette and Duncan asked Stonewall to arrange legal representation, and it led to a long battle through the courts with other gay victims of discrimination. Although the judges in the High Court of Appeal stated that they felt the ban was not justified, they were not in a position to overturn it. Consequently Stonewall took the case to Strasbourg and the European Court of Human Rights, where they won it. The judgement of the court was a vindication of the rights of lesbians and gay men. The Labour government of the time immediately announced that it would lift the ban. This historic act took place on 12 January 2000, and a new general code of sexual conduct was introduced.[1]

On 19 May 1999 Dudley Cave, who had served in the Army during World War II, died at the age of 78. He did not live to witness the lifting of the ban. In 1942, during the fall of Singapore, he was captured by the Japanese and spent the remainder of the war as a prisoner of war. After the war he became a gay rights activist, a pioneer who, for 20 years, battled against the Royal British Legion's refusal to acknowledge that lesbians and gay men had served and died in wars defending Britain. He also challenged the Legion over its opposition to the participation of gay organisations in Remembrance Day ceremonies. Peter Tatchell wrote in his obituary of Dudley in the *Independent*:

> He was incensed in the early 1980s when the Legion's Assistant Secretary, Group Captain D. J. Mountford, condemned moves to promote the acceptance of gay people as an attempt to 'weaken our society', and declared that homosexuals had no right to complain about being ostracised by Legion members. One of Dudley Cave's final public acts was last November, when he was the keynote speaker at Outrage!'s Queer Remembrance Day vigil at the Cenotaph. After laying a pink triangle wreath honouring gay people who died fighting Nazism and in the concentration camps, Cave deplored the fact that gay ceremonies of remembrance are still – in the late 1990s – being condemned by the British Legion as 'distasteful' and 'offensive'.[2]

Dudley was born in Golders Green and was working as a cinema projectionist when the war broke out. He joined the Air Raid Precautions (ARP) and in 1940–1 lived through the London Blitz:

> You got accustomed to bombs falling. At first, perhaps, you took shelter and were frightened. Very rapidly you didn't pay much attention unless you heard one coming fairly close, when you might duck down. I didn't go into shelters. I despised them. I also looked down my snooty nose at people who slept in the Underground. I thought they were really rather cowardly and I would go home and sleep in my bed or, at worst, under the dining-room table. I was not aware they had been bombed out of their homes in the East End and I was sitting smugly in Golders Green, feeling all brave and looking down my nose at them.[3]

When Dudley was called up in June 1941 he was just 20 years old. He later recalled in the television documentary *Comrades in Arms* (1990): 'Up until the war I regarded myself as a pacifist. I felt war could never be defended. However, I was aware to some extent what was happening to the Jews in Germany and I felt a fight against Nazism was a worthy fight.'[4] He joined the Royal Army Ordnance Corps as a driver and he later recalled that men were put in the Army 'regardless of whether they were gay or not. It didn't seem to bother the military authorities. There was none of the later homophobic uproar about gays undermining military discipline and effectiveness. With Britain seriously threatened by the Nazis, the forces weren't fussy about who they accepted.'[5]

Dudley believed that there was a relaxed attitude towards gay men joining the services during the war. From the start there existed the possibility of an imminent German invasion. Operation Sea Lion, the German code name for a proposed invasion of the United Kingdom during the Battle of Britain, was postponed indefinitely on 17 September 1940, but the threat remained. Consequently the military could not afford to be selective about who they recruited. Throughout the war there was a need to maximise combat strength, so the military's top brass unofficially lifted the ban on gay men. In the Army, soldiers who were discovered having same-sex encounters rarely faced severe punishment. Instead they were reprimanded by their commanding officer or transferred to another unit. Dudley recalled that neither the top brass nor his heterosexual comrades showed any concern about gay recruits: 'There were none of the anti-gay witch-hunts we had after the war,' he told Peter Tatchell:

> Homosexual soldiers were more or less accepted. The visible gays were mostly drag performers in concert teams. Regarded with considerable affection, their camp humour helped lift the men's spirits. All the gays and straights worked together as a team. We had to because our lives might have depended on it.[6]

Dudley expected to fight the Nazis but, on 7 December 1941, when the Japanese entered the war with their military strike on the American naval base at Pearl Harbor, he found himself posted to the Far East. During the fall of Singapore in 1942, Dudley was captured by the Japanese and marched north in a prisoner-of-war labour detachment: 'I felt very much that this wasn't happening to me. Disbelief [...] I'd assumed that I would be a prisoner-of-war Geneva Convention-wise. Little did I know what was to come as we went ahead.'[7] Said Peter Tatchell in the *Independent*:

> his unit was put to work on the Thai–Burma railway, 10 miles beyond the bridge on the River Kwai. Three-quarters of Cave's comrades in H force perished. He was lucky. After he suffered a bad bout of malaria, the Japanese declared him unproductive and ordered his incarceration in Changi Prison, Singapore.[8]

Before he was captured, Dudley had known about a soldier who was renowned for providing sexual favours in the mangrove swamps:

> He was well liked. Even supposedly straight men made use of his services. You could say he did a lot to maintain the unit's morale. When a zealous sergeant attempted to charge him with being out of barracks after lights out, the commanding officer, who knew exactly what went on in the mangrove swamps, dismissed the charges. He had the wisdom to know that it was all harmless fun and a useful relief from the stress of war.[9]

Dudley was aware that some of his comrades gossiped about him behind his back, referring to him as a 'nancy boy'. He recalled an incident in *Comrades in Arms*: 'I overheard a soldier refer to me as a nancy boy but another soldier immediately protested that I wasn't because "he was terribly brave in action". You notice you couldn't be gay *and* brave.' He stressed that the worst comment he ever heard was being criticised for holding a broom like a woman! In

Changi Prison, Dudley began to accept his homosexuality when a British Army medical officer loaned him a copy of the book *Sexual Inversion in Men*, written by the sexologist Havelock Ellis, enlightened and eye-opening for 1920, when it was published. In spite of making Dudley laugh, he said he also found it an 'immense revelation'.

Changi Prison was a nightmare of physical deprivation and, when Dudley was liberated in 1945, he was almost dead from malnutrition, down from 12 stone to less than 8. He said that he would not have survived if the war had gone on one more month:

> It was mainly a question of day-to-day survival. I'm fairly even-tempered, and I'm fairly philosophical. I'm reasonably sensible [...] I saw somebody die of beriberi malnutrition after I'd been a prisoner for about three months and I realized that it was worth making an effort to get vitamins, eat rice polishing, and it was very important to keep alive. So I was fairly sensible that way. I stopped smoking and used my cigarettes to buy vitamin pills. I'm not a dramatic sort of person, so I was able to cope. And there is luck, of course. We were liberated about ten days after Hiroshima.[10]

After being demobbed in 1945, Dudley became a manager of the Majestic Cinema in Wembley:

> I did have sex with people at work, never imposing on them. And when it subsequently became rumoured that I was gay, my district manager got to hear about it, asked me, and I couldn't or didn't deny it. I was suspended and hauled up to Head Office and they decided I should go. In fact he suggested I might like to resign and I, thank goodness, said 'no', I didn't feel like that. I eventually left Odeon theatres with three months' pay in lieu of notice. I felt absolutely dreadful about it. I felt dreadful because I had to tell my father I had been sacked or was leaving, without telling him the reason. I felt totally friendless and alone and very demoralised.[11]

Dudley's feeling of isolation did not last. In 1952 he met Bernard Williams, who in wartime had been one of the ground staff working for Fighter Command in the RAF. After the war Bernard became a schoolteacher. The two men fell in love and remained together as partners and gay rights champions for 40 years until Bernard died in 1994. Among the many important gay organisations supported by Dudley and Bernard were the information and advice service Gay Switchboard and the Lesbian and Gay Bereavement Project.

In spite of his own wartime suffering as a prisoner of war, Dudley became a leading light in the promotion of peace and reconciliation with Japan, which made him unpopular with some of his former comrades. 'I will never forget what the Japanese did to us, but the time has come for forgiveness,' he said. In the television programme *Comrades in Arms* Dudley returns to the Far East and to the Peace Temple near the River Kwai: 'I came back from the war hating the Japanese. Then I heard that a Japanese soldier was building a shrine at the River Kwai. A temple of peace. It was an act of reconciliation for his part and a memorial to all who had died.' Dudley helped to raise funds to pay for a large bronze bell for the temple and he attended the dedication ceremony in person:

> I had some reservations and I concluded that my friends who were dead had not had the chance to give [money for the temple], but I had to feel that they would have done and should have done. Not all prisoners share my view. I feel sitting in the temple a feeling of tranquillity and peace and remembrance too. Many of my friends died.

However, Dudley remained angry with the powers-that-be that refused to lift the ban on gays and lesbians in the armed services. He said:

> They used us when it suited them, and then victimised us when the country was no longer in danger. I am glad I served but I am angry that military homophobia was allowed to wreck so many lives for

over fifty years after we gave our all for a freedom that gay people were denied.[12]

Keith Howes remembers Dudley as:

a lovely, gentle, *genuine* man who worked very hard for truth and freedom. He was one of our assets in the UK. Very quietly but forcefully spoken, always well groomed but never ostentatious, probably a practising Christian in the true sense. He was well liked by *all* strands of the gay movement.[13]

8

Prisoners of War Part 2

For prisoners of war, there was a choice: abstinence or same-sex relations. For many heterosexual POWs the *fear* of homosexuality was a reality of their everyday life in a camp. For those who had been imprisoned for long periods there was an anxiety that they might *become* homosexual. At a time when homosexuality was a criminal offence and considered a sickness by most people, the Canadian Bob Prouse was concerned he could be 'affected'. Imprisoned in an all-male work camp attached to Stalag IXC at Bad Sulza in Germany, he said: 'A few soldiers wouldn't wait for freedom and indulged in homosexuality. Fortunately, they were a very small minority but disturbing all the same when you realized that some were otherwise tough soldiers. It made you wonder if you, too, could be affected someday if the war went on endlessly.'[1] In *POW: Allied Prisoners in Europe, 1939–1945* (2006), Adrian Gilbert said that Reverend J. Ellison Platt 'worked himself up into a lather over what he suspected were unseemly goings on in Colditz. "Homosexualism", he reported, "has occupied an increasingly large place in contemporary prison humour." He also added, "Jocular references to masturbation, too, are freer than is usual among healthy minded adults."'[2] Gilbert wrote:

> The actual prevalence of homosexuality within the camp system is hard to discern. In officer and other non-working camps homosexual

activity seems to have been minimal, and a number of chroniclers confidently asserted that there were no instances of homosexuality in their camp (although as heterosexuals they may have been unaware of what was usually a very covert activity).[3]

But then we are talking about the love that dared not speak its name. Regarding the prisoners of war interned in Colditz Castle, 'Is it really likely that a bunch of banged-up ex-public school boys weren't going at it like knives?'[4]

Adrian Gilbert acknowledged that in the other, larger ranks' camps there were instances of 'quite overt' homosexual behaviour: 'Many prisoners seem not to have been particularly concerned, and if some were censorious others were tolerant. Ballroom dancing and theatrical activities became a focus for homosexual interest.'[5] Private Geoffrey Ellwood, a Canadian soldier in Stalag VIIIB at Lamsdorf, quoted by Gilbert, described same-sex behaviour on the dance floor:

This is where you'd see the odd queer show up. I mean, it was one thing for guys to dance together because there's nobody else to dance with. But when they start dancing together and likin' it, and start snugglin' up, it became very, very obvious, you know. This went on, but nobody seemed to take it as serious. They'd look at it, and discuss it among themselves, and that was it. It was accepted that some people are that way.[6]

The unpublished memoir of Jim Witte offers some revealing insights into same-sex antics in a POW camp. Witte, a heterosexual, wrote a frank memoir of his sex life and service as a gunner with the 160th Light Anti-Aircraft Battery, Royal Artillery. He was just 22 when he was captured in 1941 near Tobruk, and he served part of the war as a prisoner in Sulmona, Italy. Witte recalls how homosexuality was 'rife' in the camp in Sulmona, and he vividly describes the love affairs of the 'boy friends' and their 'girl friends' (female impersonators who entertained in shows in the POW camp's theatre). He also mentions a corporal in the Military

Police who was 'violently' in love with one of the 'actresses'. When they went missing during roll call, the Italian guards found them snuggled under a blanket so they put them together into solitary for a week. 'They weren't too keen on one another after that,' said Witte, who also testifies that same-sex liaisons existed between all kinds of prisoners in the camp and took many forms, from parcel sharing, holding hands and heavy petting to full-on relationships.[7]

The writer G. F. (George Frederick) Green was not a prisoner of war, but he was a soldier who became a prisoner in wartime, arrested and incarcerated for 'conduct unbecoming'. He was the son of a working-class iron founder but graduated from Cambridge University in 1932 with an English degree and began his writing career. Called up in 1940, he served first as a private in the 3rd Suffolk Infantry Regiment. After passing out from an officer cadets training unit, he joined the Border Regiment as a second lieutenant. On being posted to Ceylon (Sri Lanka), he travelled all over the island and, according to Chloe Green in the *Oxford Dictionary of National Biography* (2004), 'found it utterly enchanting'. However, George's alcoholism and attraction to Sinhalese youths led to him courting disaster. Chloe Green said that in 1944 'he was caught *in flagrante* with a Sinhalese rickshaw puller; he was court-martialled and sentenced to two years' imprisonment. The first months of his sentence were spent in military detention in a Ceylon gaol, during which time he kept a diary.'[8]

George used his Ceylonese prison diary to write under the name of 'Lieutenant Z' an article entitled 'Military Detention' which was published in 1947 in *Penguin New Writing No. 31*. This was edited by his friend and fellow homosexual, John Lehmann, a poet and man of letters. George's article does not refer to his sexuality, nor why he was arrested, but he offers graphic and disturbing insights into the harsh and brutal treatment of prisoners. 'When a prisoner passes the iron gates,' said George, 'he is treated with total contempt for his identity as a man. He is made to strip naked and double mark time with knees up, his arms held above his head, while the sergeants watch, smoking cigarettes and yelling orders or abuse.' George described his fellow prisoners as:

young civilian soldiers, sailors and airmen who had never considered crime, their chief fault overstaying leave, neither worse nor better than those still in the ranks. But it is certain that they were better men and better fighters than the sergeants who had them in charge [...] Contempt for the Sinhalese, throughout the island, by men neither honest nor happy but totally ignorant, oppressed those who knew the friendly, innately gentle, happy and charming race. It revolted the minority who believed these virtues good.[9]

George served the rest of his prison sentence in Yorkshire's Wakefield Prison. He was released in March 1946 in an emotional state, but he was helped by the psychiatrist Dr Charlotte Wolff. He resumed his writing career but alcoholism and heavy smoking led to his death in 1977. Chloe Green said that his friends:

All spoke of the warmth and generosity of his nature, his eccentricities, his honesty in exploring human relationships, and his infectious laughter and sense of the ridiculous. Although he so often wrote about the lack of love between people, everyone who knew him seemed to love him and feel the pleasure of his companionship.[10]

In conclusion it appears that, in some cases, the military turned a blind eye to same-sex liaisons in the POW camps. Such relationships may not have had the approval of all the prisoners, but these relationships did exist and some of the couples were tolerated and even accepted. However, if caught and arrested while serving, the military could make life extremely difficult for the prisoner in wartime. The terrible experiences of G. F. Green demonstrate just how harshly homosexual prisoners were treated. Thanks to John Lehmann, Green was able to document and publish a record of his experiences as a prisoner. In his writing, Green does not acknowledge the sexual practices which led to his imprisonment, but his firsthand testimony offers the reader some idea of what befell gay men who were exposed and court-martialled.

The Navy

9

Rum, Bum and Concertina

George Hayim served in the Royal Navy during World War II, and in his autobiography he summarised the difference between the Army and the Navy during that difficult time: 'In the Army discomfort was inevitable, even if you never heard a shot go off. But in the Navy one was always clean, warm and well-fed, unless, of course, you drowned.'[1] Hayim had a wonderful sense of humour, which appears to be common among sailors, especially those who, like Hayim, were gay. Perhaps that is why sailors, gay and straight, enjoyed dressing up as women for concert parties, and entertaining their comrades. It was good for morale. So was sex, with women (if you were heterosexual) and each other (if you were heterosexual *or* gay).

The Navy has had an enduring reputation for same-sex liaisons or, as George Melly described it, 'rum, bum and concertina'. This is the title he gave to his entertaining and bestselling autobiography, first published in 1977. Melly joined the Royal Navy towards the end of the war, when he was just 18. He informed the recruiting officer that he was drawn to the uniforms because they were 'so much nicer' than the Army and RAF. However, Melly found his ship, HMS *Argus*, 'a den of skivers, misfits and lunatics, a floating, tethered thieves' kitchen'. But the young sailor soon became friendly with 'an open-faced and charming rogue nicknamed Wings'. After a short time, Melly became Wings's official 'winger'. Melly explained:

The expression 'winger' means, at its most innocent, a young seaman
who is taken under the wing of a rating or Petty Officer older and
more experienced than himself to be shown the ropes. It can also,
although far from inevitably, imply a homosexual relationship, and in
our case this was so, but on a comparatively playful and lighthearted
level, mostly confined to rum-flavoured kisses when he returned on
board.[2]

George Melly was not the only recruit who was attracted to the
uniform. George Hayim could have avoided the war. His Russian
mother and Iraqi-Jewish father were millionaires. He had been
born in Shanghai in 1920, so he was quite young, just 20, when he
joined the Navy in 1940. As he wrote in his autobiography, *Thou
Shalt Not Uncover Thy Mother's Nakedness* (1988), he was attracted to
the Navy's 'hard men' and navy blue uniform:

I never wanted to join the Navy to kill anyone, or sink the *Bismarck*.
I just thought it would be a turn on: a bunch of hard men bubbling
away together in a pot. Also, navy blue is my best colour and I love
dressing up. I chose the Navy because I'm sallow and look green in
khaki.[3]

On joining the Navy young Hayim had to endure some 'discomfort'
when the 'old hands' on board took him to see the 'golden rivet',
part of his initiation into Navy ways: 'A lot of winking and giggling
went on. One was taken down a passage and when you were all
bent down, they'd suddenly crash into your behind and scream with
laughter.'[4] On another occasion he narrowly escaped being raped by
a 'lanky giant of a marine'.

In 1942 George joined a brand-new anti-aircraft cruiser, the
Cleopatra, and this took him to Malta: 'Hurrah!' he thought. 'The
Mediterranean and sun.' But on arriving in Malta he discovered
that the island was being bombed night and day. He said he did not
care: 'I might escape a bomb, but I could never escape the vomitous
North Sea.' Lying in his hammock, George began to wonder if he

had made the right decision in joining the Navy in wartime: 'I could have stayed in Shanghai and been surrounded by servants [...] The guy in the next hammock lifted his head and gave me a wink. I leaned over and joined him. Yes! I had done the right thing.'[5] The horror of war hit Hayim as they came within sight of Malta. Dive-bombing German Stukas bombed the *Cleopatra* and he witnessed his friends being killed. He was also distressed when two of the ship's cadets were killed in a cinema in Malta which suffered a direct hit during an air raid: 'They were young, fair, beautiful. I wept for them.'[6]

On returning to England on board the *Mauretania*, Hayim felt sympathy for the Italian prisoners cramped in the bottom of the ship: 'I'd always had a love for Italy and imagined the prisoners would be beautiful, curly-haired, brown Adonises talking of food and singing. Instead, they were a batch of undernourished shaven-heads.'[7] He described the British sailors as 'shits' who would rather throw leftover food into the sea than give it to the Italian prisoners: 'I never thought of Italians as enemies. They were friends who had taken a wrong turning.'[8]

Hayim spent much of his shore leave drinking cocktails in the Lower Bar or 'Pink Sink' of the Ritz Hotel in Piccadilly. This was a popular meeting place for homosexuals, and it was here that he was picked up by the well-known dramatist Terence Rattigan, then serving as a tail gunner in the Royal Air Force. When Hayim was interviewed by Matthew Sweet for *The West End Front: The Wartime Secrets of London's Grand Hotels* (2011), he recalled that he was never afraid of air raids, but 'the thought of being caught doing something by a policeman – that worried me. The shame of it, I suppose.'[9] It was in Hyde Park that Hayim met his principal wartime lover, Lieutenant Commander Anthony Heckstall-Smith, who had joined the *Cleopatra* after Hayim had left. Stationed at the naval barracks in Southend, he informed Hayim that his father had been in charge of George V's yacht, *Britannia*. Hayim quite liked the idea of being with 'royalty' and Heckstall-Smith's royal connection endeared him to Hayim's mother, who treated her son's lover as:

any Society woman might treat a gentleman who had shown a romantic interest in her marriageable offspring. It helped that Heckstall-Smith was dashing and well connected. He had just returned from a submarine mission on Crete [...] As the host on their visits to the Lower Bar, he was required to pay for the evening. 'Fortunately', said George, 'my mother drank nothing more expensive than lemonade.'[10]

George and his mother tried to get Heckstall-Smith to tell them why he had received the Distinguished Service Cross (DSC), one of the highest honours that can be awarded in the Navy: 'He was very British about it all: he said it all had something to do with torpedo-boats in Crete.'[11]

Drama student John Beardmore abandoned his acting studies at the Weber Douglas School when the war broke out: 'I wanted to fight for my country, almost everybody did. There was a great nationalistic feeling and I wanted to go right from the word go.'[12] In 1939, at the age of 19, he joined the Royal Navy. He spent the war years on the Russian convoys, in the Battle of the Atlantic and in the invasions of North Africa, Sicily and Normandy. When John was interviewed for the BBC television documentary series *It's Not Unusual* in 1997, he said he discovered a whole new world opening up for him:

> I assumed I was the only person in the world who was gay. I went on a destroyer. I was blond, blue-eyed and had long eyelashes and I immediately became a target for young married men who were mostly active service and petty officers who invited me to become their winger, to be taken under their wing, but it really meant they were after my cherry.[13]

John also believed that the captain must have known he was gay, 'because occasionally he used to squeeze my arse'.[14] John said that living in very confined quarters on the ship inevitably led to the building of close relationships, many of them platonic, but 'some of them were sexual. Many sailors didn't want to go ashore and catch VD from a prostitute so they sought sexual relief – mutual masturbation – from fellow seamen.'[15] John recalled Freddy, a coder on his ship, a former chorus boy who was popular with the crew. At his action station it was Freddy's job to relay the captain's orders to the forward guns: 'When the captain said, "Open fire," Freddy simply repeated, "Open fire, dear," which would crack up the troops. He was immensely popular on the ship and everybody loved him and cared for him.'[16] Freddy also endeared himself to the crew when he wrote letters home for illiterate sailors.

John explained that an 'oppo' was a sailor who was the same age as a new recruit and shared the same rank. They were often on the same watch and so the pair would become pals, go ashore together and keep an eye on each other. In Alkarim Jivani's book *It's Not Unusual* (1997), based on the BBC television series, John said: 'in some cases it developed into a sexual relationship which went on after the war ended. I know of fellows who were oppos and who were having affairs at the time who went on to become godfathers to each other's children.' John added: 'Sailors were a fairly randy lot and masturbation was not at all uncommon.'[17]

John faced terror in July 1942 when he was a 22-year-old Royal Naval Volunteer Reserve (RNVR) sub-lieutenant, serving as navigating officer on board the newly built Flower-class corvette, HMS *Poppy*. *Poppy* was part of Convoy PQ17, a convoy of 35 ships which had sailed from Iceland en route to the Soviet Union, but in the Arctic Ocean they had to scatter when they were located by the Germans. Convoy PQ17 lost 24 of its 35 merchant ships during a series of heavy enemy daylight attacks which lasted a week. For his war service, John Beardmore received the Russia Star, the Africa Star, the Atlantic Star, the Arctic Star and the Malta Star as well as being mentioned in dispatches twice but, he reflected, 'I don't regard myself as a hero. I was just lucky. I don't really approve of awards as such because everyone should be awarded, I mean, we were all heroes.'[18] After the war, John resumed his theatrical career.

BBC2's *Timewatch* programme *Sex and War*, shown in 1998, featured one of the most engaging television interviews with a

gay sailor. Dennis Prattley served as a signalman on a destroyer in
the Royal Navy from 1942 to 1946. He believed he was the only
acknowledged homosexual on board: 'I became a mascot for the
crew. It was marvellous. I was treated as just one of the boys but at
night it was very different.' Sailors would climb into his bunk and
have sex with him. They told him he reminded them of their 'girl'
or wife back home. 'All these boys were heterosexual,' he said. 'And
they told me not to breathe a word of this to anyone. "This is strictly
between you and me." But everybody knew what was going on.'[19]
Dennis was very hurt when some of the men spurned him the next
day when they were on duty.

Dennis eventually faced the tragedy of war when a friend of his
was killed in front of him:

> It hit us all because up to that time we didn't think anything could
> happen to us because all the boys thought it was one big adventure.
> We never thought about death. When it did come we all hit a
> depression. And it was during that depression that the boys came to
> my bunk more than ever as if live today because tomorrow we might
> not be here.[20]

On shore leave Dennis met another gay sailor, who wore
makeup and informed him that he had named himself Bette, in
honour of the famous Hollywood movie star Bette Davis. When
Dennis enquired if he was permitted to wear makeup on board his
ship, Bette replied, 'There's no law against it. So I wear makeup
all the time. I can't do without it.' And then Bette introduced
Dennis to two more sailors: 'We call him Rita Hayworth and this
is Katharine Hepburn.' The trio of sailors who named themselves
after their favourite movie stars then christened Dennis: 'So I was
called Ann Sheridan and I became "Sherry" in the concert party
we put together.'[21]

Dennis organised the concert party with two other sailors
and then spent much of his naval career entertaining sailors by
'dragging up'. The performers proved to be such a success that

they felt confident they could leave the Navy and pursue full-time careers as entertainers. Unfortunately, the Navy did not want to let them go. Each of them was interviewed by naval psychiatrists, at which all three declared that they were homosexual. Instead of the expected discharges, they were refused! Dennis gave up trying to leave the Navy and resigned himself to the fact that the Navy would keep him and his drag queen pals right up until the end of the war because they were too valuable to be discharged. In wartime they were good for morale. Dennis said: 'I did my bit for my country and was always in action one way or the other. I think I made a lot of difference.'[22]

10

Terri Gardener: Behind Enemy Lines

Terri Gardener's story is important to *Fighting Proud* because he left a legacy. He agreed to be interviewed by Keith Howes in *Gay News* in 1983, Alkarim Jivani in *It's Not Unusual* (1997) and Steve Humphries in *The Call of the Sea* in 1997. In these interviews Terri recalled his war service as a female impersonator and gave a frank and honest account of what it was like to be a gay man at that time. In historical research, eyewitness accounts can bring out into the open details that are sometimes missed by academics who are immersed in theoretical concepts and approaches. Firsthand testimonies of gay men from history, especially *ordinary* (not famous) gay men, are rare, and hard to find. It helps if the interviewers are sensitive to the person they are interviewing. Keith Howes, Alkarim Jivani and Steve Humphries are among the best at this type of information gathering, and we are fortunate that Terri Gardener was interviewed by them.

When Terri Gardener joined the Royal Navy as an officers' cook during World War II, he was unprepared for the salty language and insults that would be directed at him. Poor Terri found himself in the firing line in more ways than one. Interviewed by Keith Howes in *Gay News* in 1983, he recalled:

I was called horrendous things. If anything sent a shudder through me it was when I was first asked 'Are you a brown hatter?' But it got so that every 'brown hatter' didn't sound so bad. I used to reply: 'Yes, dear. But what goes up my arse won't give you a 'eadache.' Fight crudity *with* crudity. And if you've got the pluck to do that you'll find you make friends. Every time anyone has ever challenged me I've said 'What of it? Have I ever taken advantage of you? Do I want *your* cock?' I've found that this attitude has had the reverse effect and people respond positively to me. But if you're going to allow yourself to be shit on, dear, then blush and run away.[1]

Terri spent most of his working life as a female impersonator. His father had been the stage manager of a drag revue in World War I and Terri started dragging up between the wars. He learned how to speak Polari (gay slang) from two drag queens who went busking around London's East End with a barrel organ:

Of course being ladies they couldn't pull a barrel organ around so they paid an ome – which is another word for a man – to pull the barrel organ and because they didn't want him to know what they were talking about they talked in Polari [...] They didn't want him to know how much money they were doing because they'd perhaps only pay him duay biancsay a day. And in case you don't know what duay biancsay is, that was half a crown. And the 'palone vadas ome palone very cod' meant you were getting some very funny looks from her serving the tea.[2]

Terri came to terms with his sexuality early on. He discovered that, growing up in the East End, working-class communities were often more tolerant of gay men than the middle-classes. He settled happily into his life as a 'theatrical' and he was just getting himself established in the theatre and music halls when, at the age of 20 in 1940, he was conscripted into the Navy. This led him into the secret, illicit world of same-sex encounters, and he was eventually discharged for being homosexual:

It was exciting, the idea of being surrounded by all these butch men, but it was frightening too because I had no idea what my life would be like. A gay person who I knew at the time said they might give me a bad time and that the best way for me to be was downright outrageous.[3]

Terri's life at sea was made bearable when he volunteered to take part in entertainment shows for the sailors. In the bottom of his kit bag he always stored a wig, a dress and some makeup so that he was able to transform himself into a female impersonator within minutes:

I've always believed in making people laugh. If you make people laugh [...] they're on your side. I just went on and told some rather risqué stories and sang in my rather peculiar voice. During the war it was very different because the troops, when they were massed together, thousands of men, all at a loose end, entertainment meant a great deal to them. I had to take a few kicks, of course; not everybody likes theatrical people, or gay people, but funnily enough I don't even remember running into real unpleasantness the whole time I was in the services.[4]

At first, Terri was quite happy to enjoy same-sex encounters with fellow sailors on board: 'you're out to get every bit and have as much fun as you possibly can,' he said. However, he discovered that the married man away from home and in the Navy was the worst sort of man:

he would go out of his way for a bit of nonsense. The difficulties were finding somewhere to be intimate [...] 'One had to be a bit discreet with affairs because quite apart from it being a punishable offence, you couldn't let everybody know what was going on [...] I was absolutely surrounded by men and by temptation and this went on until I just couldn't take any more of it.'[5]

Terri went to see a naval psychologist, who reported him for homosexuality. He never set sail again and, while waiting to be discharged, he was placed under 'open arrest', which meant that he had not been found guilty of anything except simply *being* homosexual. He later discovered that there had been an inquiry. On his corvette everyone was questioned about their relationship with him: 'They were trying to get someone to admit to having sexual intercourse with me and then a prison sentence would follow. Fortunately no one spoke against me […] Eventually I was given this "dishonourable" discharge and thrown out – and they said "Away you go."'[6]

After the war, Terri teamed up with another female impersonator, the irrepressible Barri Chatt. They formed a double act called 'Chatt and Gardener' and became close friends, sharing a professional relationship that lasted until Barri died in 1971. Terri said that he did not know anyone who disliked Barri, who possessed great charm.

Barri had been born in 1907 in Bishop Auckland, County Durham, and was known for his association with the Combined Services Entertainment (CSE). In 1946 this civilian addition to the armed forces shows, backed and funded by the Ministry of Defence, replaced the Entertainments National Service Association (ENSA). The CSE's function was to maintain the morale of the many servicemen who were still stationed abroad. In Singapore the CSE included a number of gay men who would later find fame in show business. These included John Schlesinger, then a ventriloquist, who went on to become an Oscar-winning film director, and the comedy actor Kenneth Williams, who remembered Barri Chatt for Keith Howes in a 1983 interview for *Gay News*:

> I met Barri Chatt in Sing-a-poor. We were both in CSE. There was an appalling incident involving him at the Raffles Hotel. Barri Chatt had been given the status of Captain as he was the show's director and star. Now he wasn't the sort of person to be a Captain. When he met another officer he would greet them with 'Hello, Captain dear' or 'Colonel, dear' or even 'Brigadier, dear'. He wasn't well suited to

wearing a Captain's uniform because he walked in a way that was pro-voc-at-ive, in very, very short shorts that exposed the whole of his calves. When he arrived at HQ he did pirouettes in front of the brigadier. He turned round five times on point and said to the startled officer 'Tell your mother we're here, dear, and put the kettle on.' Another of his phrases – which everybody took up – was 'It's life, love; it's the the-a-ter!'[7]

In his diary in 1952, Williams described seeing Barri at Collins Music Hall in a '5th rate variety show, which was appalling in every way. Saw Barri after in dressing room. Shocking really. Pathos here, covered in dusty gags.'[8] A few years after he died, Barri was the inspiration for the flamboyant and very out gay Captain Terri Dennis in Peter Nichols's play with songs, *Privates on Parade*. This was first staged at Stratford by the Royal Shakespeare Company before receiving its London premiere at the Aldwych Theatre on 17 February 1977 with Denis Quilley as the Captain. The play was set around the exploits of a mostly gay British military concert party stationed in Singapore and Malaysia in the late 1940s during the Malayan emergency. In the 1982 film version Quilley memorably recreated his stage role.

In 1983 Keith Howes described Terri Gardener as 'imposing and rosy-cheeked' and as someone who 'exudes home-fire warmth and generosity.' His flat in East London was filled with movie and theatre memorabilia. Greta Garbo was his idol. Terri spoke to Keith about Barri Chatt with love and affection. Their relationship was strictly professional. He told Howes: 'I feel his presence all the time. Sometimes when I'm about to go out onstage, I'll say "Dear God, Barri, I need you tonight."'[9]

Terri died on 15 August 2000 at the age of 80. In 2016 I asked Keith Howes to recall his meeting with Terri. He said:

Terri and I had a mutual friend – Barry Conley – and it was Barry who persuaded Terri to be interviewed by *Gay News* in 1983. Twisted his arm, actually. Terri was not into self-advertisement, or the 'out there' 'broadcasting it' stance of gay liberation and newspapers like *Gay News*. That first half-hour in Terri's cramped flat on a cold March day, electric fire at full suffocating power, elicited his basic life story without much rapport or enthusiasm. He made tea for photographer Bob Workman and myself, and we dutifully applied ourselves to the bought cake and biscuits. Then something happened, sun through the clouds. He spoke of his late partner Barri Chatt and asked if I would like to see some photographs. There, in a ragged scrapbook, was Terri's drag persona – a square-jawed Jezebel in a jet black wig, false eyelashes, lacy dress. I said, 'Terri, it's Jane Russell!' Ice broken, I gasped and gestured at every scrap of Terri and Barri's glamorous, clamorous past. It was joyous and camp ... and gay! The three of us sat down again, this time with the Full Terri – a beautiful, modest, loving man with many friends and a philosophy of gentle kindness which would break down the defences of the most committed homophobe. He loved people, he loved life, he loved his past and his present. What struck me most was his voice – smokey tendrils in the air, slightly breathless, hypnotic. Bob and I left in a state of merriment. Terri was life-loving and it was catching! A few weeks later, when I was preparing to go and interview the writer and barrister John Mortimer for *Gay News*, I received a call from my friend and colleague Alison Hennegan. She told me that the paper had folded. The issue containing Terri's interview would be the last. *Gay News*, 'the world's largest newspaper for homosexuals', was dead. Part of my life, part of my identity, part of my family. I didn't meet Terri again, but I heard from Barry Conley that he liked the piece as published and was sorry to hear of the demise.

Terri was a combatant in a war – the official war and the ongoing one. As a gay man like me he was always, to some extent, fighting 'behind enemy lines'. He did it with makeup and humour, and courtesy and gentleness. I have been involved in that fight, too – using different weapons, including the pen. As I tried to make sense of why *Gay News*, so vibrant, so multi-faceted, so NECESSARY, had met such a sudden end, I was becoming involved in another fight. My oldest friend, Howard, was diagnosed with what we called then 'the gay cancer' but had recently been given the acronym AIDS. He was the 33rd person in Britain to be listed. He died two years later. Over the next few years I lost Bruce, Ken, Adrian, John and Louis from my personal circle, Monty Python's Graham Chapman, film director and artist Derek Jarman, writer and director Gerald Chapman of Gay Sweatshop, journalist Roger Baker, 'King of Leather' Bryan Derbyshire, actors Ian Charleson and Gary Bond from my professional world and, from *Gay News*, founder-editor Denis Lemon, news reporter Jeff Grace and film critic Jack Babuscio. The next interview I did after Terri's was for *Capital Gay*. It involved a man whose lover died of AIDS and whose body was shipped back to his country of birth in a body bag.

People are remembered in different ways. In Terri Gardener's case we can be thankful that he was interviewed, by three different social historians, about his war service and gay life. Their focus was on firsthand testimony, which is integral to historical research. Over time, though, there have been regrettable cuts to local funding which has meant that the good work undertaken throughout the 1980s and 1990s to document the lives of 'ordinary' people at grass-roots level has all but vanished.[10]

The RAF

11

The Killing Skies

The Royal Air Force was generally considered to be the more 'glamorous' option of the three armed services. This was best explained by Ulric Cross, a Trinidadian who became one of the most decorated black West Indian airmen in World War II. In 1944 he was awarded both the Distinguished Flying Cross (DFC) and Distinguished Service Order (DSO). Interviewed on television in 1990, Ulric said he had joined the RAF because he was young, adventurous and idealistic. He added: 'The whole idea of being a member of the Royal Air Force was romantic. To me that was the height of anybody's ambition, to be a flight lieutenant in the Royal Air Force and to get the DFC. Most of my friends thought I was mad.'[1]

Ulric was mainly drawn to the RAF for adventure and glamour. This was probably what attracted some gay men to join. Patrick Bishop said in *Bomber Boys: Fighting Back 1940–1945* (2007) that gay airmen were more likely to keep their sexual preferences to themselves and 'pretend to be heterosexual' but, he added, alcohol had a way of exposing the truth. He referred to a story told by Willie Lewis about an American crew that had been rescued from the Channel after ditching and spent the night with his squadron on their way home:

> The three officers were made very welcome in the officers' mess, and we stood shouting, and howling, through the usual list of nice songs,

and then filthy ones, and back to nice ones again. And then the incredible happened. One of our chaps continued to keep holding the hands of one of the Americans. And yet I'd never thought he was a nancy boy before [...] The American was terribly distressed [...] We grabbed our man and took him back to his bedroom and said 'Don't come back.' And that was that.[2]

In 1975 Michael Bentine, the comedian and founder member of the Goons, published *The Long Banana Skin*, the first book in his three-part autobiography. This first volume covered his attempts to join the RAF in wartime Britain and his subsequent service as an intelligence officer on a Polish Wellington squadron, to his time with the 2nd Tactical Air Force (2nd TAF). 'Let the leaders bear any burden of guilt,' he said, 'and not the young men, whose bodies and minds I saw broken, in that [...] holocaust.'[3] Bentine described one of his comrades who, under Bomber Command, flew over occupied Europe, where the targets included Berlin and Hanover, Hamburg and Bremerhaven. The comrade, a commissioned air gunner called Roy, took great delight in telling the crew he had been a chorus boy before the war. He was 'as "gay" as Caesar's Camp', said Bentine who also described him as tall and willowy, a 'one-off' who was one of the bravest people he had ever met. Not only had Roy received the Distinguished Flying Medal (DFM) when he was a sergeant air gunner, as an officer he later received the DFC. During bombing missions, Roy kept up his 'gay' banter to the amusement of the air crew, especially when they faced immediate danger. On being caught in the German searchlights he would cry 'Jesus! Skipper! They want a bloody encore!' Bentine recalled, 'as he squirted his four chattering guns down into the blue-white burning beams in a hopeless attempt to shoot them out: "For Christ's sake give us a pink, duckie – this colour shows my bloody age!"' Bentine grieved when he learned that Roy had been killed in action: 'cut to pieces by a cannon shell in his rear turret – keeping up his "gay" banter, according to the crew, for the whole of the long and agonizing return trip.'[4]

In 1977 Squadron Leader Jack Currie's *Lancaster Target* was published. It is generally considered to be one of the finest books ever written about life on a bomber station during the war. Praised for its authenticity, Currie's book relates the fears and anxieties of flying Lancaster bombers over occupied Europe while facing the threat of anti-aircraft flac from the Germans. Currie described Rory, one of the aircrew he befriended, a mid-upper gunner, 'neat and well groomed, with a face like that of a contented cat. He spoke with a lisp and a lilting, feminine diction, and he used scented soaps and lotions. He occasionally dabbed his nose with a small, silk handkerchief.' Currie explained that Rory wore a DFM ribbon and a wound stripe, 'so his manner escaped the abuse which it might have otherwise attracted, in the aggressively masculine society in which he moved.'[5] Currie also recalled the evening he spent in the officers' mess when Rory described his luxurious apartment in London's West End:

> Lovely fitted carpets up to your ankles, dear, and such beautiful pictures on the walls. Well, in the dreadful blitz, there was this absolute disaster when a horrid bomb came right through the ceiling into my lovely living-room. My dears, it wasn't so much the dreadful damage that the bomb did, it was the absolute havoc caused by the fire brigade.

Unfortunately, a group of rowdy inebriated and robust Australians who were in attendance starting mocking poor Rory, who 'flung himself at his nearest listener' and began to pummel his laughing face with his fists. The tall Australian was taken aback and retreated behind an even larger colleague who managed to calm the situation after Rory had screamed abuse at them, 'All you know or care about are rabbits, and sheep, and [...] and kangaroos! You only came here as an excuse to get away from your own awful, uncultured country.' After Rory had calmed down, he smoothed his hair, gave a twinkling smile and accepted the offer of a drink from the Australians: 'Thanks very much. I'll have a gin and lime.'[6]

In the 1970s Michael Bentine and Jack Currie remembered gay men who were accepted among their comrades in their wartime RAF days, and who shared in the banter and camaraderie whether facing death in a fighter over occupied Europe, or at a bar at their RAF station. However, homophobic hostility was never far away. Bentine recalled an incident involving one of his colleagues and a senior officer who had made an offensive remark about Roy. A 'blazing row' ensued, and Bentine's friend, defending the brave gay Roy, in a rage shouted at the senior officer: 'He's got more guts in his arsehole than you've got in your whole body! Christ, it must gall you to have men like him on your squadrons with D.S.Os, D.F.Cs and D.F.Ms while all you've got is a bloody little piece of lettuce leaf for shooting up the bleeding Arabs! Sir!'[7]

George Montague was unaware of the word 'homosexual' and the existence of men who had sex with other men until 1941 when, at the age of 18, he enlisted in the RAF Volunteer Reserve. Accepted as a trainee wireless operator air gunner, George later recalled,

> the very first time anything registered with me was when I was a corporal and the corporals didn't mix with the other ranks. We used to sit in the veranda at the end of the hut. They were all talking and I heard the end of the conversation: 'I've got one in my hut,' and then somebody said, 'I've got two in mine, and if I catch them together, I'll cut their bollocks off!' I said, 'What you talking about?' And they said, 'Brown hatters.' I said, 'What's that?' They told me and I was disgusted, absolutely disgusted.[8]

At the time, George was guilty of prejudice against homosexuals. Shortly after the war, in 1946, George experienced his first same-sex encounter but he kept his homosexuality a secret until 1982. By then he was almost 60, and had been married with grown-up children. Since 'coming out', he has led a happy and fulfilled life. At the time of writing George lives with his partner in Brighton, where he is known as 'the Oldest Gay in the Village', which is also the title of his autobiography.[9]

Before the war, Sue Westbury's uncle, Robert Bannister, was an undergraduate training to be a chemist when he met an architecture student named Eric Kimpton at a party in Cambridge. When war came, Sue's Uncle Bob volunteered for the RAF and applied to be a pilot, but he was diagnosed as having colour blindness and trained instead to be a navigator in Britain and Canada. During this time, Sue's 'Uncle' Eric joined the Royal Artillery and was commissioned. Sue remembers:

> Sometimes Bob and Eric were able to arrange their leave to coincide and spent happy days together away from the war. Eric was promoted to captain, and was involved in the planning for the invasion of France. He was trusted with sensitive information and was privy to the secret fuel Pipeline under the Ocean or 'PLUTO' as it was codenamed. Bob enjoyed his years in the RAF and had a 'good war', qualifying as a Pathfinder navigator and winning the Distinguished Flying Cross (DFC).

After the war, Bob was engaged by BOAC as a navigator on the prestigious De Havilland Comet fleet. When this folded in the wake of the Comet disasters, he was employed by a well-known bank. At some point in the 1950s, the bank found out he was gay and immediately dismissed him. Says Sue:

> When I was born, both Uncle Eric and Uncle Bob were named as my godfathers. I think that this was the family's way of showing that they supported their relationship and accepted Eric as a permanent member of the family. Eric and Bob gained acceptance with people because they were such a lovely couple; so charming and so likeable. Both were handsome and debonair, and Bob had dark good looks and resembled the actor Herbert Lom. Uncle Bob always wore a beautiful amethyst ring when he flew bombing operations. It was partly a lucky talisman, but it might also have been useful to sell if he was ever shot down over occupied territory. When, aged 18, I passed my nursing exams, Bob, with characteristic kindness and generosity, insisted I accept it as a gift. I still wear it today.

Eric was a trader, but in the 1960s his business failed and he was made bankrupt. Without telling him, Bob sold his prized DFC to a dealer and gave Eric the proceeds. Bob and Eric remained together for over 65 years.

Sue continues:

> They were very private people and discreet, yet fairly open, about their relationship and nobody seemed to mind because they were so very likeable. Bob remarked, however, that he was able to charm people when required. Bob and Eric enjoyed the arts, good food and travelling and they whizzed around the countryside in a very stylish yellow MG sports car. They also bred and showed whippets at Crufts. They loved their dogs and kept up to 18 at a time! One of the dogs even had a part in the film *The Day of the Jackal*. Bob and Eric lived in Bayswater for a time, moving to Bourne End, then to Stoke Poges. They loved each other very much, and when Bob died in 2007, Eric felt very alone and terribly lonely. He passed away himself in 2011. I miss Uncle Bob and Uncle Eric and I have very fond memories of them.[10]

12

Richard Rumbold: The Flyer

The Royal Air Force meant the world to Richard Rumbold. This troubled soul found a home and a family with his RAF pals. For Richard the teasing, jokes and camaraderie he shared with his friends in the mess contrasted with the civilian world, which he found bleak and competitive. In 1949, using the pseudonym Richard Lumford, the former wartime RAF pilot wrote an autobiography called *My Father's Son* in which he eloquently expressed the difficulties he faced in adapting to civilian life.

Richard was a complex man who, as a young adult, had suffered from tuberculosis and a chronic and only partially curable neurosis. He had loved being part of the RAF and, after the war, he missed the 'warm physical proximity in the mess' or 'the friendly smile of a fellow pilot'.[1] Martin Francis explained in *The Flyer: British Culture and the Royal Air Force, 1939–1945* (2008): 'Some former airmen found it difficult to cope with the break-up of the all-male camaraderie of service life', but he also identified Richard as a homosexual who:

> could not look, as heterosexual flyers could, to marriage and fatherhood as consolation for the loss of the comradeship of the wartime RAF. Indeed, life for gay men in the immediate post-war years was distinctly uncomfortable, given the homophobic temper

of the popular press and the increased victimization of male homosexuals by the police and the courts.²

Richard Rumbold had a troubled childhood, with a bully for a father, and a mother who suffered from depression. Raleigh Trevelyan described him in the *Oxford Dictionary of National Biography* (2004) as 'handsome and physically well built, with blue eyes' but noted that Richard's father constantly attacked him for being effeminate.³ William Plomer writes of Richard as someone who, when he was well and in good spirits, 'appeared genial and good-humoured, but a deep seriousness persisted. He had had little stimulus, in his early and formative years, to lightheartedness. As he grew up he was aware of his sadness, and he seriously and pathetically recorded a resolution, when only twenty, to make more jokes.'⁴

In 1933, while he was a student at Christ Church, Oxford, Richard ran a literary club, arranging talks by such luminaries as Oscar Wilde's lover, Lord Alfred Douglas, and W. B. Yeats. However, when he was just 20, Richard became a *cause célèbre* when he published a novel, *Little Victims*. Trevelyan wrote:

> This bitter, ill-judged, obviously autobiographical book was a *succès de scandale*, lashing out at the church [Richard was a Catholic], his parents, public-school homosexuality, and Oxford aesthetes. He was refused the sacrament by the university chaplain [...] Furious, he decided to abjure Roman Catholicism. Very soon afterwards he spat blood and tuberculosis was diagnosed. He left Oxford without taking a degree in 1934.⁵

At the outbreak of war, Richard was keen to do his bit, and he joined up as a private in the Royal Army Service Corps (RASC). This angered his father, who had served as a regular officer in a cavalry regiment – the Queen's Bays – in the South African War nearly 40 years earlier. Captain Rumbold was incensed that his only son had joined the ranks. Not only did the Captain write abusive and contemptuous letters to his son but he interfered, by informing the Army that Richard had TB. Consequently the young man was forced to leave. However, Richard was not deterred. Plomer says: 'He tried to enlist in the RAF, was rejected on medical grounds, pleaded for another chance, and by a combination of will-power and breathing exercises, magically passed an aircrew medical only six weeks later. "And thenceforth," he wrote, "began the most blessed, the most fruitful, period of my life."'[6]

Before he joined the RAF, Richard had already discovered the comradeship that existed among fellow servicemen. He said that his friends in the RASC were a 'wild lot' and he got on with them extremely well:

> I was known by many nicknames – Jumbo, Riccy, Sweetheart, Sunshine and Sundown were among them – and like everybody else I had 'my mate' – a person to whom one owed a loyalty which was strong and instinctive but at the same time casual and undemanding, a relationship which perfectly fitted the needs of my nature.[7]

After joining the RAF, he said,

> I was able to mix freely with the Hampden flying crews, and I would take every opportunity of flying with them […] in searches for aircraft reported missing from operations. For in those days losses amongst the crews were considerable, and as the whole issue of the war was still in doubt, men did not know whether their sacrifices would prove worthless or not – a test of loyalty and endurance indeed […] Among these unpretentious and extroverted men of action I felt myself perfectly at home: in the life of adventure, in life lived for the day's realism, one forgot oneself and the haunting insoluble problems of the human destiny […] By the spirit of the group and one's integration with it one was largely relieved of the burden of individual life […] I felt an affinity with the air – with the open airy world – like the kinship felt towards the sea; both are elementary things.[8]

In spite of his love of flying, and his sense of belonging, Richard made a fatal error which ended his RAF career:

> I had somehow or other to solve the intolerable tension, possibly because I hoped to hide from myself my own guilt by behaving even more anarchically and individualistically – I began to take unheard-of risks in the air […] I recklessly flew an Anson under the Menai Bridge; and an officer flying above reported the incident.[9]

Richard received his certificate of discharge on 3 March 1943 but it stated that he was discharged for being 'physically unfit' and that 'this airman has carried out his duties in a conscientious and entirely satisfactory manner'. He was devastated:

> My discharge from the RAF proved a terrible blow […] The RAF had provided an answer to many of my emotional problems in a way which civilian life would never be able to do, although at the time I had scarcely been aware of that fact. For the thing had been so blissfully unconscious – that was its beauty; it had stolen upon me unawares, born out of a hundred and one little touches; the warm physical proximity in the Mess or at P.T., the friendly smile of a fellow pilot as he got into his aircraft, the gay identification with that gay light-hearted attitude to life, the common language and jargon of the air which we shared, the ragging and the teasing and the jokes. The whole thing came back to me now with a nearly intolerable intensity, the more so in contrast with the bleak and competitive civilian world.[10]

After leaving the RAF, Richard's TB flared up and he was forced to spend a few months in a sanatorium. He then found employment as a war reporter, which enabled him to make several flights with his beloved RAF, including a bomber raid on Ulm in southern Germany. His diary entry for 13 September 1943 said:

> Had a drink with Flight Lieutenant M. We talked about the RAF, its slang words, its relationships. I thought, 'How pleasant it is to

belong to, to be a part of, a closed world – a world in which one's customs are not known to the outside world.' A mystique of the group, that *is* something. It is the only thing for people who, like myself, cannot believe in Christianity.[11]

On 10 March 1961 Richard Rumbold died when he fell from a window, possibly accidentally, at a hotel in Palermo, Italy.

Richard's story is a powerful one, and reveals the difficulties faced by many former airmen who found it impossible to cope with civilian life after the war. They missed the all-male comradeship and camaraderie of service life. Thankfully, Richard's memoir *My Father's Son* and his published diary extracts provide us with a revealing, honest and deeply moving account of his life and wartime experiences.

13

Ian Gleed: The Hero

In 1942 the heroic Battle of Britain Spitfire pilot Ian Gleed published a memoir called *Arise to Conquer*. It proved to be a remarkably honest account of his exploits, given the restrictions imposed on him by wartime censorship. Twice he bailed out of blazing Spitfires. Twice King George VI decorated him. Ian loved the RAF, and for his bravery he received the DFC and DSO, but he made the ultimate sacrifice in 1943 when his Spitfire was shot down over Tunisia.

When Ian's 'confirmed bachelor' status caused concern for Victor Gollancz, the publisher of his memoir, he agreed to create a fictional girlfriend called 'Pam'. She was a surprise to his family and friends because they had never heard of 'Pam', but Ian explained to them that she did not exist and that he had put her in because 'readers like a touch of romance'. What his family and friends probably never knew, or suspected, was that Ian had no desire to have a girlfriend. He was homosexual, but in those days he could not be open about this. He had to keep his sexuality private or risk being court-martialled and thrown out of the RAF. It was not until the 1990s, when one of his lovers, Christopher Gotch, was interviewed for two BBC television programmes, *It's Not Unusual* (1997) and *Timewatch: Sex and War* (1998), that the truth was revealed and made public.

Ian Gleed was a doctor's son, born in London in 1916. Educated at Epsom College, he was, remembered Ronald Gethen, a fellow pupil, 'a rather scruffy little individual, not overliked and he was usually thumped (or kicked) by some of the boys just because he was there'.[1] Ian's father had served throughout World War I as a captain in the Royal Army Medical Corps (RAMC), and Ian's sister, Daphne, also joined the medical profession. Ian was expected to follow in his father's footsteps and become a doctor, but the young man wanted a more exciting career: flying. He learned to fly privately before he joined the RAF at the age of 20, completing his 'wings' course on Christmas Day 1936. His biographer Norman Franks says that Ian was in his element during this period:

> The world was at his feet. He excelled at his chosen profession, had fulfilled his dream of becoming a fighter pilot and had become a member of 'the greatest flying club in the world', as the peacetime Royal Air Force of the 1930's was often called [...] He was able to soar like an eagle, swoop like a hawk and cavort like a swallow.[2]

Ian proved to be an exceptional pilot, and it did not take long for him to be promoted to flying officer, on 9 October 1938.

Away from the RAF, Ian's pastime pursuits included sailing and writing. Holidaying in the south of France in 1938, Ian met and befriended the homosexual novelist W. Somerset Maugham, who invited the young man to stay at his villa. He loaned him the use of his yacht, which Ian happily sailed on the blue Mediterranean. In 1942 Maugham published *Strictly Personal*, in which he related his thoughts and experiences of wartime France and Britain during the early months of the war. Maugham described some of the young airmen he met, including Ian, whom he did not name. Ian was later identified as the man by Hector Bolitho in *A Penguin in the Eyrie* (1955). Maugham said:

> I knew one somewhat more intimately; he was a little older than the others, twenty-four, and quite a little chap [...] jaunty, with

a care-free look in his impudent blue eyes [...] He was a jovial, cheery soul. He was in tearing spirits because he had two days' leave and was determined to have the time of his life. He was full of plans for the future. After the war was won, he was going to buy a sailing-boat, forty foot long, and sail with a friend to the South Seas.[3]

In February 1940 Ian was testing a Spitfire when it broke up in the air. He was thrown out of the cockpit and lost consciousness. When he came round he was falling to the ground with head injuries and a damaged leg, so he pulled his rip-cord and the parachute opened. In *Arise to Conquer* he described how he remained calm in this terrifying incident:

I was slung forward in the cockpit, my safety-straps just stopping me hitting the dashboard. I tried to lift my head, but couldn't. Bang! Blackness. 'Why can't I sleep? Wonder what the time is. Where am I?' Everything was black – very black. 'Where am I? When did I land? And what have I been doing? *Christ, I must be in the air!* Where's the rip-cord? It was very strange: there was no dropping sensation; it was absolutely dark, and I couldn't feel any rushing air. 'Now feel carefully for the rip-cord. Keep cool' [...] At last I felt the metal square. It felt queerly warm. I tugged hard. Felt a jerk. Then nothing.[4]

Thankfully Ian landed safely on the ground where he was rushed to hospital.

Ian, affectionately known as 'Widge', was loved and respected by his RAF pals and they meant everything to him. After he had recovered from his flying accident, Ian was notified of a posting to France to join 87 Squadron as a flight commander, and on 17 May 1940 he arrived in Senan, France, and immediately found himself in the conflict that would lead to the German occupation of that country. In Norman Franks's biography, Roland Beamont of 87 Squadron described Ian:

Gleed was one of our replacement pilots and he came out from the UK to tell us exactly how to run the war – all 5ft 6ins of him! He was immediately as good as his word and tore into the enemy on every conceivable occasion with apparent delight and entire lack of concern. His spirit was exactly what was needed to bolster up the somewhat stunned survivors of the week following 10 May. That is not to say that 87 Squadron's morale was not extremely high, but The Widge somehow managed to raise it further.[5]

In the summer of 1940 Ian took part in the Battle of Britain. All the RAF flyers were heroes, but not all of them survived. Ian did, and in September 1940 he was awarded the DFC. The award was made public in the *London Gazette*:

Flight Lieutenant Ian Gleed took over a flight in No 87 Squadron on arriving from England after intensive hostilities had begun. The Squadron was moved several times, and he knew neither the officers nor the airmen. He took on his task with energy and discretion, won the confidence of his flight and led them with skill and success. Throughout he showed great courage in the air and was on duty almost continuously.[6]

Ian received his DFC from King George VI at Buckingham Palace on 18 February 1941 with his parents and sister in attendance.

Ian continued to serve his King and country and on 18 November 1941 he was appointed wing leader at Middle Wallop, a large Air Force base near Salisbury. He was honoured yet again when he was awarded the DSO. This was the crowning achievement for Ian. On this occasion it was stated:

he has led his wing on 26 sorties over enemy territory. He has always displayed a fine fighting spirit which, combined with his masterly leadership and keenness, has set an inspiring example. Wing Commander Gleed has destroyed at least 12 enemy aircraft, two of which he shot down at night.[7]

In *Arise to Conquer*, Ian described his visit to Buckingham Palace to receive his DSO from King George VI:

> My name was called out. I stepped onto the dais, turned left and made a gentle bow. 'Congratulations. I hope that we shall see you here again soon.' The King neatly placed the glittering silver cross on my breast. I stepped back, turned right and marched briskly down to the foyer. The footman handed me a small jeweller's box, and placed my medal in it. We now stood and looked through the doors and watched the others being decorated. At last the last one was done. The orchestra gave a roll of drums, the audience rose and 'God Save the King' was sung, His Majesty standing at attention. Then the King said 'Good morning', and turned and walked through the doors at the back of the dais. The investiture was over [...] On the whole it was one of the most impressive ceremonies that I have ever attended. It gave me courage and increased my morale. Nazis, you may blow London and every town in our country to smithereens – if you can. You shall never rule the British Isles.[8]

Ian was posted to HQ Fighter Command on 16 July 1942 as Wing Commander Tactics, becoming Wing Commander Operations on 7 December 1942. He continued to be an inspiring leader to the pilots under his command. 'Bunny' Currant remembered during the early summer of 1942:

> He was one of the most courageous men I've ever had the privilege to know. He may have been tiny in stature but by God he had a big heart and seemed not to have any fear. He was unmoveable and unflappable with a modest, unassuming manner and always thought for his pilots and for the ground crews and staff. A caring man, I remember him warmly with gratitude. A pocket size man with care for others and courage beyond compare.[9]

Laurence Thorogood later said: 'I flew a lot with Ian and due to him I probably survived the war. He was a great inspiration to us all,

entirely unselfish and very brave. I have never known a better loved
Commanding Officer.'[10]

Posted to the Middle East on 1 January 1943, Ian was attached
to 145 Squadron in North Africa to gain experience of desert
operations before becoming wing leader of 244 Wing on 31 January.
On an afternoon patrol over the Cap Bon, a peninsula in far north-
eastern Tunisia, on 16 April 1943, Ian was shot down. He headed
for the Tunisian coast but his Spitfire was found on sand dunes
near the sea on the western coastline of Cap Bon. His body was
not found there but it is known that he was buried at Tazoghrane.
He was reburied in the Military Cemetery at Enfidaville, a town
in north-eastern Tunisia, on 25 April 1944. In addition to his DFC
and DSO, Belgium awarded Ian their Croix de Guerre in 1943, and
France its Croix de Guerre in 1946.

Christopher Gotch was born in 1923 and was a schoolboy at
Marlborough when he decided he wanted to be a fighter pilot.
Lying about his age, he managed to join the RAF and, after three
months' training in Canada, in 1942 Christopher was posted to
Middle Wallop, Ian's RAF station. He soon found himself the
object of Ian's affections. Christopher recalled: 'After I'd been
there about three months I was sitting in the mess and I felt
someone gazing at me. A curious sensation. And there was the
Wing Commander, "ops" he was called.' Christopher was in awe
of Ian because he was superior to him in rank, and a celebrated
fighter pilot who had survived the Battle of Britain. 'I walked up
to my bedroom,' he said:

> and who should be sitting there on my window sill, looking at my
> photograph album, but Commander Ian Gleed. He just leant over
> and gave me a kiss which took me by surprise but being the product
> of a public school it wasn't *exactly* strange. So we started having sex
> together. He was a great character, an incredible character. He was
> the first bloke who ever buggered me [...] He had charm, he had
> personality and he had a car and he used to take me up to London
> and introduce me to people.[11]

Though same-sex relationships could be tolerated throughout the war, they were rarely, if ever, openly discussed. Christopher explained that no one ever talked about same-sex relationships because they were against the law. In the armed services they were court martial offences, and servicemen could be discharged and imprisoned if discovered. He said homosexuality was a 'dirty word' and, if discussed, it was in 'hushed tones and absolute horror'. It was widely believed that homosexuality would destroy morale which, Christopher said, 'was a load of rubbish'. Christopher served in the RAF from 1940 to 1946 as a fighter pilot in Hurricanes, Spitfires, Typhoons and Mustangs in Europe, Canada, India and Burma. He survived five plane crashes and, in over 300 operational flights, he was twice wounded. In 1944 he was promoted to squadron leader. Christopher died in 2002.

Regarding Ian Gleed, Peter Devitt, assistant curator of the Royal Air Force Museum, London, summarises:

In the spring of 1941, Fighter Command began 'leaning into France', mounting offensive 'sweeps' over occupied Europe designed to bring the Luftwaffe to battle. Fighter aircraft at the main RAF stations were now grouped into 'wings' of three or more squadrons, and each was commanded by a carefully selected 'wing leader'. These men were veteran pilots of proven ability who possessed the knowledge, experience, situational awareness and tactical nous to read and control an aerial engagement as it developed; imposing order on the chaos of fighter combat. In practice, this meant identifying the most favourable circumstances in which to bring their squadrons into action, and then directing the optimum firepower on to the enemy while maintaining the wing's cohesion as a fighting unit. To succeed, wing leaders required the necessary strength of character to inspire confidence in the pilots they led, as well as the self-belief to make vital split-second decisions in the flush of battle. Wing leaders also had to have the emotional maturity to set aside the individualism and personal ambition that defined them as fighter pilots, and focus instead on the collective success of the wing and on minimising casualties. For them, courage – Hemingway's 'grace under pressure' – was a given. The young men who could do all of this were exceptional, and Johnny Kent, 'Sailor' Malan, Douglas Bader, 'Paddy' Finucane, Johnnie Johnson and 'Al' Deere belonged to a glamorous élite deservedly lionised by the popular press. It was clear that Ian 'Widge' Gleed also had what was necessary to inspire his men and lead a successful RAF fighter wing. In November 1941, Gleed was promoted to Wing Commander, in charge of the Middle Wallop and then Ibsley Wings, and took another step towards his place in the pantheon of air fighting heroes.[12]

Thanks to the television interviews with Christopher Gotch, and the honesty with which he answered questions about his love affair with Ian, we have on record some insight into Ian's 'secret' life as a sexually active gay man. It brings an important aspect of his character and personality out into the open, one that he had to cover up in his 1942 autobiography. It demonstrates that not all of the Battle of Britain heroes that we love, admire, cherish and respect were heterosexuals. Gay men like Ian were also fearless and brave in wartime, and some of them, like Ian, gave their lives.

14

Hector Bolitho: The Writer

Hector Bolitho wrote several outstanding memoirs and diary anthologies which include his reminiscences and observations about the war. One of these is *War in the Strand* (1942). He also made an important contribution to documenting the lives of RAF fighter pilots in books such as *Combat Report: The Story of a Fighter Pilot* (1943) and *A Penguin in the Eyrie* (1955). He wrote beautifully and eloquently about the bravery and sacrifices of the young men who fought in the Battle of Britain, and other battles in the air. Yet these books have remained largely forgotten. With the exception of *Combat Report*, which was reissued by Amberley Publishing in 2012 as *Finest of the Few*, Hector's wonderful and emotionally charged publications are barely, if ever, acknowledged in books about World War II. He is waiting to be rediscovered.

If Ian Gleed (see Chapter 13) had survived the war, he planned to sail his yacht and pursue his interest in writing. His wartime memoir, *Arise to Conquer*, had been a success and, before the war, he had befriended several literary people who took an interest in him, and encouraged him. These included Hector Bolitho, who, in *A Penguin in the Eyrie*, movingly recalled the younger pilot's prewar visits to his home in Essex: 'The picture I suddenly recall is of myself at a desk, looking out at Ian playing with my Dalmatian on the lawn. They were both at the puppy-dog stage and had much in common. His enthusiasms were enchanting."[1] In 1941 Hector was reunited with Ian when the latter was stationed at Middle Wallop:

> Ian's merriment made it hard for me to believe in the thirteen combats with German aircraft. When we relaxed into seriousness […] I realized, in the depth of his voice and the quiet of his mind, that there was wisdom behind his laughter. After dinner we strolled along the bank of the Avon, to Harnham, and we did not speak of war all the way.[2]

The following morning Hector visited Ian again:

> I walked with Ian to the aerodrome, to see his new Spitfire; past the bombed skeleton of a hangar – a great dinosaur of steel bones, with birds flying in and out. The Spitfire was fresh from the factory and ready for battle: Ian stroked its fuselage with the palm of his hand. Five airmen were working on the aircraft, tinkering and screwing and painting, poking their heads into its mysteries so that their behinds and legs hung in mid-air. We went again in the evening: the five were still working and one of them was painting Ian's mascot on the body – the cat from *Pinocchio*, smashing a swastika with its paw. We walked back to the mess – a calm, lovely Wiltshire evening; great shafts of light from the setting sun, stillness and peace.[3]

Hector was a New Zealander who, in 1921, left his country of birth. He had been shocked at the arrest and imprisonment of his boyhood mentor Charles Ewing Mackay, who had seriously wounded a man to whom he had made homosexual advances. In 1923 Hector settled in London, where he began working as a freelance journalist. For eight years he lived in the cloisters of Windsor Castle, with unrestricted access to the Royal Archives. His discovery of Prince Albert's unpublished letters to Queen Victoria led to the publication of his first international bestseller, *Albert the Good* (1932). A few years later his *King Edward VIII: His Life and Reign* (1937) was published three months after the December 1936 abdication. Hector was severely critical of the former monarch, which provoked scathing condemnation by Winston Churchill. In 1938 Hector's radio play *Victoria and Disraeli* was broadcast by the BBC and he made a major contribution to historical scholarship as the editor of *Further Letters of Queen Victoria* (1938).[4]

Hector shared his life and his home with John Simpson. Hector described John as his 'secretary', which was then a common euphemism for gay partner. It is possible that they had a relationship which lasted into the war. In 1943 Hector wrote *Combat Report* as a loving tribute to John (who is identified in the book only as 'John', his surname is omitted). In the book he described the start of their 'relationship' in 1934 when Hector was 37 and John was 21:

> It was amusing for me to see him emerge as a smart little Londoner, with bowler hat and gloves and umbrella. There was a certain clean correctness about his clothes which was a key to his inner scrupulousness. But he was not at home in the Berkeley and the Ritz. He pretended to enjoy it all, but I think that his heart was in the country.[5]

At this time Hector had started work on his biography of James MacKay, the first Lord Inchcape. John provided Hector with the help he needed, becoming his 'secretary' and librarian. In *Combat Report* Hector described the close relationship John had with his mother, 'a lovely, intelligent woman' and how, in September 1934, John took off his bowler hat, put away his folded umbrella, and set up home with Hector in a house called 'Boytons' in Hempstead, Saffron Walden in Essex:

> We made a garden and we collected furniture. His mother stayed with us and supervised my clumsy experiments at furnishing a kitchen [...] We set about making vegetable and flower beds from the neglected farmyard [...] the joy of that first summer was incomparable. I made my first home in England and I spread myself into the luxuries of a little lord of the manor. We dug and planted

and ate, and in the evening we were able to sleep from simple physical exhaustion.[6]

However, John was restless and keen to find something exciting to do with his life. In 1936 he joined the RAF and their home in Essex became 'open house' to John's RAF pals:

The pilots came to rest in the house when they were tired from flying and they brought their gramophone records to play [...] When they came in a party, they would be noisy and gay. When they came alone, they would be quiet and eager to talk before the fire. For there was never a bore among them. Their life was mine.[7]

When war came, Hector joined the RAF Volunteer Reserve as an intelligence officer with the rank of squadron leader. In September 1939 he was attached to the Air Ministry in London with another homosexual literary figure, David 'Bunny' Garnett of the Bloomsbury Group. Hector found Garnett 'bewildering but charming. Shy, I imagine. But I am shy of him. Working with somebody one has respected for so many years is a bit intimidating. I don't like seeing my writing gods too close.'[8] One year later the London Blitz began and Hector's harrowing diary description of one of the worst air raids, on 29–30 December 1940, which he witnessed with the Greek actress Katina Paxinou, was published in *War in the Strand*:

Last night I stood in Knightsbridge and watched the vast, spreading flames consuming the City. I was with Katina Paxinou and I could hear her sobbing as she clung to me. The night was hideous and we could see the dome of St. Paul's, a serene bubble, against the terrible saffron curtain of the fire. It is the first time I have become wholly selfless during the bombing. I had no fear and I found myself mumbling some sort of prayer. The human suffering seemed too vast for the abstract issues involved – that is what I thought for a little time. We walked along Piccadilly, across Trafalgar Square, to the

1 Lord Kitchener

2 'Is a Soldier Married a Soldier Spoiled?', *Home Chat*, 11 June 1910

IS "A SOLDIER MARRIED - - - - - - - A SOLDIER SPOILED"?

By DORA D'ESPAIGNE CHAPMAN.

LORD KITCHENER,
who thinks that in the Army "he travels the fastest who travels alone."

It must be very provoking to Lord Kitchener, no doubt, to have impertinent people, whether they are English great ladies or American interviewers, perpetually teasing him to know why he has never married.

To a man of such intense reticence, and whose unusual capacity for deep and superlatively faithful affection (indicated by most unmistakable traits in his handwriting) would hint, if rumour did not already do so, at some long-past, unforgotten disappointment, it must be peculiarly hateful.

But for all that it seems hardly "playing the game" for the greatest soldier of the day to shield himself from gossip at the expense of all womanhood by stating as his reason for remaining a bachelor that "a soldier married is a soldier spoiled."

* * *

Honour and Love.

The lot of the English soldier's wife is stern enough. Even in peace she is doomed to a roving life, and often to exile. And in time of war! No courage required of the soldier to *dare* can excel that asked of his wife to *endure* in war time.

In his heart Lord Kitchener must know this, and it is a blot on his scutcheon that he should press down the burden every soldier's wife has to bear, from the wife of Field-Marshal Earl Roberts of Kandahar, V.C., K.G., and so on, down to the unacknowledged bride of the private married "off the strength," by suggesting that she is a hindrance instead of a helpmeet to her husband, that

"He travels the fastest who travels alone."

If it were true, if soldiers' wives believed it, their lot would become intolerable. There are bad women everywhere, I know, but I am happy to believe that there are few wives of English soldiers who do not echo, and wish their husbands to echo, the words of Lovelace:

"I could not love thee, dear, so much, loved I not honour more."

* * *

Examples.

But, though we know this is the actual truth, Lord Kitchener's words are none the less wounding to husband and wife alike, and before he spoke them, to be flashed round the world as the deliberate opinion of the first general of the day, Lord Kitchener might well have bethought himself that his own mother was a soldier's wife, and that if his father had held this view Horatio Herbert Kitchener would never have been born!

Remembering this, it is possible to laugh Lord Kitchener out of court—at any rate, to put aside his words as mere prejudice, the single weakness of a character otherwise full of reason and common sense.

For what the soldier's wife knows in her heart all history cries aloud.

Practically every great general has been a married man—Alexander the Great wedded Roxana "out of pure affection"; Hannibal, Julius Cæsar, Charlemagne, Edward III. of England, Henri IV. of France, Cromwell, Marlborough, Napoleon, Wellington, were all husbands, many of them devoted ones.

*   *   *

Married Heroes.

Napoleon, in spite of passing infidelities, sincerely loved Josephine, and during his first and greatest campaign was writing her passionate love letters. Defeat came after his business match with Marie-Louise.

While to come to the present day, Lord Kitchener's own companions in the field— Lord Roberts, Lord Wolseley, Sir Evelyn Wood, General French—" our most brilliant cavalry leader "—Sir George White, the hero of Ladysmith, Sir Ian Hamilton, Kitchener's chief of staff, Lord Methuen, Sir. R. Pole-Carew, Sir Redvers Buller—all these were married, as were all the Boer generals, from the redoubtable and unconquered De Wet downwards.

Against these, as far as recollection and the reference books serve, one has to set only the bachelor Colonel Baden-Powell and Sir Archibald Hunter, the latter such a friend of Lord Kitchener's that he may easily have been affected with the microbe of misogyny against his better judgment!

Were all but these two "soldiers spoiled?"

*   *   *

A Suggestion.

It is a pity that one of the many ambitious, energetic, competent, but engaged-to-be-married young officers does not prepare a return of the married men in the King's Army to be illuminated on vellum (subscriptions from officers' fiancées, please!) and presented to his lordship, with a letter tactfully drawing his attention to the miserable handful he would have left if all these "soldiers spoiled" resigned under pressure of their wives' just indignation, which, in these days of women's rights, is not beyond the bounds of fancy.

Of course, there are men to-day, as always, to whom love—or what they mistake for love—comes as a weakness, instead of an

inspiration. A noble wife may save such a man from himself, but bachelorhood will not aid him, rather double the risk of his being swayed by some infatuation at a critical moment.

But not from such weaklings does Lord Kitchener—does any great general choose his lieutenants; and to other men—to real soldiers—love, a wife, "a warm hearthstone," is no stumbling block, but a guiding star.

—◦◦◦◦—

TIPS FOR HOLIDAY MAKERS.

If you are going on a very long journey, it is quite worth while to strap a small cushion into your holdall. A small cushion at one's back adds immensely to one's comfort, and really takes up very little room.

*   *   *

Close your eyes for a few minutes every now and then when on a long train journey. It rests them amazingly.

*   *   *

If you are travelling by night, rub a little cold cream well into your face, and wipe it off again before starting. Unless this is done, the close air of the railway carriage and the heat from the gas or electric light, are apt to dry the skin so much that it is very uncomfortable by the morning.

*   *   *

If you are going to Switzerland, or any other mountainous country, take a rubber hot-water bottle with you, if you happen to be one of those people who indulge in this luxury at home. Even in the height of summer, the nights are often bitterly cold in the mountain hotels.

*   *   *

Take with you, also, a blue or brown gauze veil, and smoked glasses, if you intend to go up any of the higher mountain railways. The glare from the ice is so trying to the eyes that it is impossible to see anything properly unless they are protected. It is a good plan, too, to rub a little cold cream into the face before starting on such an expedition.

*   *   *

And remember the railway company is not responsible for luggage that you take with you in the carriage. In such a case the luggage is in the passenger's own care, and he or she is responsible for its safety.

*   *   *

Some people find that if they go to one of the South Coast watering-places for a holiday, they suffer greatly from constipation. This is because the water has chalk in it. A good plan is to use distilled water—which can be bought for a few pence per gallon from any chemist—for drinking purposes.

5 The final resting place of Edward Brittain in Granezza British Cemetery, Italy

CAPTAIN
EDWARD H. BRITTAIN M.C.
NOTTS & DERBY REGIMENT
15TH JUNE 1918

AGED 22

Wills's Cigarettes

R. C. Sherriff

6 R. C. Sherriff

7 HMS *Erin*, 1917

8 HMS *Barham* visitors' day with sailors dancing

9 HMS *Bellerophon*, 11 November 1918

10 Aberdeen, 1919

11 Montague Glover

12 Soldiers photographed by Montague Glover

13 Wilfred Owen

14 Roger Casement

15 Ivor Novello

16 Fred Barnes

17 Ralph Hall

18 *Kiss Me Goodnight, Sergeant Major* music sheet

"——CAME THE DAWN!"

19 World War II postcard

20 'Christmas in the tropics, 1940'. Unidentified seamen aboard the *Queen of Bermuda*

21 'Christmas in the tropics, 1940'. Unidentified seamen aboard the *Queen of Bermuda*

22 Richard Rumbold

23 Christopher Gotch

24 Wing Commander Ian Gleed

25 The final resting place of Wing Commander Ian Gleed in Enfidaville War Cemetery, Tunisia

26 Hector Bolitho

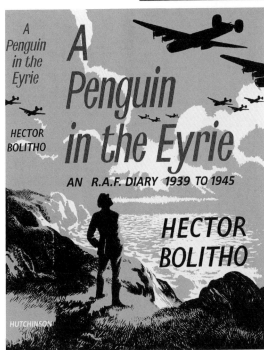

A Penguin in the Eyrie

HECTOR BOLITHO

A Penguin in the Eyrie

AN R.A.F. DIARY 1939 TO 1945

HECTOR BOLITHO

HUTCHINSON

27 The cover of Hector Bolitho's *A Penguin in the Eyrie*

28 Quentin Crisp in his Chelsea flat

29 PC Harry Daley and friend from *This Small Cloud* (1986)

30 Berto Pasuka

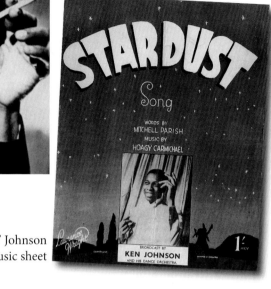

31 Ken 'Snakehips' Johnson
music sheet

32 Noël Coward entertaining the forces on BBC radio in 1943

33 Brian Desmond Hurst

34 Alan Turing

hotel. The bombing was almost over, but the American newspaper men staying at the Savoy came back with terrible stories. They always go out into the blitz. They are war correspondents. One told me that he heard a horse crying in the fire. That must have been terrible. I remember seeing a whole Polish village on fire in 1936, and the screeching of the horses was a sound from hell […] Acres of the city have been burned – early buildings and churches in which the ghosts of old London slept.[9]

On 17 April 1941 he wrote in his diary:

We have been through London's most terrible night. It is not easy to write down anything about it because I still feel as if I have been hit with a mallet. The physical reaction is like the pain of extreme exhaustion. And my brain thumps too much for my memory to be clear […] We took the sirens for granted when they sounded about nine o'clock. They are a habit now: they fit into the pattern of the City's sounds as naturally as the chiming of Big Ben.[10]

On 17 April Hector was staying at the Savoy Hotel on the Embankment when, several hours into the air raid, a bomb landed on the building. He continued in his diary:

The building staggered. One imagined that the vast stone structure was cracking, like icing sugar, and that one was living in the last second before death. Glass was flung at us, like hail through an open door. Then one smelled falling masonry. I don't remember a cry or movement from anybody. We stood still, waiting. Then I walked down to the spaces of light.[11]

During the war Hector used his journalistic skills to edit the *Royal Air Force Weekly Bulletin*, which in 1941 became the *Royal Air Force Journal*. In 1942 he was appointed editor of the *Coastal Command Intelligence Review*. He also contributed to radio programmes broadcast to the Empire and, occasionally, to the BBC journal *London Calling*. In an edition published not long after the Battle of Britain entitled 'Why I Believe in the Royal Air Force', he said:

Millions of people did not discover the Royal Air Force until the war began. Aerodromes made the countryside ugly and aircraft were noisy intruders. All this changed last summer. With a flash of courage, the pilots of the Royal Air Force caught the imagination of the world and, almost every day since we heard Mr. Chamberlain say over the wireless, 'This country is at war with Germany,' there has been some story of combat in the air to quicken our blood and to strengthen our faith in victory. The total of our day's hope is the total of enemy aircraft brought down by our pilots.[12]

Hector became a supportive friend to many of the RAF pilots he encountered and they would ask him for advice and to write letters for them: 'When John came home on leave the house was like a small Air Force mess. I think he enjoyed it because pilots are a clanny lot.'[13] In *Combat Report* Hector's love and admiration for the RAF pilots he befriended is beautifully expressed. He thought the world of them, and they clearly loved and respected him. However, as many of these RAF pilots are killed in action, as noted by the author throughout the book, the reader is gradually made aware of the impact this is having on both Hector and John. For example, Hector quotes a letter from John, who has written to him to tell him about a German pilot he has just killed in a dog fight:

I honestly did not care a bit. I hate their guts now, after so many of my friends have been killed. I found that I took this one in my stride without a tremor. But I still feel quite sick when I am on the ground, before I take off. I suppose this is some kind of fear. Once I am in the air it vanishes and I become excited instead. But I am always pleased when I land [...] I am slowly losing all my friends in 43 [Squadron] and now I am the oldest member.[14]

John Simpson had to face the horrors of the Battle of Britain but the comradeship of pilot friends was a vital factor in their survival. In *Combat Report* Hector wrote movingly of the loss of many of their friends, but miraculously John survived. In 1940 John was appointed a flight commander and for his bravery in the Battle of Britain he was awarded the DFC for showing courage and skill and for setting an excellent example. On 29 July 1941 Hector attended the presentation ceremony at Buckingham Palace with John and his mother, as well as John's sister Ruth. In *War in the Strand* Hector remembered the ceremony being simple and personal. He also recalled King George VI's smile 'engaging to see – never tiring or showing the slightest anxiety, shaking all those hands and pinning on all those ribbons'.[15] Hector remembered when his beloved John climbed the dais 'and stood before the King':

> There is only one source of honour in the land. I saw the King fix the D. F. C. on John's tunic. For me it meant that a diffident boy, who had confessed weakness and little else six years before, had played his part in the resurrection of his country. His armament had been courage, modesty and goodness of heart.[16]

If Hector and John did have a relationship it did not survive John's postings abroad to Gibraltar in 1942 as a wing commander and to North Africa in 1943 as a group captain. In 1945 John married, but in 1949 at the age of 36 he committed suicide, shooting himself in the head in London's St James's Park. Newspapers reported that at the inquest his wife told the coroner her husband was worried that headaches he was suffering following a car accident would cause him to have to give up flying, which he loved. A verdict of 'Suicide while his balance of mind was disturbed' was recorded.[17] In that same year, 1949, Hector began a long and happy relationship with Captain Derek Peel, a former public schoolboy and Army officer, who had been educated at Wellington College and wounded while serving in the war. They collaborated on a book, *Without the City Wall* (1952) and lived together in Brighton for the rest of Hector's life. When Hector died in 1974, the charity organiser Duncan Guthrie wrote to *The Times* and expanded on the paper's obituary, in which, he said:

> nothing emerges of his personality as a friend, both to young writers and to others less literary. His puckish sense of fun and the warmth of the kindness which he gave to a wide and very catholic collection of friends endeared him as much to those who were his intellectual equals as to those who, for one reason or another, were less fortunate than he had been. In his latter years, and before his final illness robbed him of many of his faculties, he helped to establish a committee for developing and providing writing and reading aids for the physically disabled. Although the protocol of committee work was far from natural to Hector Bolitho he presided over it with an almost impish humour and an immense enthusiasm [...] Those who were close to him knew how much work he undertook to help others. Those he helped often did not know, and that was the way he liked it to be.[18]

The Home Front

15

Brief Encounters in the Blackout

Dudley Cave (see Chapter 7) believed that there was a relaxed attitude towards gay men joining the services during the war, but did the authorities turn a blind eye to homosexual practices on the home front? Were the police too preoccupied with war work to concern themselves with men having brief encounters in the blackout with other men? Arrests of homosexuals did continue during the war, but figures reveal that homosexual offences were not a *priority* for the police. On the whole, on the home front, gay men like Quentin Crisp and heterosexual men looking for same-sex encounters enjoyed a certain amount of freedom. They were aware they could be killed at any moment by one of Hitler's bombs, and so they seized any opportunity that came their way for a bit of fun.

Keith Howes has described Quentin Crisp as:

the most visible – and therefore the most despised, beaten and spat-upon – gay man in Britain [...] His crusade was to make people understand that effeminate homosexual men like himself existed. His weapons were hennaed hair, long finger nails, mascara and lipstick. His philosophy was total self-absorption and passivity. His Holy Land lay between Soho and Chelsea.[1]

Not all gay men were sympathetic. When 'John' was interviewed in Kevin Porter and Jeffrey Weeks's *Between the Acts: Lives of Homosexual Men 1885–1967* (1991), he recalled:

> The bravest man in the world I know is Quentin Crisp. Even we used to cross the road and walk on the other side when he was coming towards us! It's a terrible thing to say, but he was persecuted by us as much as he was persecuted by everybody else. If we came upon him in a covered place, like a pub or a club, we would talk to him, but I can only talk about myself. There was a Bloomsbury character, a woman, and she was a great friend to all the gays, the original faggots' moll [...] he was her friend. If anybody insulted him they insulted her and she used to lash out with her handbag.[2]

In 1939 there was one gay man who befriended Crisp, the photographer Angus McBean. They also became occasional bed fellows. He described Crisp as 'one of the most beautiful people I have ever photographed', and Angus's biographer, Adrian Woodhouse, said, 'The photographs from his session in Belgrade Road endowed Crisp with the fabulous beauty of a Garbo or Joan Crawford.'[3] Towards the end of the war, Crisp was admired by the young sailor George Melly (see Chapter 9), who went on to become a popular jazz singer and critic. In 1977 Melly recalled Crisp in his bestselling autobiography *Rum, Bum and Concertina*:

> Being in Chelsea he was unshaven and rather grubby, the nail varnish on both finger and toe nails, peeping through gilt sandals, cracked and flaked, his mascara in need of attention, his lipstick of renewal. He had, however, a wistful, frail beauty and a wicked wit. His hair was henna red [...] unseen then on ostensibly male heads. I thought him extraordinary and suspected, rightly so as it turned out, that he must have the courage of a lioness to walk the streets of London.[4]

In April 1940 the flamboyant Crisp, 'blind' with mascara and 'dumb' with lipstick, was rejected by the Army's medical board on the grounds that he was 'suffering from sexual perversion' and therefore unfit for active service. In reality, Crisp had toned down his appearance, but this was in vain, for the medical examiners had the measure of him and Crisp made no secret of the fact that he was a homosexual. He told them. Eventually a young man appeared and informed him that he would never be wanted for active service, and thrust a small piece of paper at him. Crisp said:

> This described me as being incapable of being graded in grades A, B, etc. because I suffered from sexual perversion. When the story of my disgrace became one of the contemporary fables of Chelsea, a certain Miss Marshall said, 'I don't much care for the expression "suffering from". Shouldn't it be "glorying in"?'[5]

So the Army did not embrace *all* the homosexuals who wanted to do their 'bit' for King and country. However, Crisp had already been a soldier, of sorts, with London his battlefield. He later told George Melly: 'When Mr Hitler started the war, I wrote to Paris and got them to send me enough henna to last through it, however long it took. That was my war effort.'[6]

Throughout the 1930s Crisp, who had no wish to hide his effeminacy, mascara or hennaed hair, had been subjected to vitriolic homophobic verbal abuse and physical attacks. So, with the outbreak of war, he was more than equipped to face risks and dangers. However, when the London Blitz started in September 1940, Crisp discovered that everyone began to talk to each other, 'even to me'. And in the blackout there was sex, lots of it, in shop doorways, train carriages, air-raid shelters and other secret places. For Crisp, the London Blitz was a 'feast of love' laid on by 'St Adolf'. Joshua Levine described him in *The Secret History of the Blitz* (2015) emerging, one evening, from Leicester Square tube station: 'Crisp found himself disoriented in the darkness. Asking a [male] passer-by what street he was on, he received a kiss on the lips – followed by the answer.'[7]

In 1940 Crisp moved into the bed-sitting room at 129 Beaufort Street in Chelsea which would be his home for 40 years. In 1942 he left his job as an engineer's tracer and became a model in life classes in London and the Home Counties. He continued to pose for artists for 30 years. Like so many who discovered sexual freedom on the streets of London in wartime, Crisp enjoyed the war, especially when America entered the conflict in December, 1941. He was overjoyed when they began to 'flood' Britain with handsome GIs. He was impressed and seduced by their openness, kindness and affection, and this inspired his love of all things American. In 1981 he left Britain and settled in New York. In his autobiography *The Naked Civil Servant* (1968) Crisp described the arrival of the GIs as an exciting and sexually arousing event: 'Labelled "with love from Uncle Sam" and packaged in uniforms so tight that in them their owners could fight for nothing but their honour, these "bundles for Britain" leaned against the lamp-posts of Shaftesbury Avenue or lolled on the steps of thin-lipped statues of dead English statesmen.'[8]

For Crisp, the most unexpected wartime development was an enlightened attitude he encountered at Bow Street Police Court in November 1944. He had been falsely arrested by two lying policemen 'disguised as human beings' in Coventry Street, and charged with soliciting. However, the magistrate grew tired of the parade of Crisp's character witnesses singing his praises and decided that the evidence against him was insufficient to convict him. The case was dismissed. After the war, the persecution of homosexuals began to increase, and Crisp acknowledged that he had become 'a loathsome reminder of the unfairness of fate. I was still living while the young, brave and the beautiful were dead.'[9]

Another gay man who had fun in the blackout was Gerald Dougherty, a wartime ambulance and Light Rescue worker. Interviewed by Alkarim Jivani in *It's Not Unusual* (1997), Gerald recalled what he did on the first night of the London Blitz: 7 September 1940. He had spent the afternoon at a concert, but on leaving he found himself gazing at a red sky and listening to the sound of German bombers overhead and anti-aircraft guns. Gerald headed for the Fitzroy Tavern, a gay pub on Charlotte Street, where he encountered and befriended another gay man. Realising that they both needed to find their way in the blackout to Charing Cross Station, they ran along the streets of Soho down to the Strand, all the time dodging the shrapnel which landed on the pavements. At their destination they discovered that no trains were running so they took shelter from the air raid in the first-class compartment of a stationary train. Gerald recalled: 'It was most exciting with the bombs dropping and the glass shattering and I thought this is the way to spend the first night of the Blitz – in the arms of a barrow boy in a railway carriage.' Said Alkarim: 'For Gerald the earth moved both literally and metaphorically for him that evening.'[10]

Tom Driberg found the blackout a blessing, for he enjoyed quite a few brief encounters when the lights went. Driberg was a left-wing journalist and wartime member of Parliament (as an independent member for Maldon, 1942–5) who had been educated at Lancing College and Christ Church, Oxford. In 1933 he began the popular 'William Hickey' society column in the *Daily Express*, which he continued to write until 1943. The column made him nationally famous and helped to protect him because, throughout his life, he made no secret of his homosexuality. In his autobiography, *Ruling Passions* (1977), he happily shared some of the details of his many brushes with the law while pursuing attractive young men. In the book he claimed that the fear of imprisonment made him more promiscuous and that his election to Parliament in 1942 helped to get him out of 'tight corners'. He described the 'narrowest shave of my life', which occurred in wartime Edinburgh, where he had gone, as a newly elected MP, to give a speech at a by-election.

In the blackout Tom bumped into a tall figure in a 'foreign' naval uniform: 'One of us struck a match to light cigarettes.'[11] Tom described the sailor as Norwegian, flaxen-haired and smilingly attractive: 'he was eager for anything, and perhaps lonely (Loneliness is as strong an incentive, often, as lust.)'[12] Retiring to an empty air-raid shelter,

In a matter of seconds he had slipped his trousers half-way down, and was sitting on the bench, leaning well back. We embraced and kissed, warmly enough, but my interest was concentrated lower down, on a long, uncircumcised, and tapering, but rock-hard erection; and I was soon on my knees.[13]

However, the erotic joy of the encounter was shattered all too soon:

[the] blinding light of a torch shone full on us, and a deep Scottish voice was baying, in a tone of angry disgust: 'Och, ye bastards – ye dirty pair o' whoors' [...] the sailor pulled his trousers up over a prick that was rapidly losing its pride, and sat forward, his face buried in his hands; and I stood up to confront a Scottish policeman [...] with an older special constable lurking behind him.[14]

The quick-thinking Driberg saved the day when he revealed his identity to PC George Crowford, who reacted positively: '*William Hickey!*' he said. 'Good God, man, *I've read ye all my life!* Every morning.'[15] PC Crowford sent the special away, as well as the Norwegian sailor (much to Driberg's disappointment), and Driberg convinced PC Crowford that, if he let him off, he would *never* do such a thing again. Not only did he escape arrest, but, 'In twenty minutes or so, we were good friends, on a writer-and-reader basis.'[16] Having ascertained the name and address of PC Crowford, 'I sent him from London, a few days later, book-tokens to the value of six guineas.' They remained friends until 1955, when PC Crowford's wife wrote to Driberg to inform him of her husband's death at the age of 43. She spoke of his 'high regard' for Driberg.

So there was passion during the war, in the blackout. The English have a reputation for being cool and reserved but, when faced with imminent death in an air raid, thousands threw caution to the wind. It did not matter what gender you were; there was plenty of sex to be had. More so when the glamorous, sexy and gum-chewing American GIs, the 'Yanks', arrived from 1942 onwards. As Quentin Crisp summarised: 'Never in the history of sex was so much offered to so many by so few.'[17] Of course, not all English people lost their reserve. But there were those, gay and straight, who *were* tempted and dropped their inhibitions in the blackout. England would never be the same again.

16

Against the Law

During World War II arrests of gay men had continued, but not on the scale of the postwar years. In 1952 in the United Kingdom there were 3,757 convictions of homosexual offences, compared with 956 in 1938. This shocking rise in arrests and convictions began just as the war was drawing to a close. In *The Secret History of the Blitz* (2015), Joshua Levine said that, after the war was over, 'With greater manpower now available, the police stepped up surveillance operations, and huge numbers of prosecutions resulted.'[1] Maureen Waller wrote in *London 1945* (2004):

Homosexuality was a criminal offence. As the Public Morality Council officer noted in the autumn of 1945: 'Police are again conducting a campaign against those engaged in this deplorable offence. The happy hunting ground is Piccadilly and Leicester Square.' Offenders were usually charged with being 'concerned together in committing an act of gross indecency'.[2]

There were several high-profile arrests of homosexuals in wartime but there were also cover-ups, as described in 1989 by Richard Huggett in his acclaimed biography of Hugh 'Binkie' Beaumont. Binkie was the powerful and influential managing director of the theatrical production company H. M. Tennent, and in 1942 he saved

a famous actor from public humiliation. The actor was touring with
ENSA through the West Country and was invited to a private
gathering. A party of servicemen were also in attendance. The police
raided the party and arrested the actor and the servicemen for 'acts
of gross indecency'. Binkie intervened on the actor's behalf in an
attempt to save him from scandal. He made a series of telephone
calls to his contacts in Parliament, the royal household, the Home
Office and finally the police. It was not only the actor's career that
faced ruin, but Binkie's organisation. In 1964 Huggett was cast in
the film *The Yellow Rolls-Royce*, where he befriended the gay actor
Tom Gill, who was also in the cast. Gill described for Huggett his
wartime role in the cover-up which led to him acting as a scapegoat
for the famous actor, and serving a prison sentence:

> A deal was suggested. The actor of fame and distinction would be
> released at once, no charges would be preferred, his name would
> be erased from the charge book and other official documents and
> nothing would be said to the press or anybody. In exchange, Binkie
> offered two scapegoats who had been at the party; they would be
> arrested, charged and imprisoned. He pointed out that this was a
> form of justice very popular in the Middle and Far East where it is
> believed that if a crime has been committed then somebody must be
> punished but it doesn't have to be the guilty party. It doesn't matter
> who because justice will have been done and seen to be done. Binkie's
> delicate and persuasive argument was convincing and the authorities
> agreed. One of the two scapegoats was a young actor named Tom
> Gill, well known for playing breezy service and establishment types.
> He declared himself willing to go to prison for a year in exchange
> for £2,000 cash, £1,000 before and the other £1,000 afterwards, and
> the promise of permanent employment for the rest of his life. He
> wasn't newsworthy and with small newspapers as a result of wartime
> newsprint control, the matter was not reported. Binkie was as good
> as his word: the money was paid and the work flowed in whenever
> he wanted it. He had only to call at the office or telephone. 'I took
> Binkie up on his promise and he always gave me a part: nothing very

big or important but something,' said Gill later. 'But there was always such an air of embarrassment when I called on his office or met him in the street or at first nights that I eventually stopped. So I never again worked for Binkie after the war. But that was my decision, not his.' Gill had been sworn to secrecy but, like Binkie, he was a born gossip and chatterbox. He would tell the story to anybody in earshot while he propped up the bar at the Salisbury in St Martin's Lane, his favourite watering hole and second home. Inevitably, the news leaked out since a secret which is known to a dozen people has a limited lease of life, but it was common knowledge only within the narrow circle of their profession. It was never mentioned in the press and the identity of the famous actor (and the second scapegoat) has remained a secret.[3]

Tom Gill was arrested in November 1941 during a police raid, but Huggett fails to mention that it was at the home in Bath of the well-known theatrical photographer Angus McBean. This may have something to do with the fact that McBean was still alive when Huggett's book was published in 1989. McBean was arrested and charged with three counts of gross indecency. Six others, including Gill, were also charged with homosexual offences. Reports of the trial and verdict at Winchester Assizes in March 1942 were published in various newspapers, including the *News of the World* (8 March 1942) and *Bath Weekly Chronicle and Herald* (14 March 1942). McBean's biographer Adrian Woodhouse says that he was dismayed to find that, contrary to what he had been told about the advantages of admitting guilt, 'the prosecution rehearsed the details of the case in great detail. He was deemed to be the ringleader.'[4]

McBean was found guilty of gross indecency and sentenced to four years' penal servitude. It was an extremely harsh sentence that, 'with the added nastiness of hard labour out in the open, rather than sewing mailbags or the like inside a prison workshop – caused an audible gasp in the court. Angus collapsed in the dock.'[5] For McBean, 'It was a moment of terrible weakness. Everything that I had been going through in the previous fifteen weeks just came in on top of me and I went down. I wasn't faking it.'[6] He served two years and six months and was released in September 1944, just in time to appear courageously as a witness at the trial of his friend and former lover Quentin Crisp in November 1944. At the trial in 1942, Mr Cyril Williams, appearing for McBean, told the judge that, if he went to prison, his career as a theatrical photographer would be ruined forever, 'and I don't put it too high when I say that perhaps the whole of his life now lay in ruins'. Nothing could have been further from the truth, for in the event McBean's imprisonment did not harm him or his career. Happily for him, after the prison term, he successfully picked up where he had left off, and continued to be loved and respected in theatrical circles for his remarkable and innovative photographic work until he died in 1990 at the age of 86.

The servicemen who were arrested with Angus included Tom Gill, who was described as a 25-year-old lieutenant in an Armoured Division. He was sentenced to 15 months' imprisonment. Theodore Parker, aged 18, was sent to borstal for three years. Parker had been found in the possession of 36 letters written by Gill, letters which could be described as love letters. A Harley Street psychiatrist told the judge that in his view there had been considerable emotional retardation in the accused's case. That opinion was born out of the extravagant and fantastic language in the letters Gill had written to Parker; they were evidence of a state of 'emotional imbalance'.[7] Gill's eldest brother, an officer in the RAF, remarked that his brother Tom had always shown a certain retrogression, and was easily led. Adrian Woodhouse confirms that it was McBean who was also 'sacrificed' for the famous actor, the 'second scapegoat' unidentified by Richard Huggett. The identity of the famous actor, he says, was probably the bisexual Emlyn Williams.[8]

Angus McBean successfully rebuilt his life and career after being released from prison. Others who were incarcerated in wartime did not fare so well. In 1931 the Oxford-educated Paul Latham not only inherited his father's wealth and baronetcy but was also elected Conservative MP for Scarborough and Whitby. However, the charming Latham had a dark, sadistic side. Michael Bloch describes him in *Closet Queens* (2015) as someone who:

> delighted in causing pain and discomfiture to others; he was also a promiscuous and predatory homosexual. For more than a decade he conducted a sado-masochistic affair with Eddy Sackville-West (later 5th Baron Sackville) […] a talented writer and musician, who was finally driven (in 1937) to a nervous breakdown by the relationship.[9]

Latham married in 1933 but he took pleasure in humiliating his wife in public. 'You bore me an heir,' he had told her. 'That's all I want and expect.'[10] In 1939, despite being exempt from military service, Latham volunteered to join the Army. He became an officer in the 70th Searchlight Regiment, Royal Artillery, and later attained the rank of acting major. However, in 1941 Latham 'entered the history books as the only serving MP of modern times to go to prison because of homosexuality'.[11] He was arrested for 'improper behaviour' with three gunners in his own regiment and a civilian. Latham attempted suicide (then illegal) by riding his motorcycle into a tree, but this just made the situation worse. He was court-martialled and found guilty of ten charges of indecent conduct and of an attempted suicide. He was discharged dishonourably from the Army and imprisoned for two years without hard labour, of which he served 18 months. In 1941 Latham resigned his seat in Parliament and his wife divorced him two years later.

After Latham was released from prison, his friend James Lees-Milne visited him in May 1943 and observed:

> He talked incessantly of himself […] his conversation is more depraved than anyone's I have ever heard. He is obsessed by sex and already haunts the most dangerous places, as he told me […] He is a sadistic man. He had the grace to acknowledge Eddy [Sackville-West]'s great kindness in helping him, yet he is irritated by Eddy's devotion. I am terribly sorry for him but would pity him more if he were less wayward and less egocentric.[12]

Three years later Lees-Milne discovered a different Latham: 'He was giggly and rather endearing [...] He is greatly improved. Far less hysterical and more reconciled. Less sex mad. Seems to take a saner view of life.'[13] Latham died in 1955 at the age of 50. In 1967 Godfrey Winn reflected on his former Eton schoolboy friend:

> he had been born with the seeds of arrogance in his make-up, for which the Greeks had a word which cannot be bettered. Hubris. To imagine yourself above the power of the wrath of the gods. No one is. Unfortunately, Paul Latham was to grow up believing that there was one law for him and another for his fellows. There isn't.[14]

17

Lily Law Goes to War

The relationship between the police ('Lily Law') and the gay community has always been a difficult one. It has taken tragic incidents, like the 1999 bombing of The Admiral Duncan pub in London's Soho, to encourage the police to work more closely with gay men in ways that would have been unthinkable before that event. At the time of the bombing, groups such as the Gay London Police Monitoring Group and the Gay Police Association (GPA) were mobilising to help build bridges and improve the hostile relationship that existed between the police and the gay community.

When the GPA was founded in 1990 by serving police officers they risked persecution and being thrown out of the service if they were found out to be gay. So, for a number of years, they met in secret. Until then, gay police officers remained firmly in the closet, with the exception of PC Harry Daley. When his autobiography *This Small Cloud* was published posthumously in 1986, it offered a rare glimpse into the life of a serving gay police constable. When Harry walked the beat in London from 1925 to 1950, he happily continued to engage in unlawful acts while upholding the law. Harry's story is extraordinary.[1]

It is humorous, endearing and self-deprecatory. When Peter Burton wrote about Harry Daley and *This Small Cloud* in *Gay Times* in 1987, he commented that Harry acknowledged himself as a champion of the underdog and the oppressed. In this respect *This Small Cloud* presents a heart-warming portrait of the old-fashioned bobby on the beat, close kin to Dixon of Dock Green, rather than the harassed and computerised policemen we know today [...] Daley's ruthless self-improvement led to the writing of this rare record of working-class gay experience.[2]

In the book Harry is refreshingly indiscreet about his homosexuality and life as a London 'bobby on the beat'. He said: 'My sexual inclinations were clearly defined. I was attracted to normal men, older, rougher and stronger than myself. Youthful innocence and freshness of outlook I found delightful, but never connected it with sexual desire.'[3] Regrettably, he did not acknowledge the friendships and love affairs he enjoyed with the famous figures he encountered in the literary world.[4]

Harry was born in Lowestoft, Suffolk in 1901 into a close-knit, working-class family. His father, Joseph, was the skipper of a fishing smack and his family originated from Bermondsey in South London. He was lost at sea in the Lowestoft fleet disaster of 1911. Harry's brother, also known as Joseph, served in World War I but was tragically killed in action on 7 November 1918, just a few days before the war came to an end. After leaving school, Harry found work as a Post Office telegraph boy. When the family moved to Dorking in Surrey in 1916, he worked as a grocery delivery boy but craved the bright lights of London. He would spend his weekends in the metropolis, exploring theatres, cinemas, art galleries and concert halls. He was 24 when he decided to join the Metropolitan Police and make London his permanent home. In his autobiography, Harry described himself at this time as 'sexually both innocent and deplorable; honourable if not exactly honest; trusting; truthful; romantic and sentimental to the point of sloppiness.'[5] In 1978, P. N. Furbank, in his biography of Harry's lover, the celebrated novelist E. M. Forster, described the young policeman as 'plump, curly-headed, genial and rather cocky in manner: very intelligent, with a taste for music and opera, and a brilliant *raconteur.* He was homosexual and made no secret of it; indeed he was wildly indiscreet. His closest friends, and lovers, were mainly criminals.'[6]

At work, Harry was open about his sexuality, and another of E. M. Forster's biographers, Wendy Moffat, described his fellow officers making a 'clear distinction between the behaviour of one of their own and the "nancy boys" brought into the station on charges of soliciting. These men were routinely harassed and humiliated: their faces were rubbed with toilet paper to detect makeup' while Harry 'endured oblique slights: a knothole in the main office wall was graffitied to look like an anus, and "love from 308" – Harry's badge number – was pencilled below. But on the whole, Harry was let be.'[7]

In 1925, on his Hammersmith beat in 'T' Division, Harry met the dramatist J. R. Ackerley. His groundbreaking play *The Prisoners of War* was then running at the Lyric, Hammersmith. This encounter is described by Wendy Moffat: 'One Sunday morning Ackerley went out into the river mist of Hammersmith Terrace at dawn to get the milk bottle off his stoop, and came back inside with the milk bottle and a brilliant young policeman who had been walking the beat.'[8] The homosexual theme of Ackerley's play, set in World War I, had intrigued Harry and the two men enjoyed a long-lasting intimate friendship.

Before Ackerley served his King and country in World War I, he had had a student reputation for effeminacy and was nicknamed 'Girlie'. However, on the battlefields of France, he demonstrated his bravery. As a second lieutenant he was assigned to the 8th Battalion of the East Surrey Regiment and in June 1915 he was sent to France, where he proved to be a courageous officer, far removed from the prewar 'Girlie'. He was wounded at the Battle of the Somme on 1 July 1916, recovered, returned to the front line, wounded a second time, and then taken prisoner in 1917. His older brother, Peter, was killed in action in 1918. In 1925 censors failed to identify the homosexual theme of his play *The Prisoners of War*, and it found its way onto the London stage.

In the summer of 1926 Ackerley introduced Harry to E. M. Forster, who became Harry's lover, but it was a troubled relationship. Ackerley and Forster introduced the young policeman to members of the literary world and in 1931, wearing his uniform, Harry's portrait was painted by the homosexual artist Duncan Grant. However, Harry was too indiscreet for the closeted Forster and the Bloomsbury Group or Bloomsbury Set (writers, intellectuals, artists), who also befriended him. Forster was so alarmed by Harry's lack of discretion and his friendships with rough lads from the criminal underworld, that the couple eventually broke up in 1932. Forster then had a more satisfying and long-term relationship with another – discreet – police officer called Bob Buckingham. For several years Harry and Bob lived in the same section house in Paddenswick Road, Hammersmith, overlooking Ravenscourt Park. Though at first jealous of the relationship, Harry acknowledged that, temperamentally, Bob and Forster, known as 'Morgan', were good together: 'Bob was the man for Morgan, much more suitable than me, and I am glad that's how it ended.'[9]

Bob Buckingham, born in King's Cross, London, came from a poor, working-class background but, according to P. N. Furbank, 'he had survived with great resilience, becoming a warm-hearted, broad-minded, responsible man, with a patronizing manner [...] He loved to be in the know (a *trait* of the police generally).'[10] Bob served with the Metropolitan Police from 1926 to 1951, and Furbank offers an insight into Bob's relationship with Harry: 'Bob, for his part, treated Harry as a sort of licensed lunatic. He refused to countenance Harry's gaolbird friends, but not censoriously, merely treating Harry as a hopeless case. He would put his arm around him affectionately, sighing "Oh Harry, you *are* a fool."'[11]

According to Bethan Roberts in the *Guardian*:

> For 40 years, E. M. Forster and the policeman Bob Buckingham were in a loving relationship. Buckingham was 28, Forster 51, when the two met. They shared holidays, friends, interests, and – on many weekends – a domestic and sexual life in Forster's Brunswick Square

flat [...] Buckingham was a large, good-humoured man, with a nose flattened in the boxing ring, a wide smile and a deep, loud laugh. On the day they met [in 1930], he impressed Forster with his knowledge of the Thames and told him he was reading Dostoevsky.[12]

Although Bob married in 1932, and then fathered a son, he remained close to Forster until the novelist died in 1970.

Bob was a pacifist, but the war changed his point of view. Based in the heart of the London Blitz, in September 1940 he wrote to Forster:

I just couldn't bear to be away from London as things are. I don't think it is anything to do with courage at all, rather I feel that the Police are really doing a fine job and I at least get a wonderful feeling of having accomplished something which was worth doing, and of course it is exciting.[13]

By 1943 Bob was desperate to join up. 'I shall never forgive myself if I don't go,' he told friends, but he was turned down by the RAF for defective eyesight and was then rejected by the Navy. Bob died in 1975.

In *This Small Cloud* Harry described how, at the police station and section house in Soho's Beak Street, officers were looked after by Mrs Fisher, a Jewish publican's wife. He described how her 'motherly hands' made nice things for the officers to eat, and they grew fond of her. 'How can Hitler and Mosley have made such headway when there must have been Mrs Fishers all over the world for everyone to see?' he mused.[14] Then the air raids started in September 1940. Terrorised, the Fishers were invited by Harry to share the officers' reinforced basement. However, some of the officers, described by Harry as 'Fascists', complained, and the Fishers were forced to go to the public air-raid shelter. An angry Harry confronted the officers about this, and soon made himself unpopular.

As the Blitz intensified, Harry was in the midst of things, but in spite of the horrors, he found a perverse enjoyment in what was going on around him:

The blitz now became frightful enough to be often enjoyable. When all available firemen and ambulances were engaged on the big disasters, we managed without help as best we could – one bomb, one copper. On such a night I stood alone in one of our neighbouring streets and saw the buildings on one side eaten up by flames; then the wind changed, the flames leapt across and with a roar devoured the other side of the street, and nobody could deny the spectacle was enjoyable. These were not homes, but warehouses and shops.[15]

Harry wrote movingly about the young policemen he befriended at the Beak Street section house who were given permission to leave and join the armed services: 'The first away were killed almost as soon as they could be trained [...] An atmosphere of horror now developed, with our friends gaily saying goodbye and news of their death following almost automatically.'[16]

In 1941 Harry moved to another part of London: Wandsworth or 'V' Division. By then he had been promoted to sergeant. He recalled: 'Wandsworth was full of lively, good-looking people who thought nothing of telling policemen to go and get stuffed [...] It was a marvellous place and I couldn't see myself making many arrests here.' But the horrors of the Blitz were never far away. Harry describes how a landmine killed 27 women and children in a surface shelter and he found himself at the scene, holding a handbag which was heavy with congealed blood, 'containing a sailor's address and a note – "If anything happen to me let my son no."'[17]

When J. R. Ackerley became a talks producer at the BBC, he arranged for Harry to give a series of talks about his life as a policeman and the work of Lowestoft fishermen. As the 'human face' of the British bobby in these BBC radio broadcasts, including *Children's Hour* (1929) and *While London Sleeps* (1929), Harry may have inspired the writer Ted Willis to create PC, later Sergeant, George Dixon, the friendly copper who pounded the beat in BBC TV's popular drama series *Dixon of Dock Green* (1955–76).[18] Every Saturday evening, at 6.30 p.m., Dixon welcomed viewers to the fictional Dock Green police station in London's East End and into a world of small-time thieves and petty villains. In real life, Harry retired from the Metropolitan Police in 1950 and joined the Merchant Navy as a master-at-arms.

In 1957, after leaving the Navy, Harry retired to his younger brother David's home at Hillview Cottage in Pixham Lane, Dorking. It had originally been their mother's house and it looked out onto Box Hill. During Harry's retirement, J. R. Ackerley encouraged him to write an autobiography. Harry hoped that it would be published in his lifetime, but sadly this was not to be. Harry died in 1971, and his ashes were scattered on Box Hill. It was not until 1986 that *This Small Cloud* was published.

In Dorking Harry befriended a local couple, John and Hazel Coombes. John remembers:

I had known Harry by sight for many years before I made friends with him. Physically he was a great big man, very impressive and, to my surprise, very intellectual. He read the *New Statesman* and owned a massive record collection, about 7000 records including 700 LPs. The rest were 78s. He had been buying them since the 1920s. He was very knowledgeable about classical music, conductors and opera singers. He loved chamber music and he was a member of various music societies. He also loved music hall. Harry's brother David was also gay and spent his early life as a solicitor's clerk in Dorking. Then he worked for the civil service at Bush House in London. During the war, David was a commissioned officer in the RAF. David was more 'up market' than Harry, he was a member of the Capel Tennis Club, that sort of thing. David had a long-term partner called John Kenny who was a plumber until he met David. Then he became a carpet fitter. Encouraged by David, he eventually found work as a carpet salesman in Guildford. John and Harry did not get on well, due to John's jealousy of Harry's close relationship with his brother. The day before Harry died he was still talking about his book being published but David was not keen, he didn't think it was good enough. My wife Hazel typed up the manuscript and Harry's literary contacts saw it. Some years later the book went to print in both hardback and paperback. Harry adjusted to retirement. He was friendly and sociable. I would describe him as a 'high street loiterer' because he could always be seen in Dorking chatting to people in the street. He rode a bike, and enjoyed a swim in the Mole River which was close to his home. Harry had a sense of humour and he told me he loved vulgarity.[19]

In the days when gay officers had to conceal their sexuality, Harry was an exception and happily engaged in unlawful acts while upholding the law. At the same time, his colleagues made fun of him as well as telling him how they acted as *agents provocateurs* against homosexuals. A fitting testament to Harry's popularity with the public he served came from a disgruntled member of a family of gypsy travellers who, during an altercation with two policemen, told them that all coppers were bastards. He then added, as an afterthought, 'Except Sergeant Daley.'

Entertainment on the Home Front

18

Noël Coward and In Which We Serve

Noël Coward was a national treasure, a songwriter and entertainer who weathered many professional storms but remained firmly in the public eye until his death in 1973. In spite of being a major figure in the theatrical world, he could never declare his homosexuality, although it was widely known. Coward was not alone, for many of the great men of English theatre who were his contemporaries were also closeted homosexuals: John Gielgud, Ivor Novello and Terence Rattigan, to name but a few. As long as they kept their sexuality private, no one need do anything: 'Don't ask, don't tell.'

During World War II Coward wanted to do his bit, and sought official war work, but Winston Churchill insisted that he could do more for the war effort by entertaining the troops: 'Go and sing to them when the guns are firing – that's your job!', he said. Coward became popular with the troops and, in 1942, he created – and starred in – the morale-boosting patriotic film drama *In Which We Serve*. It was inspired by the exploits of his close friend, Lord Louis Mountbatten. At first, Noël Coward was reluctant to become involved in the making of *In Which We Serve*. He said: 'I had no intention of making a film then or at any other time. I had generated in my mind a strong prejudice against the moving-picture business, a prejudice compounded of small personal experience and considerable intellectual snobbery.'[1]

Once he had been persuaded, Coward made a huge contribution to *In Which We Serve*: producer, co-director (with David Lean), screenwriter, composer and star. However, the press were hostile towards him and this mighty venture and, he said:

> [they] proceeded to sabotage the project from the moment the news broke that I was going to do it. There were sneering articles, contemptuous little innuendoes in the gossip columns, letters of protest written, I suspect, editorially, and the suggestion that I was going to portray Lord Louis Mountbatten on the screen, a suggestion for which no possible evidence had been furnished, was reiterated ad nauseam until even the Admiralty became restive and, I believe although I am not certain, protested strongly to the Ministry of Information. I only know that after a few weeks the clamour died down.[2]

In Which We Serve movingly charts the story of a destroyer, HMS *Torrin*, and the men who served on her during the early years of the war. Coward's screenplay was inspired by the experiences of his friend, Mountbatten, who described to him the service record of his own British destroyer. Not everyone was happy with the unlikely casting of Noël Coward as Captain Kinross. Charles Thorpe, who represented Columbia Pictures, withdrew the studio's support early on because they did not consider that Coward's name had sufficient power to draw audiences into cinemas. Then the Ministry of Information objected. So did the head of its Film Department, Jack Beddington, who said that the film would be bad propaganda for the Navy, as it showed one of His Majesty's ships being sunk by the Germans. Permission to make the film was refused, but Mountbatten intervened. He had friends in high places, including King George VI, who gave the film his blessing. Coward was given the green light but casting himself in the lead was not a wise decision. Thorpe and Columbia Pictures had a point. As an actor Noël was famous for appearing in lighthearted, witty comedies. He was hardly the sort of chap one would expect to play the captain of a destroyer in wartime convincingly. And yet, in wartime, the casting did not harm the film's popularity and the reviews were outstanding. In September 1942 the film critic Dilys Powell described it in her *Sunday Times* review as 'the best film about the war yet made in this country or in America'. *In Which We Serve* was highly regarded at home and abroad. In America it received the prestigious New York Film Critics Best Film Award, and Coward was honoured with a special Oscar for his 'outstanding production achievement'. He was also Oscar nominated for his original screenplay.

Wartime cinemagoers may have accepted Noël's casting as Captain Kinross, but it is a major flaw in an otherwise superb film drama. The character desperately needs a dashing, manly and sympathetic actor, a Laurence Olivier, to be believable. The foppish Coward speaks in almost incomprehensible clipped tones. He is unsympathetic and lacks warmth. His body language is all wrong. He looks awkward and uncomfortable. He goes to war in an irritatingly sporty, jolly, almost casual manner. He might just as well be saying, 'Let's play cricket on Sunday and go into battle on Wednesday.' He addresses his men like a gym mistress briefing her girls as they are about to go into battle on the hockey pitch. In 1991 Marcia Landy described Coward's portrayal of Captain Kinross in *British Genres: Cinema and Society, 1930–1960* as 'a paternal, magisterial figure, consonant with the 1940s photographic portrayal of such figures as Churchill and Roosevelt, while downplaying any erotic relationship between Kinross and his wife.'[3]

The film's main strength lies in a number of low-key, emotionally charged and beautifully acted scenes featuring the supporting cast. These include John Mills as the cockney sailor informing his friend, the middle-class chief petty officer, played by Bernard Miles, about the death of the latter's wife and mother-in-law in an air raid. There is also a young Richard Attenborough as the sailor who panics and deserts his post when the ship is torpedoed. Mills, Miles and Attenborough lack the artificiality of Coward and bring truth and reality to the screen.

In Which We Serve also inspired a generation of young men to join up, including some who lived in the colonies. Eddie Martin Noble, a Jamaican, was travelling the island as a sales representative until he joined the RAF in 1943. He later recalled: 'From the moment I saw the film *In Which We Serve*, I had made up my mind that no self-respecting able-bodied young man could honourably remain at home when the fate of the world was literally at stake in Europe.'[4]

As for Lord Mountbatten, for years there were rumours that he was bisexual and had had an affair with Coward, but his daughter, Lady Pamela Hicks, was not convinced. In the Channel 4 television documentary *Secret Lives: Mountbatten* (1995), she said:

> I was surprised the first time they suggested that he might be gay. He was a great friend of people like Noël Coward and he had a lot of gay friends. Therefore the writers seemed to indicate that he must have been gay himself because he was very fond of Noël. But he liked Noël because Noël was fun. He didn't happen to have the same fancies.[5]

Coward's remarkable success with *In Which We Serve* should have guaranteed him a knighthood, but it was not to be. Could his homosexuality have been the problem? In 1942 he appeared to have been 'sounded out' to see if he would accept a knighthood, should it be offered, that being the normal procedure:

> It was believed that His Majesty had expressed a personal interest in the matter. Although irked by the knighthood that had recently been conferred on Alexander Korda, which, Noël felt, cheapened the honor, he indicated that he would be proud to accept. But even as did so, wheels were turning within wheels.[6]

In December 1942 Winston Churchill advised the King against it.

Noël Coward entertained the troops throughout the war, including a Middle East tour in 1943. During the winter of 1943–4, following a request from Mountbatten, the newly appointed

Supreme Commander of South East Asia, Coward agreed to become the first artist to entertain the troops through the war zones of Assam and Burma at the height of the monsoon season. On the whole the suave and sophisticated Coward went down well, but for one disastrous appearance on the main route between Burma and India. He tried to entertain the audience, mainly African American GIs, but he was defeated by the deafening sound of monsoon rain battering onto the tin roof of the stage. 'I'm most frightfully sorry,' he told the audience, who hadn't heard of him and were getting soaked and restless, 'but it's the fucking awful weather!'[7] In July 1944 Colonel Philpotts, an ENSA entertainments officer, complained in a letter: 'Noël Coward has been with us. He was an infernal nuisance throughout his tour but all the first-hand accounts of his performances I have had were that he had a very good reputation.'[8] Noël's devoted accompanist, Norman Hackforth, later recalled: 'You might have thought Noël would be far above the dear boys heads but don't you believe it. He was tremendously popular and they adored him.'[9] In a letter to Coward dated 29 July 1944, Lord Mountbatten expressed his gratitude:

how really deeply grateful I am. I realise that it was at great personal inconvenience that you came on to South East Asia from South Africa and that the tour you undertook was terribly strenuous. You have the satisfaction of knowing that you are the first British star to have come and entertained our troops at the front [...] the greatest value your visit will have is to make the men feel that they are not forgotten by the people back home.[10]

Coward later reflected on these times:

Right up until the end of the war, by which time I had visited hundreds of hospitals and become accustomed to the sight of sickness and suffering, I never ceased to be impressed by the endurance of those soldiers, sailors and airmen; and by their capacity for overcoming, or at least appearing to overcome, desolation,

boredom, homesickness, pain and discomfort […] It was only after I
had left them that any sadness came into my mind […] I could only
hope that by just chatting to them for a few minutes I had at least
temporarily mitigated their boredom and given them something to
talk about in their letters home.[11]

And yet, in spite of his theatrical achievements and contribution to
the war effort, he had to wait until he was 70 before he was given
the knighthood he was denied during the war. It came in the 1970
New Year's Honours List.

In Which We Serve was a monumental achievement for Coward
and, even though he was miscast, he has had a huge influence on
screen actors. Writing about Coward's legacy to cinema, David
Thomson says in *The New Biographical Dictionary of Film* (2014):

There was a time, in the last fifteen years or so of his life, when
you could believe – if you were inclined – that a vigorous, manly
and rough-spoken generation of actors were sweeping 'Cowardy
custard' off the English stage. And a good thing too? For some
people growing up then, Coward was a bit of a mystery […] And
yet, if you take a film like *North by Northwest* (1959), it's hard to
think that Cary Grant or James Mason could have carried on as
they do but for Coward's example and legacy. It may be argued that
Grant and Mason – and others, not least Olivier – actually played
the Coward type more intriguingly than the master ever managed.
So he wasn't that good an actor […] For Coward, it may have had
as much to do with the need to veil gay yearnings as with the wish
to suppress vulgar emotionalism; still, Coward more than anyone
created (as author as much as actor) the manner of speaking that
left us to read between the lines. Grant was actually much better
at it than Olivier […] the influence is intimate and actorly, and it
affects ideas of what a man, or a gentleman, is, and you will find the
rhythms of Noël Coward, as well as the same awkward fascination
with gayness. And now that the lust for male authenticity that so
spurred the Method seems quaint, it's much easier to see gender

ambiguity in, say, Kevin Spacey, Johnny Depp, Ralph Fiennes, Rupert Everett, Jude Law, Matt Damon, Hugh Grant ... and how about Anthony Hopkins in *Hannibal*?[12]

If Hitler had invaded Britain, Coward was on his list of people to be arrested by the Gestapo. In Hitler's 'Black Book', a copy of which is available to view at the Imperial War Museum in London, Noël Coward can be found with other homosexuals, such as E. M. Forster, and such famous figures as Virginia Woolf, Paul Robeson, Bertrand Russell, C. P. Snow and H. G. Wells. Coward found out about this after the war, and later reflected:

> If anyone had told me at that time that I was high up on the Nazi black list, I should have laughed and told him not to talk nonsense. In this, however, I should have been wrong, for, as it ultimately transpired, I was. In 1945, when the Nazi list of people marked down for immediate liquidation was unearthed and published in the Press, there was my name. I remember that Rebecca West, who was one of the many who shared this honour with me, sent me a telegram which read: – 'My dear – the people we should have been seen dead with.'[13]

19

'Snakehips' Swings into the Blitz

In the American journal *Jazz Times* in 2001, James Gavin wrote about the homophobia that has existed in the jazz world:

> The jazz world is one of the last cultural frontiers of old-fashioned macho, and in it, homophobia runs rampant. I've met a multitude of jazz figures who pride themselves on soulfulness and sensitivity, yet are as sensitive as rednecks on the subject of homosexuality – especially its presence in jazz, which is not inconsiderable. Many of the same musicians who would flatten anyone who called them or a friend of theirs a 'nigger' haven't hesitated to tag somebody a 'faggot,' if that person threatened their standards of masculinity.[1]

Gavin also drew attention to the African American arranger-composer Billy Strayhorn (1915–67), one of the very few openly gay jazzmen of his (or any) time. Billy was Duke Ellington's right-hand man, his creative partner. Duke called Billy 'my right arm, my left arm, all the eyes in the back of my head, my brain waves in his head, and his in mine.'[2] The same description could also be applied to Lawrence Brown (1893–1972), another gay African American arranger-composer who, in the 1920s, befriended the singer Paul Robeson and introduced him to spirituals and the concert platform.[3] Brown became Robeson's lifelong musical collaborator and yet the homosexuality of Strayhorn and Brown has not been fully acknowledged in the many books and articles written about Ellington and Robeson, two of the most famous African Americans of the music world.

It is disappointing that, in some cases, only fragments about the lives of black gay men from history have come to the surface. Either homophobia or reluctance on the part of the interviewer or interviewee to explore the subject has meant that crucial information has been lost. For example, the Jamaican musician Leslie Thompson once referred to a British-born dancer called Stanley Coleman who toured Britain in 1929 in the show *Brownbirds*: 'He was a quiet chap, a little effeminate, and I heard that he was badly beaten up during military service during the 1940s.'[4] Further investigations have revealed nothing more about Stanley. Information about the Jamaican dancer Berto Pasuka is also sparse. He loved to dance and travelled to Britain in 1939, where he undertook a course in ballet. Throughout the war he made a living by dancing in cabaret shows in West End nightclubs, and modelling for sculptors, painters and photographers, including Angus McBean, who admired Berto's fine physique. Towards the end of the war, Berto established Britain's first black ballet company, Ballet Negres, which made its debut in 1946.[5]

Happily, Gemma Romain has published a biography of Patrick Nelson, also from Jamaica. On his arrival in Britain in 1937, he worked as a 'gentleman's valet' in North Wales. He also became an artist's model and in 1938 he met the Bloomsbury Group painter Duncan Grant and became his lover. In 1940 Patrick joined up and went to France with the British Expeditionary Force (BEF), where he was captured by the Germans. He remained a prisoner of war for over four years.[6]

Black gay men also existed in Britain outside the worlds of music and dance. The Barbadian Dr Cecil Belfield Clarke practised as a family GP at 112 Newington Causeway, near the Elephant and Castle, in South London, for 45 years.[7] British-born Ivor Cummings, who was rejected by the RAF because of his race, took on an important wartime role as the assistant welfare officer for the Colonial Office. This job earned him a reputation as someone who would assist any black person in trouble.[8]

Ivor Cummings was a friend of the bandleader Ken 'Snakehips' Johnson, who was undoubtedly one of the most famous black men in Britain when the war broke out. Born in British Guiana (now Guyana), from 1929 to 1931 Ken was a pupil at Sir William Borlase's Grammar School in Marlow, Buckinghamshire. He did well at his studies and played the violin in the school chapel. He also played for the school cricket and football teams, with his full height of six foot four inches making him an ideal choice for goalkeeper. After leaving school he was supposed to study medicine but in 1934, aged just 20, he visited Harlem in New York, where he saw the jazz giants Cab Calloway and Fletcher Henderson. This was a key element in Ken wanting to form his own swing band, even though his knowledge of music was extremely limited. In 1936, in Britain, his dream came true when he collaborated with the successful Jamaican trumpeter Leslie Thompson. Together they launched a new swing band, the Emperors of Jazz. These were the players who started to change British music by putting American-style swing into it for the first time. However, though Ken could dance, he had limited musical expertise. A colleague once commented: 'He couldn't tell a B flat from a pig's foot!' Leslie Thompson later described Ken as a charming and vivacious young man:

> I took a liking to him. We had Ken out front – he was a tall, lean fellow, and he could dance. Ken didn't know any music but he could wiggle and waggle himself to the time of the music, and so keep onlookers amused and interested. Somehow he got his name put out there on the posters [...] he was such a nice boy, but he wanted money, and he got led off without being aware of the consequences.[9]

The band was soon recognised as one of the country's top swing groups and was one of the few at the time to include black musicians from Britain and the Caribbean. This was the intention of Leslie and Ken, who were aware of the discrimination encountered by black musicians in Britain. The band enjoyed residencies at several popular nightclubs: the Old Florida Club (1936–8), Willerby's (1939) and the Café de Paris (1939–41), situated at Coventry and Wardour Streets, just off Leicester Square. The Café de Paris had opened its doors in 1924, and was the top nightspot in London. It featured an oval mirrored room and a spacious dance floor, and attracted members of the royal family and aristocracy, as well as eminent political figures and stars of the silver screen.

In 1937 Leslie quit the band and Ken took over the leadership, and the band was renamed Ken Johnson and his West Indian Dance Orchestra. At first Ken and his band were mainly known to the exclusive and fashionable elite of London who frequented sophisticated West End nightclubs. However, 'Snakehips' had a meteoric rise to fame; by the outbreak of war, the general public were familiar with Ken and the Orchestra's swing music. The elegant Ken projected an image of the gentleman about town: handsome, elegant, well over six feet tall. With his extra-long baton he led the smart white-jacketed Orchestra, providing a class act. The band became the toast of Mayfair and, because the Café de Paris was 'wired' for BBC radio broadcasts, the band's frequent appearances on the airwaves from the club helped to raise its profile further. They successfully broke through to the mainstream of British entertainment with their BBC radio broadcasts and appearances on the variety stage.

In the world of music, it was generally agreed that Ken was not a great musician, but he had the gift of imparting his terrific enthusiasm for swing music to both jazz enthusiasts and the general public. Ken's main achievement was to show that Britain could produce a black bandleader as sensational and classy as African Americans like Cab Calloway and Duke Ellington. Everyone who met Ken commented on how kind and gentle he was. He always found something nice to say about everyone. Outside of music, he loved good food, wines and, above all, a cigar. Sailing was one of his favourite pastimes.

Offstage, Ken was the lover of Gerald Hamilton, a memoirist and critic who served prison sentences for bankruptcy, theft, gross indecency and being a threat to national security. He was immortalised in Christopher Isherwood's novel *Mr Norris Changes Trains*. Infamous as 'the wickedest man in Europe' and 'a rogue laced with poison', he had, says Tom Ambrose in *Heroes and Exiles: Gay Icons Through the Ages* (2010), 'an appalling track record of deceit and swindling. He had even been imprisoned in England during World War I for his "openly expressed pro-German and anti-British sentiments" that provoked the British politician Horatio Bottomley to demand that they "Hang Hamilton".'[10]

Gerald was 20 years older than Ken and, while the younger man:

> was never more at home than when sitting in on some all-night jam session, which Gerald would have abominated because of the smoke and the noise [...] Ken, like many others, was amused by Gerald's Edwardian airs and malicious anecdotes [...] while Gerald, for his part, undertook to educate Ken's palate in the mysteries of wine.[11]

The couple met in 1940 and made a home for themselves at 91 Kinnerton Street in Belgravia. They were neighbours of Gerald's friend, the film director Brian Desmond Hurst (see Chapter 20). During the London Blitz, the couple acquired a Thames-side cottage called 'Little Basing' in Vicarage Road, Bray in Berkshire, where Ken indulged his passion for sailing. After appearing at the Café de Paris, Ken would drive to the cottage, arriving in the early hours of the morning, but still have the energy to be up and about in the morning and out sailing on the Thames until late afternoon, until it was time to return to London's West End and the club. These were happy times for Ken and Gerald.

In the first year of the war, Ken reached the peak of his popularity. The Café de Paris, situated underground, directly beneath the Rialto Cinema on Coventry Street, was thought to be impregnable. It was advertised by its owner, Martin Poulsen, as 'the safest and gayest restaurant in town – even in air raids. Twenty feet below ground.' Poulsen deluded the public into thinking there were four solid storeys of masonry above. Said Charles Graves in his history of the Café de Paris: 'all that protected the Café from a direct hit were the glass roof of the Rialto Cinema and the ceiling of the Café de Paris itself.'[12]

At 9.30 p.m. on Saturday 8 March 1941, Ken was having drinks with some friends at the Embassy Club before his show at the Café, which was not far away. It was one of the worst nights of the Blitz and an air raid was raging. No taxi was available. His friends begged him to stay, but Ken was determined to arrive on time for his appearance. He ran all the way from the Embassy Club to the Café de Paris, through the blackout, and the falling bombs. He arrived at 9.45 p.m. but five minutes later two high-explosive bombs crashed onto the dance floor, and one exploded in front of the bandstand. Charles Graves described the devastation: 'There was a flash like the fusing of a gigantic electric cable. All the lights went out. Masonry and lumps of plaster could be heard crashing to the ground.'[13] Band member Joe Deniz was there. He later recalled that the band had just started playing their signature tune, 'Oh Johnny', when the ceiling of the club collapsed:

> As we started to play there was an awful thud, and all the lights went out. The ceiling fell in and the plaster came pouring down. People were yelling. A stick of bombs went right across Leicester Square, through the Café de Paris, and further up to Dean Street. The next thing I remember was being in a small van which had been converted into an ambulance. Then someone came to me and said: 'Joe, Ken's dead.' It broke me up.[14]

Reports of the numbers of dead and injured have varied, but most reports agree that over 30 people lost their lives that night at the Café de Paris, including its owner, Martin Poulsen. Sixty others were seriously injured. Another casualty was the Trinidadian band member, saxophonist Dave 'Baba' Williams, who had been cut in half by the blast. Ken, however, was discovered without a mark on his body, his red carnation still in the buttonhole of his tailcoat. In the aftermath looters 'prowled around the floor of the shattered nightclub, ripping open handbags, tearing rings off the hands of the dead and the unconscious. There was an epidemic of looting during the blitz, so serious that Scotland Yard set up a special squad to deal with it.'[15] The actor Ballard Berkeley was working in his spare time as a special constable and he was one of the first to arrive on the scene:

> The explosion within this confined space was tremendous. It blew legs off people, heads off people, and it exploded their lungs so that when I went into this place, I saw people sitting at tables quite naturally. Dead. Dressed beautifully without a mark on them. Dead. It was like looking at waxworks.[16]

In *The People's War* (1969), Angus Calder described the macabre scenes 'among the most indelibly horrifying of the period.'[17]

The reporting of the incident in newspapers was delayed because in wartime Britain there were strict government restrictions on the reporting of air-raid casualties. Newspapers were expected to maintain a balance between news and keeping up the morale of the public. At first the incident at the Café de Paris was played down and it took time for the facts, including the tragic death of Ken, to be made known. Some early press reports gave a clue to the location in London in the song title, 'Oh Johnny'. Everyone associated this song with Ken and his Orchestra. It was their 'theme' song. If readers knew this, they could probably work out which nightclub had been hit.

On 15 March 1941 Ken's death made front-page news in the *Melody Maker*:

> The Nazi murder raids on civilians in London have caused the dance band profession to suffer some grievous blows, and it is the mournful task of the 'Melody Maker' this week to record the passing of some famous figures in the business who have fallen victims to enemy

action. First and foremost is Ken Johnson, leader of the West Indian Orchestra, and one of the most progressive disciples of modern swing in this country.[18]

Ken was survived by his mother in British Guiana. Following his funeral, she gave consent for his ashes to remain in Britain. Arrangements for Ken's final resting place were made by his friend Ivor Cummings, who contacted the headmaster of Ken's former school, Sir William Borlase's, and requested permission for the ashes to be buried in the school's chapel. On 8 March 1942, one year after he was killed, Ken's ashes were interred during a memorial service at the chapel and the order of service included the following hymns: 'City of God', 'Through the Night of Doubt and Sorrow', 'What Sweet of Life Endureth' and 'Praise My Soul the King of Heaven'.

Britain's first black swing band was no more; its surviving members went their separate ways. While he was alive, Ken Johnson's fame may have only lasted a few years, but he made a big impact on the British public, who mourned his tragic death. The fact that his name is still remembered by older generations who were around at that time is a testament to his legendary status in British show business. As for his partner, Gerald Hamilton, he was devastated. Early on Sunday morning, 9 March 1941, he was awakened at 'Little Basing' by a telephone call from the police in London asking him to come to a mortuary to identify his beloved Ken. He later recalled, 'Again that awful feeling of nausea which I had felt when France fell, and again that sensation of the ground slipping from beneath my feet.' Thereafter, Gerald never travelled anywhere without the photograph of the young man he called 'My Husband' – and the photograph of a woman he referred to as 'My Wife'. She was his close friend, the wealthy Suzy Renou, whom he had married in 1933 for a payment of £20,000. It was a marriage of convenience. 'Like household gods these two in their silver frames adorned the mantelpiece of every Hamilton dwelling, Suzy looking demure like the ingénue of a 1930s musical comedy, and Snakehips in a white tuxedo with white satin facings.'[19]

Before the war, in Britain, many black gay men were drawn into the world of music and the arts. For some of them it was a case of survival. They could earn money as artist's models or in the choruses of cabaret shows in London's West End. In most cases very little is known about them. They have been marginalised or, in the case of someone popular and famous, like Ken 'Snakehips' Johnson, their sexuality has not been acknowledged. There was no mention of it in 2013 in *Swinging into the Blitz*, BBC2's *Culture Show* television documentary about 'Snakehips'. It was not until 2014, and the publication of Tom Cullen's *The Man who Was Norris: The Life of Gerald Hamilton*, that there was public confirmation of 'Snakehips's homosexuality. Until then it was only discussed in hushed tones, behind closed doors.[20]

20

Brian Desmond Hurst 'Old Twank'

Although gay men in the worlds of film and theatre worked hard to keep their private lives private some, like Noël Coward (see Chapter 18), were known to be gay, but it was not a subject that was openly discussed. To some degree, the theatrical world protected them, partly because there were gays working in the field with friends who were supportive and believed that the draconian law was outdated and needed to be changed. However, although they were 'protected', some gay men in the arts were dangerously indiscreet and took great risks in their pursuit of sexual gratification and fulfilment. An example of this is the film director Brian Desmond Hurst, who made no secret of his homosexuality and somehow managed to avoid law enforcers (except the ones he bedded), detection and imprisonment.

Brian told his biographer, Christopher Robbins: 'Some people have asked me whether I'm bisexual. In fact, I am trisexual. The Army, the Navy and the Household Cavalry.'[1] Brian's home in Bradbrook House, Studio Place, around the corner from Kinnerton Street in Belgravia, conveniently placed him close to the barracks of the Household Cavalry, and Brian enjoyed greeting (and bedding) a succession of guardsmen. They willingly presented themselves at his house for 'active service'. Robbins explained that homosexual prostitution in the Brigade of Guards had been one of the 'less hallowed' traditions of the British Army:

It has a long history, stretching back many generations. Young guardsmen from the provinces on poor pay suddenly find themselves living in the best areas of London, as the barracks of the oldest and smartest regiments tend to have fashionable addresses. A certain percentage have always made themselves available, at a price, to the Old Queens of Belgravia – referred to by the soldiers as 'Old Twanks' [...] One young captain complained to Brian that he needed to be warned in advance if there were likely to be any of his soldiers in the house. 'Why, pray?' Brian asked, affronted. 'It undermines discipline.' 'Nonsense.' 'The last time I was here I ran into the lance-corporal who brings my charger from the stable every morning when I go riding in Hyde Park.' 'What of it?' 'The next morning he brought me my horse and as he handed me the reins, he looked up and said, 'Have a nice gallop, darling!'[2]

Robbins added that Brian also welcomed the occasional 'copper' (policeman) into his home, but whether his conquests were in uniform or not, they had to be masculine, physically fit and preferably working class. Brian was described by the actor-turned-film director Bryan Forbes as 'an amiable but wicked old queen'[3] and by the film star Diana Dors as someone who 'always insisted that in order to gain his favour, *everybody* must be pretty, witty or rich!'[4]

Brian's life had not always been one big party. In August 1914, at the outbreak of World War I, when he was just 19, he left his Belfast home and joined the 6th Battalion Royal Irish Rifles. He served in the Middle East, the Balkans and at the Battle of Chunuk Bair in Gallipoli. Robbins later documented the horrors faced by Brian during the 1915–16 Gallipoli campaign, in which around 100,000 men were killed. Brian told Robbins that, years later, when he made a pilgrimage to a war memorial in France:

I thought of war cemeteries all over the world – and my dead comrades left in the gorse and rock of Gallipoli, and the epitaph to a young gunner killed there in 1916: 'Only a boy but a British boy,/The son of a thousand years.' And I remembered the words of Pericles: 'For the whole earth is a sepulchre of heroes. Monuments will rise and be set up to them, but on far-off shores a more abiding memorial shall be kept. It is graven not on brass, not on stone, but on the living heart of all humanity.'[5]

Robbins also related Brian's bitterness at the sentiment famously expressed by the World War I poet Rupert Brooke: 'If I should die, think only this of me:/That there's some corner of a foreign field/That is for ever England.' Brian reacted: 'The rocky earth of Gallipoli is stuffed with Irish, Scots, Welsh, Gurkhas, Australians, New Zealanders and Indians as well.' Robbins added:

> Rupert Brooke died of blood poisoning before he even reached Gallipoli, his illusions intact. In old age Brian did not quote Brooke, who wrote of the romance and adventure of war, but Wilfred Owen, the poet who chronicled the slaughter and horror of it: 'What passing-bells for these who die as cattle?'[6]

During World War II, Brian made several important contributions to British cinema, the most famous being the melodrama *Dangerous Moonlight* (1941). The film's popularity was helped by Richard Addinsell's emotionally charged Warsaw Concerto, played on the soundtrack by the Hungarian pianist Louis Kentner with the London Symphony Orchestra. *Dangerous Moonlight* was one of the most popular films released in wartime Britain and Brian filmed it during the London Blitz of 1940–1. The producer, fearing that Brian would be killed in an air raid, extracted a promise from Brian that, during the filming, he would avoid returning home to Belgravia at weekends. Brian, of course, disobeyed. One weekend he returned home and went to have dinner at the Ritz with some friends:

> We were in the downstairs dining room when the bomb fell that destroyed Green Park station. The dead and dying from the station

were carried into the foyer of the hotel which was soon awash with blood. The women were tearing their dresses and underwear to make bandages for the wounded. We finally got everyone away in ambulances […] some thirty or forty ranks of young people, ten deep, in uniform and out of uniform, moved towards us up Piccadilly from the Circus. They were singing, and at first we couldn't make out what, and then we heard it – 'There'll Always Be an England.'[7]

In addition to Brian and Addinsell, *Dangerous Moonlight* involved a number of gay men. Brian co-scripted the film with Rodney Ackland, Cecil Beaton designed the 'gowns', and its star was the handsome Anton Walbrook. He played Stefan Radetzky, a Polish musician and pilot who sees his country occupied by the Nazis and seeks refuge in the United States. When Simon Callow reviewed Robbins's biography of Brian, he described *Dangerous Moonlight* as a 'masterpiece of the higher schmaltz' and Walbrook's performance in the film as 'Preposterously romantic, hair tumbling over his noble brow, moustache quivering with sensitivity, the great Austrian actor passionately pounded the ivories while the eponymous moonlight washed over him, dangerously.'[8]

During the filming of *Dangerous Moonlight* Anton Walbrook was desperately unhappy because his boyfriend, a Norwegian, had been sent to Canada. Brian was troubled by his performance in one scene where he said to his leading lady, Sally Gray: 'I'm handsome, full of charm and a wonderful musician.' Brian later recalled:

I thought he was doing this in an extremely feminine way and tried every word I could to explain that to him – the word 'camp' had not yet been invented. Walbrook pretended not to understand. The camera man hid himself in the black cloth. I turned my back and said to the camera man: 'You go and tell him it's too sissy.' 'But I've never addressed a star in my life,' he replied. Finally, I had to say it was too sissy. Anton said, 'No'. I said, 'Yes'. I got my way and because he was a very good actor, he ended up playing the scene very well.[9]

In 1942 Brian featured his friend and neighbour, the singer Elisabeth Welch, as a Parisian cabaret entertainer in the thriller *Alibi*. New York-born Elisabeth had settled in Knightsbridge in the 1930s, moving to the Kinnerton Street area to be close to her friends, who included Brian and others, such as Hermione Gingold:

> Brian gave fantastic parties and everybody came. He lived in a private mews in a beautiful studio which had a gallery all around the inside. Brian and Hermione were lovely people and persuaded me to move into a flat in Capener's Close, just off Kinnerton Street. That's how we became neighbours. It was a well-known and very exclusive artist's residential section of Knighstbridge. Many big names lived there, including Lord and Lady Mountbatten. We had pianists, musicians, painters – a real 'colony' of creative, elegant people. You could say it was London's equivalent of New York's Greenwich Village! A lot of people who didn't live there envied us. It was a wonderful place to live – secluded, respectable, but fun.[10]

Theirs is the Glory (1946) was Brian's personal favourite among his films. This much-admired documentary reconstructed the landings at Arnhem in 1944 and the subsequent battle for the Rhine bridge. Said Brian McIlroy in *Re-Viewing British Cinema 1900–1992* (1994): 'Hurst movingly reinforces the loss of many soldiers by a slow, eerie, pan across the empty beds of a previously full dormitory. The full dramatic developments of the Arnhem operation are followed with precision and with outstanding verisimilitude.'[11]

The journalist Patrick Newley recalled befriending Brian in the director's later years, after his career was over:

> I knew Brian very well – and I am not ashamed to say so! I first met him when I was working with Robin Maugham. Brian had directed Robin's film *The Black Tent* many years ago. This, however, was in the late 1970s and Brian was a regular at Maugham's notorious luncheon parties in Brighton. Notorious because everyone got wonderfully drunk and many were carried out. One Christmas I stayed there in

Brighton with Robin as did Brian, who had his latest young man in tow – there were many, as you probably know – and on Christmas morning all the guests were assembled in Maugham's living room and were proposing various festive toasts. There were the usual good wishes for health and happiness and fortune and then Brian raised his champagne glass and said very loudly to the ensemble, 'I propose a toast to oral sodomy, something which I have been engaged in all night.' I sometimes used to go and visit Brian at his invitation at his house in Kinnerton Street – not a stone's throw from the guardsmen's barracks – and he always promised lunch. There never was any at all save a tin of soup. So every time I visited I ended up lugging a hamper for his 'lunch' and well out of pocket. Brian had expensive tastes and he never paid for anything. He really was a great character and full of energy – both mental and the other – well up until he was 90-odd. If you managed to stop him talking about sailors and soldiers and who was on the game he was dazzlingly knowledgeable about the film business. I loved him. Expense and all.[12]

Brian Desmond Hurst died in London on 26 September 1986 at the age of 91. In his heyday as a film director, including the war years, he had avoided arrest because he was, according to the film producer Michael Relph, 'protected':

In those days film directors like Anthony Asquith and Brian Desmond Hurst, as well as Noël Coward and Ivor Novello, were protected by the theatrical world. There wasn't any harassment of gay people in our profession. Asquith was a very sweet, nice person but he was not open about his homosexuality. In fact, I don't think it was dominant in his life. So he was quite happy and safe working within the protected world of film and theatre. On the other hand, Hurst was quite flamboyant and did venture outside the theatrical world. He walked a very dangerous path by picking up guardsmen, but I don't think he was ever caught! However, a cat-and-mouse game existed with the police if gays stepped outside their particular world. I remember when John Gielgud was caught cottaging in the early

1950s. Sometimes the police turned a blind eye because the law was transparently ridiculous and hypocritical as far as homosexuality was concerned. From their point of view, provided you didn't overstep the mark, they were quite tolerant. But the law that existed [until 1967] seemed distasteful and out-of-date to me.[13]

PART III
NOT FORGOTTEN

21

1914–1918

It is explained in the Preface that the life stories of some of the iconic gay figures from the two world wars would not be the main focus of *Fighting Proud*. Legendary figures such as Wilfred Owen, Lawrence of Arabia, Roger Casement, Ivor Novello and Alan Turing are well-served by biographers and other media. However, *Not Forgotten* does acknowledge them and a number of other gay men from diverse backgrounds who lived through the two world wars. Some of them were directly involved in the conflicts – for example, in the armed services – others were not.

FRED BARNES (1885–1938)

Fred Barnes was a popular light comedian and character vocalist in British music halls who made his professional debut in 1906. He made his name with a song he wrote and composed for himself called 'The Black Sheep of the Family'. In 1908 he was contracted by the impresario Oswald Stoll, for whom he became a star of the major London music halls: the Coliseum, Alhambra, Canterbury, Tivoli and Oxford. He also took part in pantomimes every Christmas and pierrot shows each summer. On stage he captivated audiences with his charm and good looks. He was considered to be an Adonis, with blue eyes and wavy hair, and he usually appeared as a debonair man-about-town in white tie and tails, with monocle and cane. He appealed mainly to older women and was effeminate. In the *Oxford Dictionary of National Biography* (2004), Jason Tomes comments:

> There was something almost dainty about his dancing, and he wore a pink and white make-up more common among female artistes. Some people may have detected a double meaning in the sentimental lyric of his signature song: It's a queer, queer world we live in/And Dame Nature plays a funny game –/Some get all the sunshine/Others get all the shame. Fred seemed quite unabashed when audiences greeted him with cries of 'Hello, Freda!' In the profession, his homosexuality was an open secret – and rumours spread.[1]

When Fred inherited £10,000 in 1913 he spent the money extravagantly and entertained friends at his grand apartment near London's Regent's Park. He became more flamboyant, walking about London in white plus-fours and pink stockings, with a marmoset perched on his shoulder. At night he picked up male prostitutes in his Rolls-Royce. At the outbreak of World War I in 1914 Fred wanted to join the Army but was rejected on account of a 'nervous condition', a euphemism for homosexuality. Throughout World War I his music hall career flourished. Says Paul Bailey in *Three Queer Lives* (2001): 'He was featured on picture postcards, and during the First World War he sang the rousingly patriotic "Boys in Khaki, Boys in Blue" to cheer the spirits of wives, mothers and sweethearts.'[2] However, after the war, Fred was banned from the annual Royal Tournament for being 'a menace to His Majesty's Fighting Forces'. In 1924 he was arrested for drunken and negligent driving in London's Hyde Park after he had knocked down a motorcyclist. Jason Tomes writes:

> He tried to bribe the police officer (since he had a half-naked sailor in the car) and ended up spending a month in Pentonville

Prison. Released in February 1925, he found his fans forgiving. There appeared to be some truth in the title of his song 'The Worse You Are the More the Ladies Like You'.[3]

Alcoholism and tuberculosis destroyed Fred's health and in 1938 he was found dead by John Senior, the theatrical manager who had been his lover from 1929. During his lifetime and for years after his death, gay men would seek each other out by asking, 'Do you know Fred Barnes?'

ROGER CASEMENT (1864–1916)

Roger Casement, a British diplomat and human rights activist of Anglo-Irish descent, was knighted in 1911 following a distinguished career in the British consular service. He then became a passionate Irish Nationalist and visited Berlin in 1914 seeking German aid for Irish independence and the Easter Rising of 1916. David Parris writes in Robert Aldrich and Garry Wotherspoon's *Who's Who in Gay and Lesbian History* (2001):

> The German episode had elements of swashbuckling adventure but ended in farce as Casement landed from a U-boat in Kerry, was swiftly apprehended, taken to London and imprisoned in the Tower. Casement was stripped of his knighthood and was hanged in Pentonville Prison in 1916. It has never been entirely clear whether Casement's infamy was his treachery or his sexuality.[4]

In 1965 Casement's remains were repatriated to the Republic of Ireland, where an estimated half a million people filed past his coffin. He was given a state funeral and his remains were buried with full military honours in the Republican plot in Glasnevin Cemetery in Dublin, with other militant republican heroes.

LIONEL CHARLTON (1879–1958)

Air Commodore Lionel Charlton, CB, CMG, DSO, was a British infantry officer who, shortly before World War I, transferred from the Army to the Royal Flying Corps, where he held several command and staff posts, finishing the war as a brigadier general. In 1923 Air Commodore Charlton took up the post of chief staff officer at the headquarters of the RAF's Iraq Command, but he strongly opposed the bombing of civilians in Iraqi villages which led to the killing of women and children. Within a year of accepting the post of chief staff officer, Lionel resigned. A few years later, in 1928, he retired from the Air Force and became a successful author of children's adventure stories. His partner, Tom Wichelo, was a shy, working-class former airman. Lionel was friends of the homosexual circle that included the writers E. M. Forster and J. R. Ackerley, as well as the actor John Gielgud. It is said that Lionel's London home boasted an indoor swimming pool where he would entertain young cadet officers of the Royal Flying Corps in whom he was interested.

T. E. LAWRENCE (1888–1935)

T. E. Lawrence, popularly known as Lawrence of Arabia, is generally regarded as one of the most heroic and legendary figures of World War I. At the start of the war this Edwardian scholar-gentleman joined the British Intelligence Service in Cairo and was soon sent to Mesopotamia. Seeking to further British war aims, Colonel Lawrence succeeded in overseeing the difficult but triumphant Arab revolt against the Turks, entering Damascus in 1918. On returning home to Britain, Lawrence wrote his famous memoirs *Seven Pillars of Wisdom*. Said Robert Aldrich in *Who's Who in Gay and Lesbian History* (2001):

> Lawrence admitted having no attraction to women and shied away
> from sexual contacts. In Syria in 1911, he formed a close friendship

with a handsome 14-year-old Arab, nicknamed Dahoum, a donkey-boy, with whom he shared his quarters. Eyebrows were raised when Lawrence sculpted a figure of a naked Dahoum and mounted it on his roof. Dahoum accompanied Lawrence to Britain in 1913 and to the Sinai the following year. It is possible that Lawrence's reconnaissance behind enemy lines in 1917 was partly an effort to see his friend. The young man died of typhus behind Turkish lines. Lawrence was distraught at his death.[5]

In *Gay Life Stories* (2012), Aldrich said:

Behind Lawrence's heroic, if enigmatic, public persona lurked several homosexual secrets – or rather half-secrets, since he intimated his proclivities and experiences in his writings. The first pages of *Seven Pillars of Wisdom* reveal Lawrence's erotic interest in young Arabs and the sexual tensions of his desert life with them. He explicitly mentions their sexual play and his empathy with their frolicking [...] Lawrence, like many other homosexual men – [André] Gide and [E. M.] Forster among them – found in the Arabic world the seductiveness of attractive men and the pleasures of erotic friendship.[6]

IVOR NOVELLO (1893–1951)

The versatile Ivor Novello was a successful actor, dramatist and composer who was devoted to his mother, a domineering Welsh singing teacher called Clara Novello Davies ('Madame Clara'). From 1913 they lived in a flat above the Strand Theatre in Aldwych, London. During World War I Ivor's greatest achievement was to compose 'Keep the Home Fires Burning' (1914), arguably the most famous song of the Great War. Its huge success brought him both fame and a regular and substantial income from royalties. Strikingly handsome, Ivor attracted the attention of a female audience who remained devoted to him for the rest of his life. His greatest successes were his roles in a series of self-penned, lushly romantic stage musical extravaganzas with titles such as *Glamorous Night* (1935) and *The Dancing Years* (1939 – sometimes referred to as '*The Prancing Queers*'). The singer Elisabeth Welch was featured in two of Ivor's shows and remembered him as:

> a great romantic. I don't think Ivor would be accepted now, because of what some people would call his schmaltz but I don't say schmaltz. I call it romance. Ivor was a man who was in love with love. I'm a singer that goes around the house singing all the time and I never know what I've been singing until I've stopped, and I always find myself singing Ivor's 'Shine Through My Dreams.' It's so romantic, and it's stayed with me all though the years. So his music has lasted, for me anyway.[7]

In 1944 Ivor was imprisoned for one month for evading the wartime petrol restrictions. The sentence was extremely harsh, and it was noted that the judge who imposed this was known to hate homosexuals. Ivor never recovered from the public humiliation of his imprisonment, and his health suffered. Privately he would have liaisons with actors from the casts of his shows, chorus boys, and any other presentable gentleman who happened to stray into his circle. His 1987 biographer, James Harding, said:

> Bizarre stories were told about him in London society. Somerset Maugham once remarked in old age to Winston Churchill: 'Winston, your mother often indicated that you had affairs in your youth with men.' 'Not true!' said Churchill. 'But I once went to bed with a man to see what it was like.' 'Who was it?' 'Ivor Novello.' 'And what was it like?' 'Musical', replied Churchill committing a pun, since 'musical' was then the cant word for gay.[8]

WILFRED OWEN (1893–1918) AND
SIEGFRIED SASSOON (1886–1967)

The war poet Wilfred Owen enlisted in the Artists' Rifles in 1915, commissioned into the 2nd Battalion Manchester Regiment in 1916 and was sent to the Battle of the Somme. Suffering from shell-shock, Wilfred was invalided home in 1917. While recuperating at Craiglockhart War Hospital in Edinburgh, Scotland, he befriended another poet, Siegfried Sassoon, who decided to mentor him. Siegfried had enlisted in the Sussex Yeomanry at the start of the war and he was commissioned into the Royal Welch Fusiliers in 1915. He earned a Military Cross in 1916. Invalided home in 1917 he wrote a public protest against the war and published his collections of war poems, *The Old Huntsman* (1917) and *Counter-Attack* (1918). Siegfried was homosexual (though only in his early years) and encouraged Wilfred to develop his graphically descriptive style, which is noticeable in some of his more powerful poems, such as 'Dulce et Decorum Est' and 'Disabled'. Wilfred hero-worshipped Siegfried. Pat Barker's novel *Regeneration* (1991), the first volume in her World War I trilogy, acknowledges the homoerotic character of the friendship between Wilfred and Siegfried. Discharged from Craiglockhart, Wilfred returned to the Western Front and earned a Military Cross before he was killed in action on 4 November 1918, just one week before the Armistice was signed. Siegfried was devastated and years later wrote: 'W's death was an unhealed wound & the ache of it has been with me ever since. I wanted *him* back – not his poems.'[9] Wilfred wrote to Siegfried between November 1917 and October 1918, but sadly Siegfried destroyed most of the letters. One that has survived – dated 5 November 1917 – was published in Rictor Norton's *My Dear Boy: Gay Love Letters Through the Centuries* (1998); it is very revealing and deeply moving:

> Know that since mid-September, when you still regarded me as a
> tiresome little knocker on your door, I held you as Keats + Christ

+ Elijah + my Colonel + my father-confessor + Amenophis IV in
profile. What's that mathematically? In effect it is this: that I love
you, dispassionately, so much, *very* much, dear Fellow, that the
blasting little smile you wear on reading this can't hurt me in the
least. If you consider what the above Names have severally done for
me, you will know what you are doing. And you have *fixed* my Life
– however short. You did not light me: I was always a mad comet;
but you have fixed me. I spun round you a satellite for a month, but
I shall swing out soon, a dark star in the orbit where you will blaze.[10]

Said George Piggford in *Who's Who in Gay and Lesbian History*
(2001),

Owen is arguably the most significant poet of World War I, and
his main theme, 'the pity of war' rather than its heroism, mirrors
the pessimism of the modern movement. As Paul Fussell has
persuasively contended [in *The Great War and Modern Memory*,
1975], Owen occupies as well a firm place in the tradition of
homoerotic war poetry, epitomised by his early 'It was a Navy Boy'
and the more mature 'Sonnet: To My Friend, with an Identity
Disc' and 'Strange Meeting'.[11]

Only five of Wilfred's poems were published in his lifetime. His
war poetry was posthumously published first by Edith Sitwell in
1920 and later by Siegfried Sassoon. In 1964 a selection of Wilfred's
war poems were read by the actor Michael Redgrave in BBC
Television's epic series *The Great War*.

SIR PHILIP SASSOON (1888–1939)

The enigmatic and wealthy Philip Sassoon was a politician, art
collector and social host. He was also a cousin of the poet Siegfried
Sassoon. During World War I (1915–18) he served as the private
secretary to Field Marshall Haig. Philip was present at the

meeting on 1 December 1914 at the Chateau Demont at Melville in France when King George V and Edward, Prince of Wales, met with Raymond Poincaré, the president of France, and Generals Joffre, Foch and Rawlinson. At that meeting the Allies showed their determination to fight Germany. Philip was then a second lieutenant in the Royal East Kent Yeomanry and it was because of his numerous social and political connections that he was in attendance at that historic meeting. In 1917 he was appointed a Companion of St Michael and St George (CMG) and on 7 October 1919 it was announced that he had been awarded the French Croix de Guerre 'for distinguished services rendered during the course of the campaign'. In 1923 he was knighted. Philip's homosexuality does not appear to have affected his military career.

ERNEST THESIGER (1879–1961)

Ernest Thesiger once described the Battle of Ypres: 'My dear, the noise and the people!' He passed the time doing petit-point embroidery, which distracted him from both the noise of the shelling and guns *and* the people. Ernest was a stage actor when the war broke out and he interrupted his theatrical pursuits to join the Queen Victoria Rifles. In 1915 he was wounded while serving on the Western Front and invalided home, where he resumed his acting career. This lasted until his death in 1961. An obituary in the *Observer* described him as 'an eccentric blend of satanic impishness and good breeding [...] He never moved without grace or spoke without elegance, but implicit in his performance there was a quizzical mockery of these qualities. It was a contradiction that gave his work its ironic edge.'[12] Ernest was an English eccentric and sometimes wore outlandish garb, including a string of pearls, green-painted toenails and blue velvet shorts with matching blouse. In *The Pink Plaque Guide to London* (1986), Michael Elliman and Frederick Roll acknowledged his needlework accomplishments and said: 'In later life he modelled himself on Queen Mary [they were reported to have embroidered together] and grew more and more to resemble her, with his pursed lips, regal bearing and haughtiness of manner.'[13] In addition to his long and distinguished stage career, Ernest was one of cinema's great character actors. As an actor he embodied intelligence with wit and, occasionally, as a hostile alien in a horror film, such as James Whale's *Bride of Frankenstein*, he could instil sheer terror in an audience. In 1960, a few months before he died, he was created a Commander of the British Empire (CBE).

22

1939–1945

ANTHONY ASQUITH (1902–68) AND
TERENCE RATTIGAN (1911–77)

Charming, gentle, effeminate, closeted and probably celibate, the
film director Anthony Asquith was affectionately known to his
friends and colleagues as 'Puffin'. He collaborated several times
with the dramatist Terence Rattigan, a troubled, self-conscious
homosexual, but Terence was not forthcoming when he was asked
if Puffin was also a homosexual. 'There was an impenetrable side
to Puff,' he said, 'however close one was to him. He certainly liked
being with young men, but it never went further than talking
or going to a concert, or playing cards.'¹ Puffin and Terence's
professional association was long and happy. Terence informed
Puffin's biographer, R. J. Minney: 'I more or less fell for him –
fell for his personality, fell for his charm, fell for his enthusiasm
and for his eagerness, for his way of life. This led to a friendship
which lasted until his death.'² Unlike Puffin, Terence did have
sexual relationships with other men, including Kenneth Morgan.
That liaison ended in tragedy (Morgan's suicide) and inspired one
of Terence's most famous plays, *The Deep Blue Sea*, though the
relationship he depicted had to be heterosexual. During the war,
Terence served in the RAF as a tail gunner and his experiences

led to one of his most successful plays, *Flare Path*, first staged in 1942. The RAF then decided to release him from active duty so he could concentrate on writing. Towards the end of World War II, Puffin and Terence collaborated on one of their most popular films, *The Way to the Stars* (1945). Though set in and around a wartime RAF station shared by British and American airmen, it is not a war film, for there are no battle scenes. The emotional impact of the war on the men and women depicted in the film is movingly explored instead. Because the film was released a few weeks after the war in Europe had ended, the scene opens in the deserted RAF station in 1945 before going back to 1940, the time of the Battle of Britain. We are introduced to a new pilot, Peter, played by John Mills, arriving at the station. He is assigned to a room with the quiet, sensitive David, played by Michael Redgrave, a lover of poetry and the recipient of the DFC. In *The Way to the Stars*, Puffin directs Mills and Redgrave, two of Britain's finest actors, with great sensitivity and, together with Terence Rattigan's script, they create a powerful study of the frailty of masculinity.

W. H. AUDEN (1907–73) AND CHRISTOPHER ISHERWOOD (1904–86)

W. H. Auden is regarded as one of the greatest poets of the twentieth century. After studying at Cambridge, he journeyed to Spain to fight fascism during that country's Civil War. In 1939 he emigrated to the United States with his friend, the novelist Christopher Isherwood. Says Tom Ambrose in *Heroes and Exiles: Gay Icons Through the Ages* (2010):

> Their flight on the eve of the Second World War was seen by many as an act of cynical self-preservation that made a mockery of their political posturing. By choosing the safety of America they particularly shocked their many left-wing friends who had been their keenest supporters, although Isherwood was at least quite open about his own

motives for leaving Europe when he wrote in his diary for 11 January 1940: 'Am I afraid of being bombed? Of course, everybody is [...] If I fear anything, I fear the atmosphere of the war, the power that it gives to all the things I hate – the newspapers, the politicians, the puritans, the scoutmasters, the middle-aged merciless spinsters. I fear the way I might behave, if I were exposed to this atmosphere. I shrink from the duty of opposition. I am afraid I should be reduced to a chattering enraged monkey, screaming back hate at their hate.'[3]

Auden and Isherwood became American citizens in 1946.

CECIL BEATON (1904–80)

In 2012 the Imperial War Museum's major exhibition of Cecil Beaton's wartime photography, 'Cecil Beaton: Theatre of War', provided a rare opportunity to assess the diversity of his work. While best-known for his postwar work as a stylish set and costume designer on the Hollywood films *Gigi* (1958) and *My Fair Lady* (1964), for the duration of World War II the effeminate dandy Beaton set aside his glamorous portraits of royals and movie stars to work for the Ministry of Information (MOI). Before his MOI work took him to the battlefields of North Africa, Beaton recorded the destruction of Wren churches and the heroism of Londoners under attack. His photographs of the devastation caused by the London Blitz of 1940–1 are particularly striking. A well-known diarist, in 1965 his wartime diaries were published in a volume entitled *The Years Between*. When he described a location that he visited to photograph the aftermath of an air raid, he said:

Went to Croydon to see real air raid damage. It is pathetic! The sirens didn't go off and 300 women and girls were killed in factories there. The relics are poignant: a picture of the King and royal family among the white cocaine-like debris! [...] Along one road, where a stick of bombs dropped, they've made a guy of Hitler.[4]

Asked in the 1970s what kind of man he found attractive, Beaton replied that, in his work, he looked for a beautiful man with masculine qualities. The Imperial War Museum's exhibition did not shy away from presenting some of Beaton's most impressive and homoerotic images of sexually attractive male servicemen. These included the handsome sailor, naked from the waist up, using a sewing machine on board a merchant cruiser. Beaton was knighted in 1971.

MARC BLITZSTEIN (1905–64)

The innovative and influential left-wing American composer, lyricist and librettist Marc Blitzstein won national attention in America in 1937 when his pro-union musical *The Cradle Will Rock*, directed by Orson Welles, was shut down by the government. Openly gay throughout his life, during World War II he served in the US Army Air Force. Assigned to the film unit attached to the Eighth Army Air Force, Marc reported for duty at its base in England in 1942. In London he worked as the music director for the American broadcasting station, broadcast for the BBC and worked on his 'Airborne Symphony'. He also helped prepare the 200-voice US Army Negro Chorus, a singing group from the segregated African American engineer aviation battalions, for two magnificent concerts with the London Symphony Orchestra on 28 and 29 September 1943 at the Royal Albert Hall. Part of the concert was broadcast on BBC radio. During the concerts Marc's symphonic poem 'Freedom Morning' was premiered. After attending the Wigmore Hall premiere of Benjamin Britten's 'Serenade for Tenor, Horn and Strings' on 15 October 1943, sung by Benjamin's partner Peter Pears, Marc commented that Britten avoided him because 'I was going to ask him how he squared his conscientious objection to the war with doing propaganda work for the BBC.'[5] In 1945 he worked on the music score for the Oscar-winning documentary *The True Glory*. In October 1944 he met a young American Ninth Air Force radio-gunner in a Soho pub. He was the blond, blue-eyed and handsome William 'Bill' B. Hewitt. Bill was an avid reader and music-lover and impressed Marc when he revealed that he owned a recording of *The Cradle Will Rock*. They became romantically involved, though Bill was bisexual and later married.

Douglas Byng (1893–1987)

Douglas 'Dougie' Byng was one of the busiest entertainers of World War II. He happily divided his time between West End revues, variety, cabaret and entertaining the troops for ENSA at home and in the Far East. Dougie enjoyed a long residency at London's most famous nightclub, the Café de Paris and, when the war began, he asked the management to change his billing from 'The One and Only Douglas Byng' to the more patriotic 'Dougie Byng – Bawdy but British!' Dougie was famous for performing songs with outrageous titles such as 'I'm Millie a Messy Old Mermaid' and 'I'm Doris the Goddess of Wind', but the risqué lyrics often got him in trouble and during the war he was banned by the BBC. When the war broke out Dougie wrote a new song for his cabaret and variety act, 'Blackout Bella', which he also sang to acclaim at every troop concert. Dougie's bawdy material proved popular with the troops. His biographer, Patrick Newley, said:

> In 1944 Dougie was sent by ENSA on a gruelling tour of the Far East to entertain troops in India, Burma and Singapore. It was no mean feat for a man then aged 51. Kitted out with a mosquito net and toilet rolls, he sailed on a troopship convoy and after four weeks docked in Bombay [...] Said Dougie: 'You sweated like mad. But it was all very worthwhile.'[6]

Brigadier Michael Calvert (1913–98)

The Army officer Michael Calvert, affectionately known as 'Mad Mike', had been educated at the Royal Military Academy,

Woolwich, before being commissioned as a second lieutenant
in the Royal Engineers in 1933. He read mechanical sciences
at St John's College, Cambridge, and later he was the Army's
middleweight boxing champion. Michael dedicated his life to the
Army, and during World War II he fought in northern Norway
before joining the first commando training centre at Lochailort,
as an explosives expert. Michael then joined forces with Orde
Wingate to set up and train the Chindits, a 'special force' formed
to carry out Wingate's newly developed guerrilla warfare tactic
of long-range penetration behind the Japanese lines in Burma.
The Chindits served in Burma and India in 1943 and 1944 during
the Burma campaign. Michael proved to be the most successful
column commander, leading a brigade behind enemy lines in
Burma from March to August 1944. He never expected his men
to take a risk he would not take himself. His most famous victory
was to recapture Mogaung from the Japanese. He was invalided
home in late 1944, but was fit enough to be given command of the
Special Air Service (SAS) in March 1945. In addition to receiving
the DSO, Michael was honoured with both the French and the
Belgian Croix de Guerre. However, although he was considered
to be a great soldier and leader of men, Michael was also an
alcoholic, opinionated and dangerously outspoken. His men
loved him, but the military establishment did not. In 1952, after
a court martial that lasted seven days, Michael was convicted of
'gross indecency with male persons' and dismissed from the Army.
Michael protested his innocence to the end of his life. David
Rooney has written in the *Oxford Dictionary of National Biography*
(2004) that his biography, *Mad Mike* (1997):

> contained dramatic evidence that the court martial verdict was unjust
> [...] In spite of this evidence, an appeal, supported by more than
> one MP, was rejected. On 26 November 1998 Calvert, who had been
> called 'the bravest of the brave', died in penury at the Star and Garter
> Home, Richmond, Surrey, his character still unjustly besmirched. He
> was unmarried.[7]

ALBERTO CAVALCANTI (1897–1982)

When the film director Alberto Cavalcanti joined Ealing Studios in 1940 he supervised both the documentary and feature output of the studio. He also directed several feature films of his own, including the surreal wartime thriller *Went the Day Well?* (1942). This is now regarded as the finest home front film made in Britain during World War II. It cleverly depicts the occupation of a peaceful English village by disguised Nazi soldiers. Cavalcanti brought a documentary realism to the film, without losing its dramatic impact. At the end of the war, he directed the chilling 'Ventriloquist's Dummy' segment of *Dead of Night* (1945) in which Michael Redgrave gave a brilliant performance as a repressed homosexual ventriloquist who descends into madness.

DUDLEY WRANGEL CLARKE (1899–1974)

Dudley Wrangel Clarke was a brigadier in the British Army who was behind several deception operations during World War II and founded the British Army's Commando force. He is described by Ben Macintyre in *Operation Mincemeat: The True Spy Story that Changed the Course of World War II* (2010) as 'Unmarried, nocturnal and allergic to children', having 'a flair for the dramatic that invited trouble. For the Royal Tournament in 1925, he mounted a pageant depicting imperial artillery down the ages, which involved two elephants, thirty-seven guns and fourteen of the biggest Nigerians he could find. He loved uniforms, disguises and dressing up.'[8] In 1940 Dudley was summoned to Egypt and ordered to set up a special section of intelligence for deception operations in the Mediterranean. The Cairo-based section was known as the 'A' Force. In October 1941 Dudley was bailed out of a Spanish jail dressed as a woman. Ben Macintyre said, 'A Spanish police photograph shows this master of deception in high heels, lipstick, pearls, and a chic cloche hat, his hands, in long opera gloves, demurely folded in his lap. He was not supposed to even be in Spain, but in Egypt.'[9] His fellow spy chiefs were unimpressed. Guy Liddell of MI5 noted: 'he was dressed as a woman complete with brassiere [...] What on earth was the blighter thinking of? A chap might go in disguise, if needed, but in a brassiere?'[10] The incident was brought to the attention of the prime minister, Winston Churchill, but there is no record of how he reacted. As for Dudley, there was no long-term damage to his career in the British Army.

REGINALD FORESYTHE (1907–58)

After Reginald Foresythe's untimely death in 1958, obituaries celebrated him as one of the most innovative jazz composers of the 1930s. At the height of his fame, in 1941, Reginald curtailed his illustrious career in jazz music to join the RAF. He had been born in the Shepherd's Bush area of London in 1907, the son of a Nigerian barrister and an Englishwoman. He received a public school education and, throughout his life, he used his upper-class British accent to achieve some measure of acceptance as a black Briton. In the 1930s he won respect in jazz circles for his bold and dazzling compositions and among the most famous were 'Deep Forest', 'Serenade for a Wealthy Widow' and 'Dodging a Divorcee'. When the American singer Elisabeth Welch made London her home in 1933, she was offered cabaret engagements and befriended Reginald, who was more than happy to work as her accompanist. Elisabeth later recalled: 'He was a sweet, simple, charming person. His appearance was always immaculate and elegant. He loved good food and talked with that wonderful English upper class accent. When we made fun of his accent, he didn't mind at all. He had a great sense of humour about himself.' A 'confirmed bachelor', no woman was ever romantically associated with him. Elisabeth said: 'His liaisons with other men were always very discreet.'[11]

When the war broke out, Reginald was over-age for active service, but he volunteered for the RAF anyway. Drafted into the Royal Air

Force in 1941 with an officer's ranking, he became an intelligence officer and served at remote Scottish air bases and in North Africa. He had his battledress uniform tailored by his usual tailor. This was not all that unusual among officers, and those who could afford to do so opted for having a more comfortable uniform made. In the RAF Reginald addressed every airman, from commanding officer to newest recruit, as 'dear boy'. In the 1930s, he had been ahead of his time but, when he left the RAF in 1946, time seemed to have passed him by. In the 1950s he could be found playing solo piano in drinking clubs in London's Soho and Kensington. His career ended in obscurity and alcoholism, and he died from heart failure at the age of 51. After he died, the BBC producer John Burnaby said that Reginald was to jazz what

> Stravinsky is to classical music. He was constantly changing in mood from the lush to the cheeky witty counterpoint of, for instance, 'Dodging a Divorcee'. As a person, he was without doubt the most lovable musician of his time. Witty, gay, imperturbable, he couldn't care less if he were rich or poor. Music was the most important thing in his life.[12]

Myles Hildyard (1914–2005)

The Army officer Myles Hildyard was educated at Eton and at Magdalene College, Cambridge, where he read law. He was called to the Bar, but the war intervened. A soldier and aesthete, after the war he devoted his peacetime life to improving his magnificent Victorian ancestral home, Flintham Hall, near Nottingham, as well as his garden, his paintings, and handsome young men. Myles looked on World War II as the most interesting years of his life. In 1939 he was commissioned into the Nottinghamshire (Sherwood Rangers) Yeomanry, a cavalry regiment. He saw action in Palestine, the Battle of Crete, North Africa, Italy, the D-Day landings and finally Berlin in 1945. In 1941 he fought and was captured at the Battle of Crete and then, with his comrade, Captain Michael Parish, Myles embarked on a dramatic escape from a German POW camp at Galatos on the island. The escapees helped themselves to food from German stores and, carrying a bucket and spade in an effort to look like a working party, they set off across the Mediterranean to Turkey. For his daring escape, Myles was awarded the Military Cross. He was not ashamed to be homosexual in the Army. In 1944 he fell in love with 'Jimmy', an attractive young officer in the 11th Hussars. In his introduction to the collection of Myles's engaging wartime letters, entitled *It Is Bliss Here: Letters Home 1939–1945* (2005), Antony Beevor says that the references to 'Jimmy' reveal a romance that was both touching and clear-sighted: 'a wonderful corrective to the preposterous notion that such things never happened in the British Army'.[13] Myles was known to bring his male partner to regimental dances. Braving the postwar hostilities towards gay men, Myles ordered a statue of Michelangelo's David, dazzlingly white in his nakedness and life-size, to be placed at the head of his swimming pool at Flintham Hall.

DENIS RAKE (1901–76)

The World War II secret agent Denis Rake, like many other secret agents, continually embroidered and camouflaged the details of his life, but his wartime experiences have been documented and verified in various books including Geoffrey Elliott's biography *The Shooting Star* (2009). Before the war Denis worked as an actor but in June 1939 he left the cast of Ivor Novello's *The Dancing Years* to begin his military career with the RASC as a translator. His wartime experiences were eventful: he was successfully evacuated with the BEF from France in June 1940, only to find himself on board the doomed liner *Lancastria*, which was attacked and sunk by enemy aircraft. He survived and on his return to England was transferred to the RNVR. Denis then survived another sinking while serving on board a French minesweeper. His enthusiasm for dangerous assignments continued. In an interview he gave many years later, Denis explained that part of the reason he felt the need to prove himself and test the limits of his courage came from the anxieties he felt about his homosexuality. Denis's fluency in the French language and Morse Code led him into the Special Operations Executive (SOE), in spite of him being considered 'a trifle effeminate' and 'a drug addict' (actually nothing more than a reliance on sleeping tablets). SOE badly needed Morse operators and consequently Denis found himself undertaking two dangerous missions in Nazi-occupied France. He was eventually captured by the Gestapo, from whom he escaped, and he told the story of his three years in SOE in *Rake's Progress* (1968). Denis was a courageous man and, in addition to the Military Cross (1945), he was awarded the Croix de Guerre avec Palme (1946) and made *chevalier* of the Legion d'honneur (1948). When Denis died in 1976 he asked for a donation from his estate to be made to the Campaign for Homosexual Equality.

ALAN TURING (1912–54)

Alan Turing, one of Britain's most influential mathematicians and computer scientists, has been described as one of the greatest civilian heroes of World War II. Born in London, Alan studied at King's College, Cambridge, and throughout World War II he worked for the Government Code and Cypher School at Bletchley Park. Known to his colleagues as 'Prof', Alan was central to the breaking of the German naval cipher, Enigma. After the war he joined the National Physical Laboratory, where he led the work to develop a large-scale electronic digital computer. In March 1952, when Alan was brought to trial for having a sexual relationship with a man, his position as a government consultant was ended. In 1954 he was found dead. The inquest ruled suicide by cyanide. In September 2009 the prime minister, Gordon Brown, apologised

– on behalf of the government and, we presume, the nation – for Alan Turing's prosecution. 'He was a quite brilliant mathematician,' said Mr Brown, praising his contribution to:

> Britain's fight against the darkness of dictatorship. The debt of gratitude he is owed makes it all the more horrifying, therefore, that he was treated so inhumanely [...] Alan deserves recognition for his contribution to humankind [...] it is thanks to men and women who were totally committed to fighting fascism, people like Alan Turing, that the horrors of the Holocaust and of total war are part of Europe's history and not Europe's present.[14]

In 2013 Alan was granted a royal pardon for having been convicted of being homosexual, but at the very least he should have been honoured with a knighthood before his untimely death. In November 2013 the gay lifestyle magazine *Attitude* honoured Alan with its Icon Award for Outstanding Achievement. In the magazine, Simon Edge commented:

> Alan Turing has now been celebrated with a Royal Mail stamp, an exhibition dedicated to his work at the Science Museum, various statues and blue plaques, and part of Manchester's inner ring-road has been named Alan Turing Way [...] We at *Attitude* are pleased to pause and pay respect to this most extraordinary of men.[15]

23

My Friend Ken

Until he was lost to dementia and admitted to a care home, my friend Ken was one of the most friendly, outgoing and big-hearted people I have had the joy of knowing. He was also a valuable source of information about the lives of gay men from the 1940s to the 1960s, the decades leading up to the 1967 Sexual Offences Act. Ken was not a campaigner, nor an activist. He did not join marches or become a member of the Campaign for Homosexual Equality. In the 1970s he was more likely to read *Movie Memories* than *Gay News*. In some respects he was rather conservative in his views. He lived with his partner in a beautiful house in Hampstead Garden Suburb and enjoyed the company of friends who shared his enthusiasm for theatre and the movies. Ken's story is a happy one, but over time he informed me about disturbing incidents that cast a shadow over his young life. Thankfully he survived them and, being Ken, he never dwelt on them.

I was still at school in 1976 when I first met Ken. It was on a Sunday afternoon at a meeting of the Judy Garland Club at the Russell Hotel in London. My best friend Gill had taken me there as her guest. When we were studying for exams in the sixth form of our comprehensive school, Gill and I shared an interest in Judy. For us, Judy was the greatest singer of all time. Ken was the editor of the club's journal, *Rainbow Review*, having been a dedicated club member since the 1950s, and he was a walking encyclopedia on anything to do with Judy and the movies. During the tea break Ken approached Gill and myself with a tray of biscuits and asked: 'Would you like a custard cream?' He was slim in stature, polite, kind, gentle and keen to engage us in conversation. He wanted us to feel at home and to share our enthusiasm for Judy.

Ken and I became friends and through the years he has shared many memories of his cinemagoing as well as his numerous encounters with movie stars. He never forgot the first film he saw. It was called *Secrets* (1933) and starred Mary Pickford. He was seven years old at the time, and hooked. 'I was so in love with the movies,' he said, 'I wanted to be a movie star. I wanted to go to Hollywood. Then, when I reached my teens and looked in the mirror, I thought, "What could you play, Kenneth? You're not a leading man type."'

Ken celebrated his thirteenth birthday on 30 August 1939 just before the outbreak of war. For safety, he accompanied his mother from their home in England to Belfast in Northern Ireland, where they made a new home for the duration but, during April and May 1941, they faced the 'Belfast Blitz'. In one of four air raids, on 15 April, 200 bombers of the German Luftwaffe attacked military bases and war factories. Over 900 people were killed as a result of the German raids and 1,500 were injured. In the United Kingdom, outside of London, this was the greatest loss of life in a single air raid during the war. Ken never forgot the terror he and his mother experienced during the raids. 'We sheltered under the kitchen table', he recalled, 'and prayed we would survive. The house shook. We shook! But we came through. The next morning we were shocked at the devastation in Belfast. It was terrible.'

A few months before celebrating his eighteenth birthday on 30 August 1944, Ken returned to England and came to London for the first time. He had been offered a place in a fashion school, but the terrors of war were far from over: 'After settling into my London digs, a V2 rocket exploded nearby and blew me out of my bed!' In spite of the war, Ken took to living in London like a duck to water. He had always been an avid cinema- and theatregoer, and

London's West End provided him with many exciting new venues to explore. For the rest of his working life, Ken did not earn a great deal of money, but from his arrival in the metropolis he learned to be thrifty and to find the cheapest cafés, while at the same time saving his pennies for his theatrical pursuits.

For young Ken, London also provided other sources of adventure and, aged 18, he enjoyed a brief encounter with an American GI on Victory in Europe (VE) Day, 8 May 1945. 'Duane was a sergeant in the American Army,' he recalled:

> Twenty-six years old. Tall, fair-haired, of Swedish descent, well built, kind and gentle. He told me he had a wife and two children at home, but that didn't matter. We had a great time, joining in the VE Day celebrations, having lunch together, enjoying each other's company. I really fancied him, and it was obvious to me that the feeling was mutual. Duane was very affectionate. He even held my hand and this was possible while we merged with the crowds and celebrated the end of the war. There was relief and happiness everywhere.

The young men fully intended to go to bed together and have sex, so Duane said he would take Ken to a hotel, but first he had to visit the American Red Cross. 'So we went to the American Red Cross building,' Ken recalled:

> but we didn't know we were being followed by two American military policemen. As Duane entered the building, the policemen followed him inside. They must have said something to Duane because then the policemen came out of the building with Duane and took him away. We didn't speak. We didn't even say goodbye. I was heartbroken, left alone on the steps of the building. I did not know there was a law against us. Who was there to tell me? I just wanted to have a bit of fun.

In 1945, still aged 18, Ken was passing the London Pavilion on his way to Leicester Square when a policeman arrested him for importuning. The policeman falsely claimed that Ken had solicited six men. Nevertheless, a solicitor advised him to plead guilty because this would result in a fine and freedom, but at court he was sentenced to six months in prison. Ken was stunned, and horrified when he found himself in Brixton Prison. Fortunately, he remained there for only one week, by which time another solicitor had successfully arranged for a retrial. Ken was found innocent and the policeman was shown to be a liar. In a situation reminiscent of Quentin Crisp's courtroom scene in the 1975 television film *The Naked Civil Servant*, Ken's employer and a succession of supportive friends stood as character witnesses. The judge quashed the sentence and Ken was told he was free to go. The humiliation of going to prison haunted Ken for the rest of his life and he rarely spoke about it.

After the war Ken worked as a dress designer, but in the early 1950s the young film buff realised his dream to 'go Hollywood' when he worked as a film extra. His first job was at a studio in Walton-on-Thames. The film was *Saturday Island*, starring Hollywood imports Tab Hunter and Linda Darnell. Ken's scene was set on a troop ship with wounded soldiers:

> The wardrobe lady put me in a khaki shirt and khaki shorts. She took one look at me and said 'No. You look as if you're going camping', but I don't think she knew what she was saying. So she gave me pyjamas and said I could be a wounded soldier. When we were filming I thought to myself, 'How's Mum and Dad going to see me?' So I did a big yawn. There's also ten seconds of my back in close up. It was all fun for anyone who loved films.

It was around this time that Ken met Brian, the man who became his lifelong partner. They began living together as a couple in 1953, but it was a dangerous time for gay men in Britain because a homosexual 'witch hunt' was underway and the arrests of gay men were increasing rapidly. They lived in fear of being discovered, arrested, criminalised and publicly humiliated. The celebrated actor

John Gielgud was one of the famous gay men who was arrested at this time. In 1953 he was arrested on the charge of 'importuning for immoral purposes' and he gave his real name, Arthur Gielgud, to the magistrate, who did not know who he was. He was fined £10 and the magistrate also ordered him to see his doctor. Unfortunately a reporter from the *Evening Standard* was in court, and recognised Gielgud; the actor found himself plastered on the paper's front page. At first it looked as if Gielgud's career was in jeopardy, but he survived the ordeal, though at a cost to his emotional well-being.

Discussions of homosexuality on BBC television and radio were practically non-existent and it was the Conservative MP, Sir Robert Boothby, who made the historic first mention of the word homosexual on television on 27 November 1953 in the BBC series *In the News*, shortly after John Gielgud was arrested. Gielgud's arrest highlighted the absurdity of the law as it stood at the time and gave the media an opportunity to debate the subject. For the BBC, however, homosexuality remained a taboo subject, unfit for broadcast.

On 3 December 1953, homosexual law reform was raised openly for the first time in the House of Commons by Sir Robert Boothby and Labour's Desmond Donnelly, and in March 1954 the journalist Peter Wildeblood was sent to prison for 18 months for 'homosexual offences'.[1] Peter later became a campaigner for homosexual law reform after writing about the experiences of his conviction and prison sentence in his book *Against the Law* (1955).

Against the Law was partly responsible for important gay law reform because it forced the Conservative government of the day to address the issue. The Conservative government had already set up the Wolfenden Committee in 1954 to review the law on homosexuals. Published in 1957, the Wolfenden Report recommended that 'homosexual practices' in private between consenting males over the age of 21 should not be considered a criminal offence. At that time gay men were being subjected to the most vicious forms of blackmail; in fact, around 90 per cent of blackmail cases involved gay men. In spite of the report's recommendations, the law was not changed until 1967.

In 1956 the intensity of the homosexual 'witch hunt' alarmed and distressed Ken. This is hardly surprising when public figures made nasty homophobic comments. These included the World War II hero Lord Montgomery of Alamein who made this contribution to the debate for law reform: 'I regard the act of homosexuality in any form as the most abominable bestiality that any human being can take part in and which reduces him to the status of an animal.'[2] Ken put pen to paper and composed a response to some of the homophobic newspaper reports that were being published at that time. In later life he gave me a copy and explained that he had not sent it to any newspaper for publication because he feared being exposed and subjected to harassment. In fact, Ken's response had remained secret until he shared it with me in the 1990s. In Ken's handwritten note, I discovered what it must have been like to live as a homosexual in Britain in the mid-1950s.

> I was most interested in your article but as a homosexual I feel that none of the people who have expressed themselves recently in the press or on the radio can really know much about the situation. Only those involved know what it really means. We have had to make the best of our lives and more or less manage to get along quietly and without interference but these past few weeks have been intolerable with the subject so widely discussed. Those who can show real light on the problem are unable to speak because they cannot afford to let themselves be known. You say there can be no real happiness for us. The obstacle to this is not ourselves but society and the law. We can have partnerships too where we are tied not by marriage vows or children but by mutual love, need and devotion. I have seen few normal marriages you could claim were made in heaven!
>
> It is no easy matter to make a union last between us with all the obstacles in the way but next month I celebrate the third anniversary with my partner and I intend to make this thing last despite everything. I never dared discuss my problem with anyone and I did not know of any literature on the subject. In fact I thought I was the only one so stricken until in my teens I met another who felt the

same and eventually more and more until I was able to join a circle of people who had the same interests and thoughts as I did.

I did not know there were laws against us. All my life I have lived this Jekyll and Hyde existence pretending to be someone I am not in front of family, friends and fellow workers, and only able to relax and be myself in the company of my own kind. I had always hoped to meet my Mr Right but before I did there was quite a lot of desperation and disillusionment. When I finally did meet my partner we had both reached a low spot in our lives – deep depression – but in each other we found love, loyalty and understanding and a great need for each other. With our different personalities we complemented one another. After 15 months we moved in together, two rooms in a boarding house and how we enjoyed creating and building up our first home. You say this is not possible but you are so wrong. Once again with all this talk I am made to feel again that we are criminals, a bad influence and likely to be a bad example to young people.

If we are born this way what can we do about it? We can but live with it and make the most of our lives. Surely if two young men who could not find a future in a normal life and live together as we do it cannot harm others but rather give hope of a happy future. If you are homosexual you can't do anything about it. Are we expected to go through life without ever daring to experience love and understanding from another? Who can say true love is a sin or a crime? I am quite sure that in God's eyes no real love is a sin and God knows there is little enough of it about now.

Through the years, in addition to being a friend, Ken was a never-ending source of information about the movies. He shared numerous anecdotes about movie stars he had met, mostly when he politely requested their autographs. Ken was also extremely informative about his life as a gay man in Britain from the 1940s. As a younger gay man, I learned so much from him about the difficulties of living in a country where his sexuality was against the law, as well as the freedom he enjoyed after the 1967 Sexual Offences Act. When I needed information for a gay-related history book or a project, Ken was more than happy to help. In 1996 he willingly contributed to my book *Brief Encounters*. I still have the copy of his handwritten statement about his memories of seeing the groundbreaking film *Victim* on its initial release in 1961. Ken agreed that this film – and Dirk Bogarde's participation – helped to break down barriers and lead to the decriminalisation of homosexual acts. Here is an extract:

> I first saw *Victim* at the Odeon cinema in Leicester Square, the day it opened its initial run in 1961. I went along straight from work at about 5.30pm only to find a long queue stretching round the alley beside the cinema. As I walked to the end of the queue I found myself nodding to numerous acquaintances I had made during my then, fourteen years in London. It was rather amusing but they had also rushed to see this film, full of curiosity as to how it would deal with its subject matter, homosexual life in London, then very rare on screen [...] Most homosexuals seemed to find it both helpful and sympathetic [...] Bogarde was playing a bisexual, a married barrister who tried to hide a relationship he had with a young man. His playing of the part did seem honest and sincere and he was praised in the press for his courage for taking on such a role and risking the loss of his adoring female following and for displaying hitherto hidden depths as an actor [...] I wouldn't say there was a gay sub-culture in Britain at this time. From my experience, provincial cities from as far back as the 1940s had their bars frequented by homosexuals as had London where there were also several gay clubs. As far as I know there were no gay newspapers or magazines. There were gay novels and most gays (of all classes) heard of them and, if they were readers, read them. There didn't seem to be any class barriers in the gay world and in these bars and clubs you would find men from all walks of life mixing happily.

Ken and his partner Brian remained devoted to each other for 55 years. They worked hard until their retirements. They were loved and respected by their friends and neighbours. Ken was devastated when Brian died in 2008 at the age of 79. In spite of having a large group of friends, and being a socially active person, Ken started to become withdrawn. He missed Brian, the love of his life. In 2014, with his health in decline, Ken was admitted to a care home. On 30 August 2016 he celebrated his 90th birthday, surrounded by his friends and numerous birthday cards.

Conclusion

Even before the centenary of World War I began on 4 August 2014, British television and radio began commemorating with specially commissioned documentaries and dramas. Among those earlier programmes that I found particularly outstanding were *Hidden Histories: WW1's Forgotten Photographs* (BBC4, 13 March 2014) and *I Was There: The Great War Interviews* (BBC2, 14 March 2014). However, it soon became apparent to me that gay men's lives during the conflict were conspicuous by their absence in the programmes and other commemorations. An exception was the front-line hospital orderly Peter Foley in the drama series *The Crimson Field* (BBC1, 2014). He was not a major character in the series, but nevertheless a risk-taker who kept sneaking off to the woods, and not to catch rabbits! However, there was no reference to Edward Brittain's homosexuality in the film *Testament of Youth* (2015) (see Chapter 3).

In 2014 ITV produced *The Pity of War: The Loves and Lives of the War Poets*, a fact-based drama telling the story of poets Siegfried Sassoon, Wilfred Owen and Robert Graves. The three young men, all aspiring poets and secretly gay, are thrown together in the trenches, and each has to find his own way of dealing with all the chaos and slaughter that surrounds them. This production was beautifully realised by Jenny Ash, its writer/producer/director. However, *The Pity of War* was not given a peak-time slot in 2014. For reasons which have not come to light, Jenny Ash's production was not shown until 13 November 2016, in the Sunday evening 'graveyard slot' of 11.05 p.m. It was most likely the first film or television production made for the centenary to give centre stage to the existence of gay men in the Great War. It makes me angry that this production was so ill served by ITV, postponed for over two years, and then 'lost' in the schedules.

Similarly, the contribution of African and Caribbean servicemen to the Great War has been overlooked in the centenary commemorations, in spite of the publication, on 4 August 2014, of my book *Black Poppies: Britain's Black Community and the Great War.* I have read a number of books about the two world wars. However, though some of them are outstanding, they tend to focus on the same campaigns and characters, such as the Battle of the Somme, Battle of Britain, Monty, Churchill, Eisenhower and Hitler. Two of my personal favourites are John Costello's *Love, Sex and War: Changing Values 1939–45* (1985) and Joshua Levine's *The Secret History of the Blitz* (2015), but over time I have had to dig hard to find stories of black British servicemen or the presence of gay men in the conflicts. They are barely mentioned. Readers have told me they found my books *The Motherland Calls* and *Black Poppies* refreshing because they did not know that black men and women from Britain and across the former British Empire had participated in the two world wars. There was very little acknowledgement or recognition.

In *The Motherland Calls* I quoted the historian Ray Costello from an interview in the *The Voice* newspaper (31 May 2004). Ray said that Britain had been reluctant to show the world that black servicemen and women from Britain and the colonies had played a part in freeing the oppressed 'because they were afraid that it would feed the desire for independence'. With apologies to Ray, I would like to adapt his quote for *Fighting Proud* by replacing the word black with gay. In doing so it sums up how I feel about the way Britain has failed to acknowledge the gay servicemen who played a part in freeing the oppressed:

> If gay men are shown to have the capacity for bravery it makes
> them human, heroes even. And heroes should have freedom and

independence. Britain did not want that. It was more difficult to conceal their contributions at the end of World War II because of the sheer numbers who fought. The omission of the contribution of gays to the British armed services is a crime.

Cinema and Television

Although British cinema and television have rarely acknowledged the existence of gay men in the two world wars, there are a handful of dramas that I found interesting and engaging. In *The Naked Civil Servant* (Thames TV, 1975) Quentin Crisp, brilliantly played by John Hurt, attempts to join the Army with hilarious results. 'Anyone can get killed,' he explains to the bemused recruiting officer when he is asked why he should want to join. This acclaimed and award-winning television film also revealed that some of the Yanks (American GIs) were not fussy about who they had sex with in the wartime blackout.

There followed another outstanding television drama called *Something for the Boys* (1981), shown nationally in Scottish TV's *House on the Hill* anthology series. It was written by Drew Griffiths, one of the most talented dramatists in the radical theatre company Gay Sweatshop. This was the first time a gay romance was depicted on British television. The plot revolves around a young Scottish soldier who loses his virginity to a Yank after a night in an unofficial gay club in Glasgow. When Emmanuel Cooper reviewed the play in *Gay News*, he described it as 'a happy blend of romance and excitement, as well as a gentle lesson in how people, gay or heterosexual, can be kind, generous and accepting'.[1] Keith Howes described it in *Broadcasting It* (1993) as:

A much longed-for variation on the stock GI with an eye for the main chance: good-looking, self-possessed, sexy, a regular guy. There's a particularly nice ending. The American requests a farewell kiss at the station. Shyness gets the better of the Scot. 'How about a nice brotherly hug instead?' persists the American. They embrace, causing a male passer-by to comment favourably: 'That's what I like to see – the allies getting on together!'[2]

Granada TV's epic mini-series and BAFTA-laden *The Jewel in the Crown* (1984), based on Paul Scott's Raj Quartet novels, focused on the final days of the British Raj in India during World War II. The story featured two contrasting gay men: the nasty, sadistic policeman Ronald Merrick (Tim Pigott-Smith) and Corporal 'Sophie' Dixon (Warren Clarke), a cockney orderly who looks after Merrick during his stay in hospital. 'Sophie' is a revelation. In addition to winning a medal for risking his life to save wounded soldiers, he is bitchy, quick-witted and funny. He goads Merrick into asking: 'Are you a hero or a bloody pansy?' to which 'Sophie' gleefully gives as good as he gets: 'I don't think that's a question *you* ought to be asking, sir.'

Troubled gay characters surfaced in two war dramas in 1987. In BBC TV's adaptation of Olivia Manning's novels, *Fortunes of War* (BBC1), set in World War II, Aidan Pratt (Greg Hicks) is a young Army officer who was once a great stage actor. A closeted 'queer', he makes sexual advances to Guy Pringle (Kenneth Branagh) but, when these are rejected, Pratt commits suicide. In the film version of J. L. Carr's novel *A Month in the Country*, set in 1920, Kenneth Branagh played the archaeologist and World War I veteran James Moon, who had been decorated for bravery on the front line. When Moon was serving in the war, he was caught buggering another man, for which he was court-martialled. For this misdemeanour he served a prison sentence and was thrown out of the Army. It is not the main focus of the book or film, but Branagh creates a sympathetic character who in peacetime is the equal of the story's main character, his friend Birkin (Colin

Firth), who has also been emotionally damaged by the war and seeks peace and quiet in the countryside.

The 1980s ended with Derek Jarman's *War Requiem* (1989), an extraordinarily powerful cinematic visualisation of Wilfred Owen's war poems set to Benjamin Britten's music. In *War Requiem* Jarman, an openly gay experimental artist and film director, draws upon the work of a gay composer (Britten) and a gay poet from World War I (Owen). By combining these elements, Jarman succeeds in creating an evocative anti-war statement which is in keeping with the sentiments of Britten and Owen. Britten, a pacifist, grieved for many of his friends who were killed in World War II. Like Wilfred Owen, Britten was outraged by the waste of men's lives hastened by human stupidity and violence. *War Requiem* is beautifully realised and includes the return to the cinema screen of the frail 81-year-old acting legend Laurence Olivier as the wheelchair-bound 'Old Soldier'. On the soundtrack his thin, tired voice reads Owen's powerful 'Strange Meeting'. At the climax to the film, it is a German soldier who is seen placing a wreath of poppies on the Tomb of the Unknown Soldier. However, it is the sheer magnificence of Britten's music and the real horror of documentary footage of twentieth-century wars, made available by the Imperial War Museum, that make this a profound and disturbing cinematic experience.

In 1999 a fine feature-length World War I drama called *All the King's Men* was shown on BBC1. It starred David Jason as the manager of King George V's Norfolk estate who is appointed captain of the Sandringham Company. In 1915 the Captain and his company disappeared without trace at Gallipoli. If viewers blink they will miss the unexpected *frisson* in a *pas de deux* between the upper-class, classics-quoting Lieutenant Radley (Stuart Bunce) and the handsome, blond stable hand Private Will Needham (James Murray). In the chaos at Gallipoli there is another brief and tender moment between the two men when Radley tells Needham he hasn't 'done any living', in other words, he is still a virgin. Needham replies: 'We'll have to get you a bit close then!' No ambiguity there. The two men share only fleeting moments in the drama, but they are important, for, until then, World War I dramas had rarely touched upon such possibilities.

Troubled gay characters continued to surface, this time in two popular ITV television dramas set in World War II. In 'Among the Few' (23 November 2003), an episode of *Foyle's War* written by Anthony Horowitz and Matthew Hall, a friend of Foyle's son Andrew is revealed to be gay. Andrew Foyle and Rex Talbot (Mark Umbers) are RAF pilots and Rex's secret crush on his friend inadvertently leads to the accidental death of Rex's girlfriend Connie. Rex commits suicide rather than face the consequences, but afterwards Foyle reassures his distraught son that Rex was a 'good man'. *Housewife, 49* (10 December 2006) was based on the wartime Mass Observation diaries of Nella Last and starred the comedienne Victoria Wood as Nella. In the drama, written by Victoria Wood, Nella's soldier son Cliff (Christopher Harper) expresses his love for James, who has been killed in action, but war wounds make him incapable of having a sex life (albeit an illegal one) after the war. The real-life Clifford Last (1918–91) was a sculptor who made Australia his home in 1947.

In 2014 Benedict Cumberbatch gave a critically acclaimed and Oscar-nominated portrayal of the computer pioneer Alan Turing in the film *The Imitation Game*. Though Turing's life and remarkable achievements had been the subject of several documentaries and at least one television drama, the BBC's *Breaking the Code* (1997) starring Derek Jacobi, the 2014 feature film made the biggest impact. The film switches between 1952, when Turing was arrested for homosexual offences ('gross indecency'), and his wartime secret work at Bletchley Park on breaking the Enigma code used by the Nazis. With the exception of, perhaps, Winston Churchill, Roosevelt and Joseph Stalin, Alan Turing did more than anyone to ensure the defeat of Hitler and the Nazis. Aaron Hicklin described the film in the *Radio Times* as:

> elegantly made, beautifully filmed and loyal to its source material (in
> this case, Andrew Hodges's excellent 1983 biography *Alan Turing:*

The Enigma), but what brings the whole to life is Cumberbatch's immensely accomplished performance as Turing, a misfit at ease with his homosexuality (he named his computer Christopher after an unrequited schoolboy crush), but utterly at odds with the world around him.[3]

Notes

Preface

1 Tom Ambrose, *Heroes and Exiles: Gay Icons Through the Ages* (New Holland, 2010), pp. 156–7.

2 Antony Beevor, introduction to Myles Hildyard, *It Is Bliss Here: Letters Home 1939–1945* (Bloomsbury, 2005), p. 9.

3 'Timeline of LGBT History in the United Kingdom', Wikipedia, available at: https://en.wikipedia.org/wiki/Timeline_of_LGBT_history_in_the_United_Kingdom (accessed 19 January 2017).

4 'Frightening the Cavalry', *The Times*, 18 February 1992.

Introduction

1 John Costello *Love, Sex and War: Changing Values 1939–45* (Guild Publishing, 1985), p. 173.

Part I: World War I: 1914–18

1 Lord Kitchener

1 Max Arthur, *Forgotten Voices of the Great War* (Ebury Press, 2002), p. 9.

2 Jeremy Paxman, *Great Britain's Great War* (Penguin/Viking, 2013), p. 35.

3 Peter Tatchell, 'Inside the Gay Museum', *Guardian*, 8 June 2004.

4 Jeremy Paxman, 'A Great British Hero, Rumours that he Was Gay – and Conspiracy Theories Galore', *Daily Mail*, 15 November 2014.

5 Jad Adams, 'Was 'K' Gay?', *History Today*, November 1999.

6 H. Montgomery Hyde, *The Other Love* (William Heinemann, 1970), p. 182. In 1970 H. Mongomery Hyde was not the first to describe Kitchener as a homosexual. In 1964 the presenter Bryan Magee informed television viewers that Kitchener was a homosexual in the opening of *This Week: Homosexuals* one of the first actuality programmes to focus on the subject.

7 Trevor Royle, *The Kitchener Enigma* (Michael Joseph, 1985), pp. 221–2.

8 John Pollock, *Kitchener* (Constable, 2001).

9 Rictor Norton, review of *Kitchener* by John Pollock, available at http://rictornorton.co.uk/reviews/kitchen.htm (accessed 19 January 2017).
10 Pollock, *Kitchener*, pp. 486–7.
11 Paxman, *Great Britain's Great War*, p. 179.
12 Pollock, *Kitchener*, p. 489.
13 Ibid., p. 488.
14 In spite of Lord Kitchener being one of the best-loved and most celebrated military leaders of World War I, the centenary of his death on 5 June 2016 passed unnoticed.

2 Unfortunate Fellows

1 Niall Ferguson, *The Pity of War* (Allen Lane Penguin Press, 1998), p. 349.
2 Richard Holmes, *Tommy: The British Soldier* (HarperCollins, 2004), p. 597.
3 John Jolliffe (ed.), *Raymond Asquith: Life and Letters* (William Collins and Sons, 1980), p. 290
4 Ibid., p. 295.
5 Richard Smith, *Jamaican Volunteers in World War I: Race, Masculinity and the Development of National Consciousness* (Manchester University Press, 2004), p. 21.
6 Imperial War Museum Sound Archive, Oral History 730, Reel 3: Joseph Harry Vine interviewed on 16 January 1976.
7 'Young Soldier's Suicide', *Dover and East Kent News*, 4 August 1916.
8 'Soldier's Masquerade – Disowned by Sisters for his Effeminate Ways', *North-Eastern Daily Gazette*, 15 June 1916.
9 The National Archives, MH 106/2297.
10 Imperial War Museum Sound Archive, Oral History 9428, Reel 7: Tommy Keele interviewed in 1991.
11 Joshua Levine, 'The Tommy who Wore a Frock', *Telegraph*, 14 September 2013.
12 Ibid.; Note: Tommy Keele died in 1992 at the age of 99.

3 Edward Brittain

1 Nigel Jones, 'Testament of Tortured Youth: Vera Brittain's Heartbreaking WWI Memoir of Love and Loss is Now a Major Movie', *Mail on Sunday*, 20 December 2014.
2 Richard Holmes, *Soldiers: Army Lives and Loyalties from Redcoats to Dusty Warriors* (HarperPress, 2011), p. 590.

3 Ibid.

4 Mark Bostridge, *Vera Brittain and the First World War: The Story of Testament of Youth* (Bloomsbury, 2014), p. 204.

5 Vera Brittain, *Testament of Youth: An Autobiographical Study of the Years 1900–1925* (Gollancz, 1933), p. 404.

6 Bostridge, *Vera Brittain*, p. 204.

7 Ibid., pp. 209–10.

8 Mark Bostridge, email to author, 31 May 2016.

4 James Whale, R. C. Sherriff and *Journey's End*

1 Robert Gore-Langton, *Journey's End: The Classic War Play Explored* (Oberon Books, 2013), p. 70.

2 Russell Davies (ed.), *The Kenneth Williams Diaries* (HarperCollins, 1994), p. 431.

3 Gore-Langton, *Journey's End*, pp. xi–xii.

4 Roland Wales, *From Journey's End to The Dam Busters: The Life of R. C. Sherriff, Playwright of the Trenches* (Pen and Sword Military, 2016), p. 55.

5 Mark Gatiss, *James Whale: A Biography or The Would-Be Gentleman* (Cassell, 1995), p. 4.

6 *New York Times*, 8 September 1929.

7 Elsa Lanchester, *Elsa Lanchester Herself* (Michael Joseph, 1983), p. 135.

8 *Picturegoer*, 29 September 1934.

9 Michael Elliman and Frederick Roll, *The Pink Plaque Guide to London* (Gay Men's Press, 1986), p. 212.

10 Vito Russo, *The Celluloid Closet: Homosexuality in the Movies* (Harper and Row, revised edn 1987), p. 50. See also Stephen Bourne, 'Dangerously Indiscreet – James Whale in Hollywood', *Gay Times*, December 1988.

11 Lanchester, *Elsa Lanchester Herself*, p. 137.

5 Ralph and Monty: The Man I Love

1 James Gardiner, *A Class Apart: The Private Pictures of Montague Glover* (Serpent's Tail, 1992). See also Rictor Norton (ed.), *My Dear Boy: Gay Love Letters Through the Centuries* (Leyland Publications, 1998).

2 Gardiner, *A Class Apart*, p. 82.

3 Ibid., p. 11.

4 Ibid., p. 94.

Part II: World War II: 1939–45
The Army

6 Kiss Me Goodnight, Sergeant Major

1 John Costello, *Love, Sex and War: Changing Values 1939–45* (Guild Publishing, 1985), p. 162.

2 Jeremy Seabrook, *A Lasting Relationship: Homosexuals and Society* (Allen Lane, 1976), p. 79.

3 Thanks to Mark Fuller for informing me about 'Bunny'. See also John Windsor, 'Family Values: At Home with Sandy, Bunny and Alan', *Independent*, 24 January 1998, and Simon Mills, 'All Mouth and Trousers', *Guardian*, 17 June 2006.

4 Bruce Copp, with Andy Merriman, *Out of the Firing Line ... Into the Foyer: My Remarkable Story* (The History Press, 2015), p. 65.

5 Ibid., pp. 65–6.

6 Ibid., p. 64.

7 *Out on Tuesday: Comrades in Arms*, Channel 4, 1 May 1990.

8 Matt Houlbrook, *Queer London: Perils and Pleasures in the Sexual Metropolis, 1918–1957* (University of Chicago Press, 2005), pp. 151, 159.

9 Kevin Porter and Jeffrey Weeks (eds), *Between the Acts: Lives of Homosexual Men 1885–1967* (Routledge, 1991), p. 140.

10 Professor Paul Baker, Department of Linguistics and English Language, Lancaster University, says: 'I think Sharpy Omi comes from a form of slang called Parlyaree, influenced by Italian and various Mediterranean dialects from the 19th century and probably earlier. The term sharper meant to steal, and it probably developed out of another word, charper (a charpering carsey was referred to as a police station). However, charper also meant "to look" (most likely from Italian acchiappare – to catch), so there's probably been a bit of confusion with regard to the word's meaning, pronunciation and spelling, and over time it changed from charpy to sharpy to sharpy (steal). A majority (57%) of the Polari speakers I interviewed knew what sharpy meant, although it wasn't a huge majority.' Email to the author, 10 December 2016.

11 National Sound Archive, C444 03 30a–32a: Alex Purdie.

12 *Out on Tuesday: Comrades in Arms*.

13 Andy Merriman, *Greasepaint and Cordite: How ENSA Entertained the Troops During World War II* (Aurum Press, 2013), p. 234.

14 *Out on Tuesday: Comrades in Arms*.

15 Porter and Weeks, *Between the Acts*, pp. 31–2.

16 Hall Carpenter Archives Gay Men's Oral History Group, *Walking After Midnight: Gay Men's Life Stories* (Routledge, 1989), pp. 45, 49.

17 Mike Malyon, *Seems Like a Nice Boy: The Story of Larry Grayson's Rise to Stardom* (Apex Publishing, 2015), pp. 20–1.

18 Michael Parkinson, *Parky's People* (Hodder, 2011), p. 384.

19 Costello, *Love, Sex and War*, p. 163.

20 Ibid.

21 Ibid.

7 Prisoners of War Part 1: Dudley Cave

1 'Sexual Orientation and the Military of the United Kingdom', Wikipedia. Available at: https://en.wikipedia.org/wiki/Sexual_orientation_and_the_military_of_the_United_Kingdom (accessed 19 January 2017).

2 Peter Tatchell, obituary of Dudley Cave, *Independent*, 31 May 1999.

3 Hall Carpenter Archives Gay Men's Oral History Group, *Walking After Midnight: Gay Men's Life Stories* (Routledge, 1989), p. 26. Dudley Cave was interviewed in May 1987 by Paul Marshall.

4 *Out on Tuesday: Comrades in Arms*, Channel 4, 1 May 1990.

5 Peter Tatchell, 'A Gay Soldier's Story', BBC, WW2 People's War – An Archive of World War Two Memories – Written by the Public, Gathered by the BBC, Article ID: A2688636, 1 June 2004. Available at www.bbc.co.uk/history/ww2peopleswar/stories/36/a2688636.shtml (accessed 19 January 2017).

6 Ibid.

7 Hall Carpenter Archives, *Walking After Midnight*, p. 28.

8 Tatchell, obituary of Dudley Cave.

9 Tatchell, 'A Gay Soldier's Story'.

10 Hall Carpenter Archives, *Walking After Midnight*, p. 32.

11 Steve Humphries, *A Secret World of Sex* (Sidgwick and Jackson, 1988), p. 205.

12 Tatchell, 'A Gay Soldier's Story'.

13 Keith Howes, email to the author, 1 February 2015.

8 Prisoners of War Part 2

1 A. Robert Prouse, *Ticket to Hell Via Dieppe: From a Prisoner's Wartime Log 1942–1945* (Webb and Bower, 1982), p. 113.

2 Adrian Gilbert, *POW: Allied Prisoners in Europe, 1939–1945* (John Murray, 2006), p. 117.

3 Ibid., p. 118.

4 Jay Rayner, review of *Colditz: The Definitive History* by Henry Chancellor, *Observer*, 12 August 2001.

5 Gilbert, *POW*, p. 118.

6 Geoffrey Ellwood, in Daniel D. Dancocks (ed.), *In Enemy Hands: Canadian Prisoners of War 1939–45* (Hurtig, 1983), p. 107.

7 Imperial War Museum, Documents: 1279: Private Papers of J. H. [James Hendrik] Witte.

8 Chloe Green, 'George Frederick Green (1911–1977)', in *Oxford Dictionary of National Biography* (Oxford University Press, 2004).

9 'Lieutenant Z' [G. F. Green], in John Lehmann (ed.), *Penguin New Writing No. 31* (Penguin Books, 1947), pp. 146–63.

10 Green, 'George Frederick Green'.

The Navy

9 Rum, Bum and Concertina

1 George Hayim, *Thou Shalt Not Uncover Thy Mother's Nakedness* (Quartet Books, 1988), p. 78.

2 George Melly, *Rum, Bum and Concertina* (Weidenfeld and Nicolson, 1977), p. 64.

3 Hayim, *Thou Shalt Not*, p. 78

4 Ibid., p. 79.

5 Ibid., pp. 82–3.

6 Ibid., p. 84.

7 Ibid., p. 88.

8 Ibid., p. 89.

9 Matthew Sweet, *The West End Front: The Wartime Secrets of London's Grand Hotels* (Faber and Faber, 2011), p. 200.

10 Ibid., p. 202.

11 Hayim, *Thou Shalt Not*, p. 97–8.

12 *It's Not Unusual*, BBC2, 18 May 1997.

13 Ibid.

14 Ibid.

15 Ibid.

16 Ibid.

17 Alkarim Jivani, *It's Not Unusual: A History of Lesbian and Gay Britain in the Twentieth Century* (Michael O'Mara, 1997), p. 66.

18 Jivani, *It's Not Unusual*, p. 82.

19 *Timewatch: Sex and War*, BBC2, 29 September 1998.

20 Ibid.

21 Ibid.
22 Ibid.

10 Terri Gardener: Behind Enemy Lines

1 Keith Howes, 'Queen's Jubilee', *Gay News* 263 (1983).
2 Alkarim Jivani, *It's Not Unusual: A History of Lesbian and Gay Britain in the Twentieth Century* (Michael O'Mara, 1997), pp. 14–15.
3 Steve Humphries, *The Call of the Sea: Britain's Maritime Past 1900–1960* (BBC Books, 1997), p. 92.
4 Ibid., p. 93.
5 Ibid., pp. 93–4.
6 Ibid., p. 94.
7 Kenneth Williams, interview with Keith Howes, *Gay News* 261 (1983).
8 Russell Davies (ed.), *The Kenneth Williams Diaries* (HarperCollins, 1993), p. 71.
9 Howes, 'Queen's Jubilee'.
10 In a number of London boroughs in the 1980s and 1990s, various local community projects existed which enabled people to have their life stories recorded, and published. The Peckham Bookplace and Hammersmith and Fulham's Ethnic Communities Oral History Project were among those at grass-roots level that had success with this; a useful resource for this book has been the interviews conducted by the Hall Carpenter Archives Gay Men's Oral History Group in the 1980s. However, with the technological advances of recent times, people should still be encouraged to continue the oral tradition of documenting history by undertaking face-to-face interviews.

The RAF

11 The Killing Skies

1 *Hear-Say*, BBC2, 7 August 1990.
2 Patrick Bishop, *Bomber Boys: Fighting Back 1940–1945* (HarperPress, 2007), p. 275.
3 Michael Bentine, *The Long Banana Skin* (Wolfe, 1975), p. 98.
4 Ibid., p. 99.
5 Jack Currie, *Lancaster Target* (New English Library, 1977), pp. 151–2.
6 Ibid.
7 Bentine, *The Long Banana Skin*, p. 99.

8 Sue Elliott and Steve Humphries, *Britain's Greatest Generation: How Our Parents and Grandparents Made the Twentieth Century* (Random House, 2015), pp. 174–5.

9 George Montague, *The Oldest Gay in the Village* (John Blake, 2014).

10 Thanks to Peter Devitt, assistant curator, RAF Museum London, for making it possible for the author to make contact with Mrs Sue Westbury, who granted permission for this information to be shared in *Fighting Proud*.

12 Richard Rumbold: The Flyer

1 Richard Lumford, *My Father's Son* (Jonathan Cape, 1949), p. 215.

2 Martin Francis, *The Flyer: British Culture and the Royal Air Force, 1939–1945* (Oxford University Press, 2008), p. 185.

3 Raleigh Trevelyan, 'Richard Rumbold (1913–1961)', in *Oxford Dictionary of National Biography* (Oxford University Press, 2004).

4 William Plomer (ed.), *A Message in Code: The Diary of Richard Rumbold 1932–61* (Weidenfeld and Nicolson, 1964), p. 14.

5 Trevelyan, 'Richard Rumbold'.

6 Plomer, *A Message in Code*, p. 61.

7 Lumford, *My Father's Son*, p. 184.

8 Ibid., pp. 194–6, 198.

9 Ibid., p. 213.

10 Ibid., p. 215.

11 Plomer, *A Message in Code*, p. 77.

13 Ian Gleed: The Hero

1 Norman Franks, *Fighter Leader: The Story of Wing Commander Ian Gleed* (William Kimber, 1978), p. 15.

2 Ibid., p. 39.

3 W. Somerset Maugham, *Strictly Personal* (William Heinemann, 1942), p. 37.

4 Ian Gleed, *Arise to Conquer* (Victor Gollancz, 1942), pp. 17–18.

5 Franks, *Fighter Leader*, p. 56.

6 *London Gazette*, 13 September 1940.

7 *London Gazette*, 22 May 1942.

8 Gleed, *Arise to Conquer*, pp. 203–4.

9 Franks, *Fighter Leader*, p. 112.

10 Ibid., p. 95.

11 Alkarim Jivani, *It's Not Unusual: A History of Lesbian and Gay Britain in the Twentieth Century* (Michael O'Mara, 1997), pp. 67–9; *It's Not*

Unusual, BBC2, 18 May 1997; *Timewatch: Sex and War*, BBC2, 29 September 1998.

12 Peter Devitt, assistant curator of the Royal Air Force Museum London, email to the author, 3 July 2016.

14 Hector Bolitho: The Writer

1 Hector Bolitho, *A Penguin in the Eyrie: An R.A.F. Diary, 1939–1945* (Hutchinson, 1955), p. 109.

2 Ibid.

3 Ibid.

4 Michael Thornton, 'Hector Bolitho (1897–1974)', in *Oxford Dictionary of National Biography* (Oxford University Press, 2004).

5 Hector Bolitho, *Combat Report: The Story of a Fighter Pilot* (B. T. Batsford, 1943), p. 14. *Combat Report* was reissued as *Finest of the Few: The Story of Battle of Britain Fighter Pilot John Simpson* (Amberley Publishing, 2012).

6 Bolitho, *Combat Report*, pp. 15–16.

7 Ibid., p. 29.

8 Hector Bolitho, *War in the Strand: A Notebook of the First Two and a Half Years in London* (Eyre and Spottiswoode, 1942), p. 18.

9 Ibid., pp. 54–55.

10 Ibid., p. 77.

11 Ibid., p. 79.

12 Hector Bolitho, 'Why I Believe in the Royal Air Force', *London Calling* 52 (29 September–5 October 1940).

13 Bolitho, *Combat Report*, pp. 29–30.

14 Ibid., pp. 56–7.

15 Bolitho, *War in the Strand*, p. 117.

16 Bolitho, *Combat Report*, p. 86.

17 'Worried About His Flying', *Derby Evening Telegraph*, 16 August 1949.

18 Duncan Guthrie, letter to *The Times*, 30 September 1974.

The Home Front

15 Brief Encounters in the Blackout

1 Robert Aldrich and Garry Wotherspoon (eds), *Who's Who in Contemporary Gay and Lesbian History: From World War II to the Present Day* (Routledge, 2001), p. 96.

2 Kevin Porter and Jeffrey Weeks (eds), *Between the Acts: Lives of Homosexual Men 1885–1967* (Routledge, 1991), p. 140.

3 Adrian Woodhouse, *Angus McBean: Face-Maker* (Alma Books, 2006), p. 167.

4 George Melly, *Rum, Bum and Concertina* (Weidenfeld and Nicolson, 1977), pp. 75–6.

5 Quentin Crisp, *The Naked Civil Servant* (Jonathan Cape, 1968), p. 118.

6 Paul Bailey (ed.), *The Stately Homo: A Celebration of the Life of Quentin Crisp* (Bantam Press, 2000), p. 65.

7 Joshua Levine, *The Secret History of the Blitz* (Simon and Schuster, 2015), p. 220.

8 Crisp, *The Naked Civil Servant*, p. 160.

9 Ibid., p. 177.

10 Alkarim Jivani, *It's Not Unusual: A History of Lesbian and Gay Britain in the Twentieth Century* (Michael O'Mara, 1997), pp. 56–7.

11 Tom Driberg, *Ruling Passions: The Autobiography of Tom Driberg* (Quartet Books, 1977), p. 144–6.

12 Ibid., p. 144.

13 Ibid.

14 Ibid.

15 Ibid., p. 145.

16 Ibid.

17 Crisp, *The Naked Civil Servant*, p. 160.

16 Against the Law

1 Joshua Levine, *The Secret History of the Blitz* (Simon and Schuster, 2015), p. 236.

2 Maureen Waller, *London 1945* (John Murray, 2004), p. 251.

3 Richard Huggett, *Binkie Beaumont: Eminence Grise of the West End Theatre 1933–1973* (Hodder and Stoughton, 1989), pp. 350–1.

4 Adrian Woodhouse, *Angus McBean: Face-Maker* (Alma Books, 2006), p. 191.

5 Ibid., p. 193.

6 Ibid.

7 *Bath Weekly Chronicle and Herald*, 14 March 1942.

8 Woodhouse, *Angus McBean*, p. 186.

9 Michael Bloch, *Closet Queens: Some 20th Century British Politicians* (Little, Brown, 2015), p. 180.

10 Matthew Sweet, *The West End Front: The Wartime Secrets of London's Grand Hotels* (Faber and Faber, 2011), p. 198.

11 Bloch, *Closet Queens*, p. 180.

12 Ibid., p. 182.

13 Ibid.

14 Sweet, *The West End Front*, pp. 198–9.

17 Lily Law Goes to War

1 Stephen Bourne, 'Boys in Blue', *Gay Times*, June 2015.

2 Peter Burton, 'Across the Great Divide', *Gay Times*, February 1987.

3 Harry Daley, *This Small Cloud: A Personal Memoir* (Weidenfeld and Nicolson, 1986), p. 171.

4 See Peter Parker, 'Harry Daley (1901–1971)', in *Oxford Dictionary of National Biography* (Oxford University Press, 2004).

5 Daley, *This Small Cloud*, p. 78.

6 P. N. Furbank, *E. M. Forster: A Life* (Oxford University Press, 1978), p. 140.

7 Wendy Moffat, *E. M. Forster: A New Life* (Bloomsbury, 2010), pp. 206–7.

8 Ibid., p. 204.

9 Ibid., p. 223.

10 Furbank, *E. M. Forster: A Life*, p. 166.

11 Ibid.

12 Bethan Roberts, 'E. M. Forster and His "Wondrous Muddle"', *Guardian*, 17 February 2012.

13 Furbank, *E. M. Forster: A Life*, p. 239.

14 Daley, *This Small Cloud*, p. 173.

15 Ibid., p. 178.

16 Ibid.

17 Ibid., p. 183.

18 Keith Howes, 'Policemen', in *Broadcasting It: An Encyclopedia of Homosexuality on Film, Radio and TV in the UK 1923–1993* (Cassell, 1993), pp. 628–9.

19 John Coombes, interview with Stephen Bourne, Dorking, 3 December 2016. Thanks to Di Stiff, collections development archivist of the Surrey History Centre, for her help.

Entertainment on the Home Front
18 Noël Coward and *In Which We Serve*

1 Noël Coward, *The Autobiography of Noël Coward: Future Indefinite 1939–1945* (Methuen, 1986), p. 420.

2 Ibid., p. 422.

3 Marcia Landy, *British Genres: Cinema and Society, 1930–1960* (Princeton University Press, 1991), p. 159.
4 E. Martin Noble, *Jamaica Airman: A Black Airman in Britain 1943 and After* (New Beacon Books, 1984), p. 18.
5 *Secret Lives: Mountbatten*, Channel 4, 9 March 1995.
6 Barry Day (ed.), *The Letters of Noël Coward* (Methuen, 2007), pp. 470–1.
7 Andy Merriman, *Greasepaint and Cordite: How ENSA Entertained the Troops During World War II* (Aurum Press, 2013), p. 247.
8 Ibid., pp. 247–8.
9 Richard Fawkes, *Fighting for a Laugh: Entertaining the British and American Armed Forces 1939–1946* (Macdonald and Jane's, 1978), p. 167.
10 Day, *The Letters of Noël Coward*, p. 501.
11 Coward, *The Autobiography of Noël Coward*, p. 448.
12 David Thomson, *The New Biographical Dictionary of Film*, 6th edn (Alfred A. Knopf, 2014), pp. 221–2.
13 Coward, *The Autobiography of Noël Coward*, p. 362.

19 'Snakehips' Swings into the Blitz

1 James Gavin, 'Homophobia in Jazz', *Jazz Times*, December 2001.
2 Ibid.
3 Stephen Bourne, 'Lawrence Brown (1893–1972)', in *Oxford Dictionary of National Biography* (Oxford University Press, 2015).
4 Leslie Thompson with Jeffrey Green, *Swing from a Small Island* (Northway, 2009), p. 61.
5 Eric Johns, 'Negro Ballet', *Theatre World*, April 1946, p. 24.
6 Gemma Romain, *Race, Sexuality and Identity in Britain and Jamaica: The Biography of Patrick Nelson, 1916–1963* (Bloomsbury Academic, 2017).
7 Stephen Bourne, *Speak of Me as I Am: The Black Presence in Southwark Since 1600* (Southwark Council, 2005).
8 Stephen Bourne, 'Ivor Cummings (1913–1992)', in *Oxford Dictionary of National Biography* (Oxford University Press, 2015).
9 Leslie Thompson and Jeffrey Green, *Leslie Thompson: An Autobiography* (Rabbit Press, 1985), pp. 89–105.
10 Tom Ambrose, *Heroes and Exiles: Gay Icons Through the Ages* (New Holland, 2010), p. 154.
11 Tom Cullen, *The Man who Was Norris: The Life of Gerald Hamilton* (Dedalus, 2014), pp. 175–6.
12 Charles Graves, *Champagne and Chandeliers: The Story of the Café de Paris* (Odhams Press, 1958), p. 112.

13 Ibid., p. 117.

14 Joe Deniz, interview with Stephen Bourne, London, 10 August 1993.

15 Philip Ziegler, *London at War 1939–1945* (Sinclair-Stevenson, 1995), p. 148.

16 Joshua Levine, *The Secret History of the Blitz* (Simon and Schuster, 2015), p. 255.

17 Angus Calder, *The People's War* (Jonathan Cape, 1969), p. 204.

18 *Melody Maker*, 15 March 1941.

19 Cullen, *The Man who Was Norris*, p. 173.

20 Joe Deniz, interview with Stephen Bourne.

20 Brian Desmond Hurst 'Old Twank'

1 Christopher Robbins, *The Empress of Ireland: Chronicle of an Unusual Friendship* (Scribner, 2004), p. 21.

2 Ibid., pp. 22–3.

3 Bryan Forbes, *A Divided Life: Memoirs* (Heinemann, 1992), p. 307.

4 Diana Dors, *Behind Closed Dors* (Star Book, 1979), pp. 99–100.

5 Robbins, *The Empress of Ireland*, p. 253.

6 Ibid., pp. 257–8.

7 Ibid., pp. 318–19.

8 Simon Callow, 'Queen of the Higher Schmaltz', *Guardian*, 29 May 2004.

9 BFI National Archive, Brian Desmond Hurst, 'Travelling the Road', unpublished autobiography, p. 118.

10 Elisabeth Welch, interview with Stephen Bourne, London, 27 March 1995.

11 Brian McIlroy, 'British Filmmaking in the 1930s and 1940s: The Example of Brian Desmond Hurst' in Wheeler Winston Dixon (ed.), *Re-Viewing British Cinema 1900–1992* (State University Press of New York, 1994), p. 37.

12 Patrick Newley, interview with Stephen Bourne, London, 27 June 2000.

13 Michael Relph, interview with Stephen Bourne, London, 25 January 1995.

Part III: Not Forgotten

21 1914–1918

1 Jason Tomes, 'Frederick "Fred" Jester Barnes (1885–1938)', in *Oxford Dictionary of National Biography* (Oxford University Press, 2004).

2 Paul Bailey, *Three Queer Lives* (Penguin, 2001), p. 55.

3 Tomes, 'Frederick "Fred" Jester Barnes'.

4 David Parris in Aldrich, Robert and Garry Wotherspoon (eds), *Who's Who in Gay and Lesbian History: From Antiquity to World War II* (Routledge, 2001), p. 89.

5 Robert Aldrich in Aldrich and Wotherspoon, *Who's Who*, p. 258.

6 Robert Aldrich, *Gay Life Stories* (Thames and Hudson, 2012) pp. 190, 193.

7 Stephen Bourne, *Elisabeth Welch: Soft Lights and Sweet Music* (Scarecrow Press, 2005), pp. 27–8.

8 James Harding, *Ivor Novello* (W. H. Allen, 1987), quoted in *Gay Times*, February 1987.

9 Rictor Norton (ed.), *My Dear Boy: Gay Love Letters Through the Centuries* (Leyland Publications, 1998), p. 210.

10 Ibid.

11 George Piggford in Aldrich and Wotherspoon, *Who's Who*, p. 336.

12 Obituary of Ernest Thesiger, *Observer*, 15 January 1961.

13 Michael Elliman and Frederick Roll, *The Pink Plaque Guide to London* (Gay Men's Press, 1986), p. 202.

22 1939–1945

1 R. J. Minney, *Puffin Asquith* (Leslie Frewin, 1973), p. 124.

2 Ibid.

3 Tom Ambrose, *Heroes and Exiles: Gay Icons Through the Ages* (New Holland, 2010), p. 156.

4 Cecil Beaton, *The Years Between: Diaries 1939–44* (Holt, Rinehart and Winston, 1965), p. 36.

5 Eric A. Gordon, *Mark the Music: The Life and Work of Marc Blitzstein* (St Martin's Press, 1989), p. 243.

6 Patrick Newley, *Bawdy But British! The Life of Douglas Byng* (Third Age Press, 2009), pp. 59–60.

7 David Rooney, 'Michael Calvert (1913-98)', *Oxford Dictionary of National Biography* (Oxford University Press, 2004).

8 Ben Macintyre, *Operation Mincemeat: The True Spy Story that Changed the Course of World War II* (Bloomsbury, 2010), p. 153.

9 Ibid., pp. 153–4.

10 Ibid.

11 Stephen Bourne, *Elisabeth Welch: Soft Lights and Sweet Music* (Scarecrow Press, 2005), pp. 34–5.

12 *Melody Maker*, 1 March 1959.

13 Antony Beevor, *It is Bliss Here: Letters Home 1939–1945* (Bloomsbury, 2005), p. 9.

14 Sinclair McKay, *The Secret Life of Bletchley Park: The WWII Codebreaking Centre and the Men and Women Who Worked There* (Aurum, 2010), p. 298.

15 Simon Edge, 'Alan Turing: Icon Award for Outstanding Achievement', *Attitude*, November 2013.

23 My Friend Ken

1 Stephen Jeffery-Poulter, *Peers, Queers and Commons: The Struggle for Gay Law Reform from 1950 to the Present* (Routledge, 1991), pp. 13–16.

2 Ibid., pp. 86–7.

Appendix: Cinema and Television

1 *Gay News*, 22 (1981).

2 Keith Howes, *Broadcasting It: An Encyclopedia of Homosexuality on Film, Radio and TV in the UK 1923–1993* (Cassell, 1993), p. 363.

3 *Radio Times*, 15–21 November 2014.

Bibliography

Aldrich, Robert, *Gay Life Stories* (Thames and Hudson, 2012).

Aldrich, Robert and Garry Wotherspoon (eds), *Who's Who in Gay and Lesbian History: From Antiquity to World War II* (Routledge, 2001).

—— (eds), *Who's Who in Contemporary Gay and Lesbian History: From World War II to the Present Day* (Routledge, 2001).

Ambrose, Tom, *Heroes and Exiles: Gay Icons Through the Ages* (New Holland, 2010).

Bailey, Paul (ed.), *The Stately Homo: A Celebration of the Life of Quentin Crisp* (Bantam Press, 2000).

—— *Three Queer Lives* (Penguin Books, 2001).

Baker, Paul and Jo Stanley, *Hello Sailor! The Hidden History of Gay Life at Sea* (Pearson Education, 2003).

Beaton, Cecil, *The Years Between: Diaries 1939–44* (Holt, Rinehart and Winston, 1965).

Berry, Paul and Mark Bostridge, *Vera Brittain: A Life* (Chatto and Windus, 1995).

Berube, Allan, *Coming Out Under Fire: The History of Gay Men and Women in World War Two* (Free Press, 1990).

Binney, Marcus, *Secret War Heroes: Men of the Special Operations Executive* (Hodder and Stoughton, 2005).

Bishop, Alan and Mark Bostridge (eds), *Letters from a Lost Generation* (Little, Brown, 1998).

Bloch, Michael, *Closet Queens: Some 20th Century British Politicians* (Little, Brown, 2015).

Bolitho, Hector, *War in the Strand: A Notebook of the First Two and a Half Years in London* (Eyre and Spottiswoode, 1942).

—— *Combat Report: The Story of a Fighter Pilot* (B. T. Batsford, 1943).

—— *A Penguin in the Eyrie: An R.A.F. Diary, 1939–1945* (Hutchinson, 1955).

Bostridge, Mark, *Vera Brittain and the First World War: The Story of Testament of Youth* (Bloomsbury, 2014).

Bourne, Stephen, *Brief Encounters: Lesbians and Gays in British Cinema 1930–1971* (Cassell, 1996; Bloomsbury Academic, 2016).

—— 'On the Same Side', *BBC History Magazine* (February 2012).

—— 'Boys in Blue', *Gay Times* (June 2015).

Brighton Ourstory Project, *Daring Hearts: Lesbian and Gay Lives of 50s and 60s Brighton* (QueenSpark Books, 1992).

Byng, Douglas, *As You Were: Reminiscences by Douglas Byng* (Duckworth, 1970).

Cannadine, David (ed.), *Oxford Dictionary of National Biography* (Oxford University Press, 2004).

Carr, J. L., *A Month in the Country* (Harvester, 1980).

Cook, Matt (ed.), *A Gay History of Britain: Love and Sex Between Men Since the Middle Ages* (Greenwood World Publishing, 2007).

Copp, Bruce with Andy Merriman, *Out of the Firing Line … into the Foyer: My Remarkable Story* (The History Press, 2015).

Costello, John, *Love, Sex and War: Changing Values 1939–45* (Guild Publishing, 1985).

Coward, Noël, *The Autobiography of Noël Coward: Future Indefinite 1939–1945* (Methuen, 1986).

Crisp, Quentin, *The Naked Civil Servant* (Jonathan Cape, 1968).

Croall, Jonathan, *Gielgud: A Theatrical Life 1904–2000* (Methuen, 2001).

Cullen, Tom, *The Man who Was Norris: The Life of Gerald Hamilton* (Dedalus, 2014).

Currie, Jack, *Lancaster Target* (New English Library, 1977).

Curtis, James, *James Whale: A New World of Gods and Monsters* (Faber and Faber, 1998).

Daley, Harry, *This Small Cloud: A Personal Memoir* (Weidenfeld and Nicolson, 1986).

David, Hugh, *On Queer Street: A Social History of British Homosexuality 1895–1995* (HarperCollins, 1997).

Day, Barry (ed.), *The Letters of Noël Coward* (Methuen, 2007).

De Jongh, Nicholas, *Not in Front of the Audience: Homosexuality on Stage* (Routledge, 1992).

—— *Politics, Prudery and Perversions: The Censoring of the English Stage 1901–1968* (Methuen, 2000).

Driberg, Tom, *Colonnade 1937–1947* (Pilot Press, 1949).

—— *Ruling Passions: The Autobiography of Tom Driberg* (Quartet Books, 1977).

Edwards, Jimmy, *Six of the Best* (Robson Books, 1984).

Elliman, Michael and Frederick Roll, *The Pink Plaque Guide to London* (Gay Men's Press, 1986).

Elliott, Geoffrey, *The Shooting Star: Denis Rake, MC, A Clandestine Hero of World War II* (Methuen, 2009).

Elliott, Sue and Steve Humphries, *Britain's Greatest Generation: How Our Parents and Grandparents Made the Twentieth Century* (Random House, 2015).

Faught, C. Brad, *Kitchener: Hero and Anti-Hero* (I.B.Tauris, 2016).

Faulks, Sebastian, *The Fatal Englishman: Three Short Lives* (Hutchinson, 1996).

Fawkes, Richard, *Fighting for a Laugh: Entertaining the British and American Armed Forces 1939–1946* (Macdonald and Jane's, 1978).

Ferguson, Niall, *The Pity of War* (Allen Lane Penguin Press, 1998).

Francis, Martin, *The Flyer: British Culture and the Royal Air Force, 1939–1945* (Oxford University Press, 2008).

Franks, Norman, *Fighter Leader: The Story of Wing Commander Ian Gleed* (William Kimber, 1978).

Furbank, P. N., *E. M. Forster: A Life* (Oxford University Press, 1978).

Gardiner, James, *A Class Apart: The Private Pictures of Montague Glover* (Serpent's Tail, 1992).

—— *Who's a Pretty Boy Then? One Hundred and Fifty Years of Gay Life in Pictures* (Serpent's Tail, 1997).

Gatiss, Mark, *James Whale: A Biography or The Would-Be Gentleman* (Cassell, 1995).

Gleed, Ian, *Arise to Conquer* (Victor Gollancz, 1942).

Gordon, Eric A., *Mark the Music: The Life and Work of Marc Blitzstein* (St Martin's Press, 1989).

Gore-Langton, Robert, *Journey's End: The Classic War Play Explored* (Oberon Books, 2013).

Grayson, Larry, *Grayson's War: How Larry and His Friends Helped the War Along* (Macmillan, 1983).

Hall Carpenter Archives Gay Men's Oral History Group, *Walking After Midnight: Gay Men's Life Stories* (Routledge, 1989).

Hayim, George, *Thou Shalt Not Uncover Thy Mother's Nakedness: An Autobiography* (Quartet Books, 1988).

Heger, Heinz, *The Men with the Pink Triangle* (Gay Men's Press, 1980).

Hildyard, Myles, *It is Bliss Here: Letters Home 1939–1945* (Bloomsbury, 2005).

Hill, Susan, *Strange Meeting* (Hamish Hamilton, 1971).

Holmes, Richard, *Soldiers: Army Lives and Loyalties from Redcoats to Dusty Warriors* (HarperPress, 2011).

Houlbrook, Matt, *Queer London: Perils and Pleasures in the Sexual Metropolis, 1918–1957* (University of Chicago Press, 2005).

Howes, Keith, *Broadcasting It: An Encyclopedia of Homosexuality on Film, Radio and TV in the UK 1923–1993* (Cassell, 1993).

—— *Outspoken: Keith Howes' Gay News Interviews 1976–83* (Cassell, 1995).

Huggett, Richard, *Binkie Beaumont: Eminence Grise of the West End Theatre 1933–1973* (Hodder and Stoughton, 1989).

Humphries, Steve, *A Secret World of Sex* (Sidgwick and Jackson, 1988).

—— *The Call of the Sea: Britain's Maritime Past 1900–1960* (BBC Books, 1997).

Humphries, Steve and Pamela Gordon, *Forbidden Britain: Our Secret Past 1900–1960* (BBC Books, 1994).

Hyde, H. Montgomery, *The Other Love: An Historical and Contemporary Survey of Homosexuality in Britain* (William Heinemann 1970).

Jeffery-Poulter, Stephen, *Peers, Queers and Commons: The Struggle for Gay Law Reform from 1950 to the Present* (Routledge, 1991).

Jivani, Alkarim, *It's Not Unusual: A History of Lesbian and Gay Britain in the Twentieth Century* (Michael O'Mara, 1997).

Jolliffe, John (ed.), *Raymond Asquith: Life and Letters* (William Collins and Sons, 1980).

Lehmann, John, *In the Purely Pagan Sense* (Blond and Briggs, 1976).

—— *The English Poets of World War I* (Thames and Hudson, 1981).

Levine, Joshua, *The Secret History of the Blitz* (Simon and Schuster, 2015).

Lumford, Richard, *My Father's Son* (Jonathan Cape, 1949).

Magee, Bryan, *One in Twenty: A Study of Homosexuality in Men and Women* (Secker and Warburg, 1966).

Melly, George, *Rum, Bum and Concertina* (Weidenfeld and Nicolson, 1977).

Merriman, Andy, *Greasepaint and Cordite: How ENSA Entertained the Troops During World War II* (Aurum Press, 2013).

Minney, R. J., *Puffin Asquith* (Leslie Frewin, 1973).

Moffat, Wendy, *E. M. Forster: A New Life* (Bloomsbury, 2010).

Montague, George, *The Oldest Gay in the Village* (John Blake, 2014).

Newley, Patrick, *Bawdy but British!: The Life of Douglas Byng* (Third Age Press, 2009).

O'Connor, Sean, *Straight Acting: Popular Gay Drama from Wilde to Rattigan* (Cassell, 1998).

Page, Martin, *'Kiss Me Goodnight, Sergeant Major': The Songs and Ballads of World War II* (Hart-Davis, MacGibbon, 1973).

Paxman, Jeremy, *Great Britain's Great War* (Penguin/Viking, 2013).

Plomer, William (ed.), *A Message in Code: The Diary of Richard Rumbold 1932–61* (Weidenfeld and Nicolson, 1964).

Pollack, Howard, *Marc Blitzstein: His Life, His Work, His World* (Oxford University Press, 2012).

Pollock, John, *Kitchener* (Constable, 2001).

Porter, Kevin and Jeffrey Weeks (eds), *Between the Acts: Lives of Homosexual Men 1885–1967* (Routledge, 1991).

Redgrave, Corin, *Michael Redgrave: My Father* (Fourth Estate, 1996).

Renault, Mary, *The Charioteer* (Longmans, Green and Co., 1953).

Ricketts, Harry, *Strange Meetings: The Lives of the Poets of the Great War* (Pimlico, 2012).

Robbins, Christopher, *The Empress of Ireland: Chronicle of an Unusual Friendship* (Scribner, 2004).

Romain, Gemma, *Race, Sexuality and Identity in Britain and Jamaica: The Biography of Patrick Nelson 1916–1963* (Bloomsbury Academic, 2017).

Rooney, David, *Mad Mike: A Life of Brigadier Michael Calvert* (Leo Cooper, 1997).

Seabrook, Jeremy, *A Lasting Relationship: Homosexuals and Society* (Allen Lane, 1976).

Sinfield, Alan, *Out on Stage: Lesbian and Gay Theatre in the Twentieth Century* (Yale University Press, 1999).

Slattery-Christy, David, *In Search of Ruritania* (AuthorHouse, 2008).

Smith, Richard, *Jamaican Volunteers in World War I: Race, Masculinity and the Development of National Consciousness* (Manchester University Press, 2004).

Strachan, Alan, *Secret Dreams: A Biography of Michael Redgrave* (Weidenfeld and Nicolson, 2004).

Sweet, Matthew, *The West End Front: The Wartime Secrets of London's Grand Hotels* (Faber and Faber, 2011).

Taylor, Martin, *Lads: Love Poetry of the Trenches* (Duckworth, 1998).

Vickers, Emma, *Queen and Country: Same-Sex Desire in the British Armed Forces, 1939–45* (Manchester University Press, 2013).

Wales, Roland, *From Journey's End to The Dam Busters: The Life of R. C. Sherriff, Playwright of the Trenches* (Pen and Sword Military, 2016).

Warner, Philip, *Kitchener: The Man Behind the Legend* (Hamish Hamilton, 1985).

Weeks, Jeffrey, *Coming Out: Homosexual Politics in Britain from the Nineteenth Century to the Present* (Quartet Books, 1977).

Wheen, Francis, *Tom Driberg: His Life and Indiscretions* (Chatto and Windus, 1990).

Wildeblood, Peter, *Against the Law* (Penguin Books, 1955).

Woodhouse, Adrian, *Angus McBean: Face-Maker* (Alma Books, 2006).

Wright, Adrian. *John Lehmann: A Pagan Adventure* (Gerald Duckworth, 1998).

About the Author

Stephen Bourne is a writer, film and social historian specialising in black heritage and gay culture. As noted by the BBC among others, Stephen 'has discovered many stories that have remained untold for years'. Bonnie Greer, the acclaimed playwright and critic, says: 'Stephen brings great natural scholarship and passion to a largely hidden story. He is highly accessible, accurate and surprising. You always walk away from his work knowing something that you didn't know, that you didn't even expect.'

Stephen was born in Camberwell, South-East London, and raised in Peckham. He graduated from the London College of Printing with a bachelor's degree in film and television in 1988, and in 2006 received a MPhil. at De Montfort University on the subject of the representation of gay men in British television drama, 1936–79.

After graduating in 1988, he was a research officer at the British Film Institute on a project that documented the history of black people in British television. The result was a two-part television documentary called *Black and White in Colour* (BBC 1992), directed by Isaac Julien, that is considered groundbreaking. In 1991 Stephen was a founder member of the Black and Asian Studies Association.

In 1991, Stephen co-authored *Aunt Esther's Story* with Esther Bruce (his adopted aunt), which was published by Hammersmith and Fulham's Ethnic Communities Oral History Project. Nancy Daniels in *The Voice* (8 October 1991) described the book as 'Poignantly and simply told, the story of Aunt Esther is a factual account of a black working-class woman born in turn of the century London. The book is a captivating documentation of a life rich in experiences, enhanced by good black-and-white photographs.' For *Aunt Esther's Story*, Stephen and Esther were shortlisted for the 1992 Raymond Williams Prize for Community Publishing.

In 1998 Stephen researched and scripted the BBC Radio 2 series *Their Long Voyage Home*, presented by Sir Trevor McDonald, for the BBC's *Windrush* season. For his acclaimed book *Black in the British Frame: The Black Experience in British Film and Television* (2001), Stephen received the Southwark Civic Award. In 2004 Stephen began contributing biographies about black Britons to the *Oxford Dictionary of National Biography* and by 2016 Stephen's total had reached 40.

In 2008 he researched *Keep Smiling Through: Black Londoners on the Home Front 1939–1945*, an exhibition for the Cuming Museum in the London Borough of Southwark, and that same year he worked as a historical consultant on the Imperial War Museum's *War to Windrush* exhibition.

Stephen's association with the police in the London Borough of Southwark has been long and constructive. To raise awareness about homophobic hate crime, and to encourage the reporting of such incidents, in 1995 he was instrumental in setting up the multi-agency LGBT Forum, one of the first of its kind on the front line of a London borough. As a result of the bridge-building work he had already accomplished with Southwark Police, in 1999 Stephen was invited to volunteer as a member of the Southwark Independent Advisory Group, which he readily accepted. In 2003 Stephen received the Metropolitan Police Volunteer Award, presented to him by Police Commissioner Sir John Stevens at City Hall, London. The citation said: 'Stephen has discharged this responsibility with enthusiasm and conscientiousness in a number of high profile cases, most notably the tragic murder of Peckham schoolboy Damilola Taylor. In each he has provided good advice on strategy and tactics whilst informing the public of difficulties encountered within investigations and efforts made by police to achieve successful outcomes.'

In 2014 Stephen's book *Black Poppies: Britain's Black Community and the Great War* was published by The History Press to coincide with the centenary of Britain's entry into World War I. Reviewing it in the *Independent* (11 September 2014), Bernadine Evaristo said: 'Until historians and cultural map-makers stop ignoring the historical presence of people of colour, books such as this provide a powerful, revelatory counterbalance to the whitewashing of British history.' For *Black Poppies* Stephen received the 2015 Southwark Arts Forum Literature Award at Southwark's Unicorn Theatre. In 2017 Stephen was awarded an Honorary Fellowship from London South Bank University for his contribution to diversity. For further information go to www.stephenbourne.co.uk

Selected Publications

Aunt Esther's Story (ECOHP, 1991).

Brief Encounters: Lesbians and Gays in British Cinema 1930–1971 (Cassell, 1996; Bloomsbury, 2016).

Black in the British Frame: The Black Experience in British Film and Television (Cassell 1998; Continuum, 2001).

Sophisticated Lady: A Celebration of Adelaide Hall (ECOHP, 2001).

Elisabeth Welch: Soft Lights and Sweet Music (Scarecrow Press, 2005).

Speak of Me as I Am: The Black Presence in Southwark Since 1600 (Southwark Council, 2005).

Ethel Waters: Stormy Weather (Scarecrow Press, 2007).

Dr. Harold Moody (Southwark Council, 2008).

Butterfly McQueen Remembered (Scarecrow Press, 2008).

Mother Country: Britain's Black Community on the Home Front 1939–45 (The History Press, 2010).

The Motherland Calls: Britain's Black Servicemen and Women 1939–45 (The History Press, 2012).

Black Poppies: Britain's Black Community and the Great War (The History Press, 2014).

Evelyn Dove: Britain's Black Cabaret Queen (Jacaranda Books, 2016).

Index

Ackerley, J. R., 23, 129–30, 132–3, 168
Ackland, Rodney, 158
Addinsell, Richard, 157–8
Alcock, John, 49
All the King's Men (BBC, 1999), 203
Arras, Battle of, 25
Asquith, Anthony, 24, 160, 175–6
Asquith, Herbert, 8, 12
Asquith, Raymond, 11–13
Auden, W. H., 176–7

Bannister, Robert, 89–90
Barnes, Fred, 165–6
Beardmore, John, 70–1
Beaton, Cecil, 158, 177–8
Beaumont, Hugh 'Binkie', 121–2
'Belfast Blitz', 188
Belfield Clarke, Dr Cecil, 146
Bengal Entertainment Services
     Association (BESA), 48
Bentine, Michael, 86, 88
Blitzstein, Marc, 178–9
Bloomsbury Group, 130, 146
Bogarde, Dirk, 194
Bolitho, Hector, 98, 105–12
Bostridge, Mark, 20–2
Breaking the Code (BBC, 1997), 204

Britain, Battle of, 55, 100, 102,
     104–5, 110–11, 198
Brittain, Edward, 19–22, 197
Brittain, Vera, 19–22
Britten, Benjamin, 178, 203
Brooke, Rupert, 157
Brown, Gordon, 185–6
Brown, Lawrence, 145–6
Buckingham, PC Bob, 130–1
Burton, Peter, 127–8
Byng, Douglas, 179

Callow, Simon, 158
Calloway, Cab, 147–8
Calvert, Brigadier Michael, 179–80
Campaign for Homosexual
     Equality, 185, 187
Carson, Sir Edward, 12
Casement, Roger, xv, 165, 167
Cavalcanti, Alberto, 181
Cave, Dudley, xi, 53–9, 115
Charlton, Lionel, 168
Chatt, Barri, 78–9
Churchill, Winston, 107, 137, 140,
     170, 182, 198, 204
Clarke, Dudley Wrangel, 181–2
Clive, Colin, 27
Colditz, 61–2

Coleman, Stanley, 146
Combined Services Entertainment (CSE), 78
Comrades in Arms (Channel 4, 1990), xi–xii, 55
Cooper, Emmanuel, 201
Copp, Bruce, 43, 45–6
Costello, Ray, 198
Coward, Noël, 137–43, 155, 160
Crete, Battle of, 183–4
Crimson Field, The (BBC, 2014), 197
Crisp, Quentin, 115–18, 120, 124, 190, 201
Cross, Ulric, 85
Cumberbatch, Benedict, 204–5
Cummings, Ivor, 146–7, 152

Daley, David, 133
Daley, PC Harry, 127–34
Dangerous Moonlight (1941), 157–8
Davis, Bette, 72
Devitt, Peter, 103
Dougherty, Gerald, 118–19
Douglas, Lord Alfred, 92
Driberg, Tom, 119–20
Dunn, Ernest, 13

Edge, Simon, 186
Edward, Prince of Wales, 10, 173
El Alamein, Battle of, 51
Ellington, Duke, 145–6, 148
Entertainments National Service Association (ENSA), 78, 141, 179

Fitzgerald, Oswald ('Fitz'), 6–7, 9
Flers-Courcelette, Battle of, 13
Foresythe, Reginald, 182–3
Forster, E. M., 129–31, 143, 168–9

Fortunes of War (BBC, 1987), 202
Foyle's War (ITV, 2003), 204
Furbank, P. N., 128–30

Gallipoli, 156–7, 203
Gardener, Terri, 75–81
Gardiner, James, xii, 9, 32–4
Garnett, David, 108
Gatiss, Mark, 24–5
Gay London Police Monitoring Group, 127
Gay Police Association, 127
Gay Sweatshop, 201
George V, King, 10, 20, 173
George VI, King, 97, 100–1, 111, 138
Gide, Andre, 169
Gielgud, John, 137, 160–1, 168, 191
Gill, Tom, 122–4
Gleed, Ian, 97–106
Glover, Montague, 31–8
Gotch, Christopher, 97, 102–4
Grant, Duncan, 130, 146
Graves, Robert, 197
Grayson, Larry, 50
Green, G. F., 63–4
Griffiths, Drew, 201

Haig, Field Marshall, xvii, 172
Hall, Ralph, 31–8
Hamilton, Gerald, 149, 152–3
Hayim, George, 67–70
Hayworth, Rita, 72
Heckstall-Smith, Anthony, 69
Hepburn, Katharine, 72
Hewitt, William B., 178–9
Hildyard, Myles, 183–4
Hitler, Adolf, 143, 198, 204
House on the Hill: Something for the Boys (Scottish TV, 1981), 201

Housewife, 49 (ITV, 2006), 204
Howes, Keith, 9, 59, 75, 78–9, 115, 201–2
Hulme, Robert, 16
Humphries, Steve, 75
Hurst, Brian Desmond, 149, 155–61
Hurt, John, 201

Imitation Game, The (2014), 204
In Which We Serve (1942), 137–40
Isherwood, Christopher, 149, 176–7
It's Not Unusual (BBC, 1997), xii, 70, 97

Jacobi, Derek, 204
Jarman, Derek, 81, 203
Jewel in the Crown, The (Granada, 1984), 202
Jivani, Alkarim, xii, 71, 75, 118
Johnson, Ken 'Snakehips', 145–53
Journey's End, 23–9

Keele, Tommy, 16–17
Ken (friend), 187–95
Kimpton, Eric, 89–90
Kitchener, Herbert (1st Earl Kitchener of Khartoum), xvii, 5–10

Lanchester, Elsa, 27, 29
Latham, Paul, 124–6
Laughton, Charles, 27–8
Lawrence, T. E., xv, 165, 168–9
Lehmann, John, 63–4
Levine, Joshua, 17, 117, 121, 198
London Blitz, 108–9, 117, 131–2, 149–51, 157–8, 177
Lustig-Prean, Duncan, 53

Marshall, Stuart, 12
Mason, William Edward, 14
Maugham, W. Somerset, 98–9
McBean, Angus, 116, 123–4, 146
McKellen, Ian, 24
Melly, George, 67–8, 116–17
Montague, George, 88
Monte Cassino, Battle of, 45
Montgomery, Bernard (1st Viscount Montgomery of Alamein), xiii, xvii, 192, 198
Month in the Country, A (1987), 202
Mountbatten, Lord Louis, xvii, 137–8, 140–1, 159

Naked Civil Servant, The (1975), 190, 201
Nelson, Patrick, 146, 179
Newley, Patrick, 159–60
Noble, Eddie Martin, 140
Norton, Rictor, 8
Novello, Ivor, xv, 137, 160, 165, 169–70, 184

Olivier, Laurence, 139, 142, 203
Owen, Wilfred, xv, 157, 165, 171–2, 197, 203

Passchendaele, Battle of, 24
Pasuka, Berto, 146
Paxman, Jeremy, 6–7, 10
Pears, Peter, 178
Peel, Derek, 111
Pity of War, The: The Loves and Lives of the War Poets (ITV, 2014), 197–8
Prattley, Dennis, 72–3
Purdie, Alex, xvi, 46–9

Rake, Denis, 184–5
Rattigan, Terence, 69, 137, 175–6
Redgrave, Michael, 172, 176, 181
Relph, Michael, 160
Robeson, Paul, 143, 145–6
Roger, Neil ('Bunny'), 43–5
Rumbold, Richard, 91–5

Sassoon, Sir Philip, 172–3
Sassoon, Siegfried, 171–2, 197
Schlesinger, John, 78
Sexual Offences Act (1967), xvi, 193
Sheridan, Ann, 72
Sherriff, R. C., 23–9
Simpson, John, 107–8, 110–11
Smith, Jeanette, 53
Somme, Battle of the, 9, 25, 129, 198
Strayhorn, Billy, 145–6
Sweet, Matthew, 69
Swinging into the Blitz (BBC, 2013) 153

Tatchell, Peter, 6, 54–6
Testament of Youth (2015), 19–20, 22, 197
Theirs is the Glory (1946), 159
Thesiger, Ernest, 173–4
Thompson, Leslie, 146–8

Timewatch: Sex and War (BBC, 1998), xii, 71, 97
Turing, Alan, xv, 165, 185–6, 204–5

Victim (1961), 194
Victoria, Queen, 7
Vine, Joseph, 14

Walbrook, Anton, 158
War Requiem (1989), 203
Way to the Stars, The (1945), 176
Webber, John, xix
Welch, Elisabeth, 159, 170, 182
Went the Day Well? (1942), 181
Whale, James, 23–9, 174
Wichelo, Tom, 168
Wilde, Oscar, 7, 12, 92
Wildeblood, Peter, 191
Williams, Bernard, 58
Williams, Emlyn, 124
Williams, Kenneth, 24, 50–1, 78–9
Winn, Godfrey, 126
Witte, Jim, 62–3
Wolfenden Report (1957), xiii, 191
Wolff, Dr Charlotte, 64
Woodhouse, Adrian, 123–4
Wright, Frederick, 15

Ypres, Battle of, 25, 173